THE FEAST OF LANTERNS

THE
FEAST OF LANTERNS

By LOUISE JORDAN MILN

AUTHOR OF

"Mr. Wu," "The Purple Mask," etc.

A. L. BURT COMPANY

Publishers   New York

Published by arrangement with Frederick A. Stokes Company

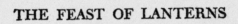

THE FEAST OF LANTERNS

THE FEAST OF LANTERNS

CHAPTER I

ALL Chinese home-life starts with one great underlying advantage—physical beauty.

And it has many others.

Every Chinese is born into surroundings of preeminent beauty—beauty of form, beauty of color, beauty of exquisite juxtapositions—natural beauty and beauty of all things that are made; into beauty, and into an almost untainted atmosphere of good-taste and intrinsic kindliness.

Consciously or unconsciously every Chinese is a sincere lover of nature and of everything lovely. No other people has so stern and uncompromising a sense of justice, so ready a sense of humor, more balance, more unflinching loyalty, or less exaggerated estimate of the importance of self. It is a proud people without vanity—a self-reliant, strong people, lacking brutality; suave without affectation, dignified without self-assertion—free from ridiculousness, industrious, contented; hard-working dreamers who, too, are shrewdly practical, honest above all other races, home-keeping, home-loving; first of all peoples in its love of children, and in its chivalrous treatment and just estimate of womanhood.

The clan of Ch'êng had all these characteristics—in-

deed few Chinese lack them—but for centuries it had
suffered from one outstanding disadvantage : prolific in
its marriages, those nuptials rarely had resulted in the
birth of a girl.   The gods had been besought and
bribed, offerings made lavishly, vows proffered, temples
built, but all to scant avail, for still the wives of the
family brought forth men children only.

Since a girl must be dowered, the Chinese poor pray
for a preponderance of sons, but for a great and rich
noble to be daughterless is to be afflicted and pitied.

A lady of the Ch'êngs had invented China's sweetest
wind instrument, and composed three of the great
classic love-songs, and at a time of sharp peril had won
back to their allegiance the revolting aborigines by her
diplomacy, her beauty and her playing of the flute.
Another had invented an imperial glaze, one had improved the telescope, and discovered a constellation, another had excelled all the other court ladies at em-
broidering, another—a poetess of the T'ang dynasty—
had enriched Chinese literature, one—when a decadence
of classical learning threatened—opened a school, and,
lecturing from behind a crimson curtain, to some hundred men and youths, averted the catastrophe, and one
had eaten the peaches of immortality that grew in the
garden of Hsi Wang Mu, the lady of the West, and
that ripen but once in three thousand years, and is
now a god with the gods.   But these were Ch'êngs but
by marriage, and had been all but barren of daughters;
and the few girls born to the family had been ordinary,
in appearance and in gifts; none of the few had
achieved distinction, done China or her own clan a
great service or made an imperial marriage.

But nearly a thousand years and more ago when
Marco Polo, the Venetian, was friend and gossip to

the great Kublai Khan, the first Mongol Emperor, a foremost soothsayer, in trance, had foretold that when in far years to come China should sink low, and threaten to pass out into international nothing, a girl should be born to a prince of Ch'êng, a girl who would journey far from home, suffer and learn from foreign influence, and return to her homeland to save and restore it. And whatever the Lis, the Sungs and the Paos thought of the old prophecy, the Ch'êngs held to it stoutly, and selected their wives with even more than the much care usual in such great families; that those brides might be worthy mothers of the girl savior of China.

Ch'êng Shao Yün, the head of the house now, had been so remarkable in person, so remarkable in ability, that she had added not meanly to the prestige of her husband's family. And when in dying he decreed that she should rule in his stead, no one resented it, and their eldest son least of all.

To be a Chinese widow is not always the best of luck. But a great Chinese lady, who has borne many sons and lived greatly, may wear her weeds with a difference. And, if the history of Chinese widowhood were written adequately, a Western world-wide misapprehension would have cause to hang its head low.

Ch'êng Yün had lived greatly, and she had borne her lord seven sons. She had known great joys and two grinding sorrows: the death of her husband, and, still sharper, that she had borne him no daughter.

Shaos had for centuries begotten more girls than boys, and that was not the least of the several good reasons why the bride of the young heir of the Ch'êng clan had been selected from the house of Shao. But the ill-luck of the Ch'êngs still dogged them, and no "lose-money-goods" came to play with and tyrannize over the seven lusty boys that Yün bore her lord.

She felt, and, to do him justice, so did Ch'êng O, her lord, that the fault should not be laid at her door, for Ch'êng Yün was one of six sisters, and the niece of almost a score of aunts.

While their youngest boy was still at her breast O, the husband, died, and the wife, still young in years, became formally what in fact she had been for some years: regnant. Neither of these two things was in the least odd—neither her potency in wifehood, nor her absolutism in widowhood—for both are of daily occurrence in China, especially among the rich and powerful caste.

Ch'êng Shao Yün was rigorous in all the obsequious observance of mourning. For O she wore the coarse colorless hempen dress of bereavement, lived in seclusion, grieved turbulently, omitting no one of the hundred hard rites of mourners, except only the fasting—since she still suckled a babe. But even in the first wild torment of her loss she set herself determinedly to end the old curse that for centuries had smirched the luster of their clan. She married her sons early and carefully, and as each daughter-in-law came into her control she received the girl and new chattel with warmth, and continued to treat her with more indulgence than a daughter-in-law can claim as a right. For Ch'êng Yün knew that while sorrowful women and women of most self-control are more apt to conceive sons, spoiled and self-indulgent wives are the more apt to bear daughters.

Six wives one after the other came into the house, and were heaped with kindness. None proved childless. Babies came thick and fast—fat, beautiful babies, born one and all with the magic triple bracelet of good luck on its wrinkled yellow wrist—and one had it twice. Soon the courtyard over-ran with babies and the soft patter of tiny plump feet and a rain of tender young laughing. But the grandmother, who adored them, sat apart and watched them askance—for when her eldest grandchild was sixteen, and the lot numbered thirty-seven, there was not a girl child among them.

The concubines that Ch'êng Yün bought for her sons would have peopled a village, and soon did people a hillside; and their purchase and keep would have strained the purse of any family but moderately rich even in China. Three of the secondary wives did have daughters, but one girl died at birth, and the others lived but a year.

To Chinese minds the pillorying of a little child is not justice, and the child of a concubine is of legitimate birth. Indeed, the concubine is of honorable, if secondary status. Ch'êng Yün would have preferred a granddaughter born of a first wife—because the young wives of her choosing were all of distinguished lineage which might fairly be expected to bequeath desirable traits even on offspring engendered from loins of Ch'êng. But failing such a granddaughter the woman would have knelt by the cradle of the concubine's daughter, and almost would have worshiped it—and had. But no girl child came to stay.

Year after year, almost month after month, the servants went forth far and wide, clad in their best liveries, carrying as gifts to kindred and friends, baskets and trays of the red eggs with which the Chinese announce the birth of a son. And Ch'êng Yün grimly watched them go. And when her favorite daughter-in-law disappointed her for the third time Ch'êng Yün shook her fist in the face of a god, and slacked it of incense. "What's the sense of paying a god who won't or can't do his part?" she said bitterly. She was a utilitarian and had little use and as little respect for a hierarchy that was purely ornamental. She believed in give-and-take and in all fair reciprocity. To her mind worship was a payment. She worshiped Confucius and Mencius—whose names she must not speak—because they had bettered China, and left guideposts to Chinese morality and sanity for all time. She worshiped her ancestors because they had given her life and China and a gorgeous heritage of good things; a love of books, and education and mind to read them, music, birds, flowers, wealth, the man of men for husband and mate —and gift and accomplishment to appreciate and enjoy —pride of race, love of country, a lien on the hereafter.

To-day she was angry with the gods, and she intended the special god who had so specially failed her to know it. She had lost her temper with heaven— and her disappointment was petulant and spiteful, and all her people avoided her, as far as they could, servants, retainers, household, her children and their children—all but Ch'êng Chü-po, her youngest son and idol, all but he and Ti-tô-ti.

The others were afraid of her in her bitterness, but not the two. Chü-po hung about her, and pressed her hands, and brought her a flower of her favorite oleander from the garden. And Ti-tô-ti crawled from his basket—where he had been licking a hurt paw—curled up on her robe's hem, and laid his tiny silk head on her tiny satin shoe.

CHAPTER II

IT was a vast domain over which this lady of Ch'êng ruled, and all in it—except her sons' wives—worked hard; and Ch'êng Yün worked hardest of all. To all intents it was a kingdom, and she ruled it a despot and supreme. In the China of that golden day there was little law and almost nothing of legal code, except the simple straight laws of principle and common sense. China was the happy land of a sane and contented people.

Every field was fertile, flowers crowded and laughed from every nook and crack, the passion flowers climbed up the great trunks of the orange trees, and the purple globes of the vines' fruitage hung pendant between the yellow orange balls. Bees sucked the honey of the clover's breath. Peacocks fattened on the meadows of scented grass. The ivory-carvers sang as they worked. The bannermen laughed and jested as they practiced hour after hour to make their wonderful archery more skillful. Peasants left their rice to play at chess. The four jewels of the scholar—paper, brushes, inkslab, ink—had pride of place in every gentle's house. The gods were docile, and the people prospered. Every month had its festival, every day its pleasant duty and its fructive toil. The looms sang their silken song, and the women sang at their spinning wheels. The children played leap-frog and blind man's buff among the bright hibiscus flowers, filched nectarines from their dripping panniers as the fruit-laden coolies passed to the kitchen doors.

"Ask us a riddle! Ask us a riddle!" the little thieves clamored, as Ch'êng Shao came suddenly among them, and the great lady laughed and said to them slowly,

" 'Little boy red-jacket, whither away?'
'To the house with the ivory portals I stray.'
'Say, will you come back, little red-coat, again?'
'My bones will come back, but my flesh will remain.' "

She said it for them thrice, and when one black-eyed urchin cried, "I know, honorable mistress, I know! A cherry! A cherry!" and all the other youngsters caught it up, and pranced about her madly, screaming, "A cherry, lady, 'tis a cherry!" she clapped her hands, and bade the servant bring the little monkey-things honey-cakes and cherries, and went her way to count the new baby pigs that had been littered in the night, and to test the quiet and the temperature in the silk-worm sheds.

And every home was happy. It was love and laughter, flowers and hard work all the way in China then—every day a day of toil, and every night a night of zither and of song.

Her coal mines were wide and deep and very rich. But they were worked so far from her house and her garden—and from the precious silkworms' sheds—that sight nor sound nor smut of them ever reached the dwelling-place, the courtyards, or the vineyards or the groves.

In the patriarchy of Ch'êng Yün the incessant laboring was a compulsion of her will, and a necessity of a place at once so teeming and so intricately crossed and counter-crossed with the industries that both fed and enriched it. And of all those industries Ch'êng Yün knew and supervised each part. She knew her mulberry trees almost to a leaf, and the output and increase of her fields almost to a millet seed. She could weave better than the master-weaver of her hundred looms, she could test the grades of tea with the light touch of a finger's tip, or guess the tea plantation's coming yield with but a glance. She knew always what her stewards should have paid—that and no more— for all the thousand things her larders stored, the grapes from Shansi and Shangtung, the pink and snow hams from Foochow, the lichees from Canton. She spent a fortune every day, but nothing was wasted or misused in all that vast, scattered place; not one little grain of rice, not one tiniest blue kingfisher's feather, not one melon seed. Everything was used to the best, and every industry was made to pay, and to pay to its utmost. The very by-products of the makings and tradings of the place, under her skillful husbandry, yielded harvest of gold. In the pretty mandarin fashion she spoke of all the common people who were her thralls, as "the babies," and if she ruled them hard, and decided for them more than many mothers do for their young, she ruled them well, and she was mother-good to them. And they loved her something as children do, and trusted her as dogs trust the human masters of their love. And well they might. Her temper was a wasp, her tongue a lash, but she was greatly bred, and her soul was fine. She gave them food and play and happiness, and she drove them to every jot of work that she deemed good for them—and her.

She drove herself hardest of all, but she drove all her underlings with no lenient hand. Her daughters-in-law had no set tasks, and no nominal compelling, but for the most part they were ceaselessly busied too with their constant and recurrent mother-craft.

And, if the concubines cost much to buy and more

to keep, their mistress saw to it that they were useful too.   Sun-fô-So was skilled in simples, U-chiao deft with her needle.   Several were fair musicians, and kept the courtyard amused and pleased.   Ping-Yang (a wife) supervised—under Ch'êng Yün—the dairy. Under Ch'êng Yün Ayuli nursed the sick, and P'an-p'an taught the babies—taught them to kot'ow, to eat their rice fitly, and later to use the tally-board, and write without spilling the smallest drop from their ink-heavy writing brushes—for P'an-p'an was clever, and had been well and delicately taught.   Still another —skilled as so many Chinese women are, in mathematics, kept the household accounts, another those of the estate—both strictly supervised by Yün herself.   For no multiplicity of affairs seemed to overtax her indefatigability.   Even in China, she was a wonderful woman.   Wearing no paint—since a widow—but gorgeously clad always and heavily jeweled, she ran like a girl on her wee feet, almost the smallest in China, romped when in the mood with her little grandsons, and outplayed them at mora, at whipping-top and at "beggar-my-neighbor," and took the first hand, and detailed, unflagging direction, at every industry on the great teeming estate.

And because she was so busy her rancor passed—or at least the ugly outer show of it—but the grief stayed. Her stubborn heart panted for a granddaughter.   And no other wish granted or dream fulfilled would slake it.

Two things, and two only, were paramount in the soul of Ch'êng Yün: to nurse a granddaughter in her arms, and to conserve and serve China.   China was her god, patriotism her religion.

This, too, was a woman of moods—but in them all

she watched, weighed and ruled. Some days she ruled
laughing and to the sound of the lute, and her servants
ran laughing to her, and laughing away to obey, and
her boys hung at her sleeve laughing, and called her
by her pet names, and the wives and concubines sang
as they served. Some days she ruled frowning, wield-
ing a stick, and to the crash of cymbals, the bellow of
drums, and the servitors rushed gravely to do her will,
and her sons and her grandsons kot'owed and were
silent, and the wives and concubines kept out of her
way. But always she ruled, and always the others
obeyed. And every year she grew richer.

The summer the nettle-rash nearly maddened her,
prickling every inch of her delicate skin with torture,
prickling her temper to ferocity, she journeyed daily
about the estate, forcing them to carry her in her litter.
A bee stung her; she swore at the bee, and beat at a
slave, but she tasted the honey, and directed its storing.
At the lime kilns she suffered an agony, but she suffered it grimly, and ordered and reordered the work-
men. And at the sheds of the silkworms she left her
litter, and moved about silent and placid among the
half-naked girls, nodding to them smiling approval; for
nothing must break the tranquillity of the cool, quiet
houses where the brooding worms spin and feed and
hatch, watched by their faithful, placid girl attendants.

But no matter what she was doing, or how seemingly
absorbed in the moment's occupation or business, always her heart ached for the girl babe, that often and
often was coming perhaps, but that never came, except
as a boy.

But she loved the boys—all of them—the boys that
she bore, and the boys that their women bore them.
And they found her their merriest playmate, and, as

they grew towards manhood, their firmest friend. She was womanly.

The little boys that were handsomest and brightest, seeming to promise most to their own future and to their country, often ran about the place dressed as girls while they were young—to deceive the evil spirits who had a special flair for boys, but rarely trouble to carry off or injure a mere girl.

And they worshiped her, her sons and her grandsons, and so did her servants; and even the wives and the concubines liked her. But it was men things that felt her thraldom soonest, surest, deepest and longest. For she had been born a Shao, and the women of that house always have been enslavers of men. To love and serve them men had but to see them. Emperors had craved them, and been denied, and one a great Manchu noble had wed in spite of the law, and held and cherished her against all odds, risking his life and his place. He had been condoned at the end—it was said because his Emperor, catching a glimpse of the girl, had envied and forgiven.

But no other Shao woman had ever given herself or been given to a Manchu, nor had ever one of the Ch'êngs. They were Chinese—and they kept it undefiled through the centuries—but for the one willful woman of long, long ago. They dwelt with the Manchus who had conquered them and been conquered by them—dwelt with them in harmony, in courtesy, even in liking; but never they let down the one barrier. Only the one woman—her name erased from their archives, and taboo—ever had wed but with one purely Chinese. And never a maiden of the Shaos or of the Ch'êngs had entered the Imperial harem. Their beauty and their charm had invited it. But the old Manchu law forbidding even the Emperor himself to seize a Chinese maiden for wife or for concubine had stood them in good stead. And to be born a Shao girl—or a Ch'êng —was to become the wife of a Chinese man, and to bear him children of race-blood unmixed.

It was a merciful law and a diplomatic one, that old decree of the Emperor—but it was a shrewd one too. Many a rebellion might have been hatched in the vermilion palace itself, and have overrun and destroyed the kingdom, through the still machinations of some slip of a Chinese girl, attached to her own people, and enthroned in the favor of the foremost Manchu—tapping state secrets, suborning state ministers, bribing the eunuchs.

But both as wife and as widow Ch'êng Shao Yün had been in Pekin. She had lived at the Court once or twice, and had life-long friends there—one in the throne-room itself.

For this was a very great lady, the tiny glittering figure with the oval unpainted face, who bent over the side of the light lacquered boat, fishing for trout, and clapping her hands, and laughing and babbling, whenever she caught one.

"Look! Chü-po, look!" she cried, holding out on her slim bamboo pole her slippery prize; and then catching it in both hands, and clasping it, all wet and wriggling, to her bosom, "The darling! What a mouthful he'll make!"

"Nay, motherling," the boy cried teasingly, "it's not much of a fish."

"You lie!"

"Not I," he retorted significantly. "It's not so long, or so heavy, or half so silvered as this one of mine. Let's measure!"

He made to take her last catch, to compare it with
the one that he boasted. She resisted, screaming shrilly. They struggled. And her fish wriggled itself
loose, or slipped from the grasp of her one hand—she
was fighting Chü-po with the other—and fell with a
splash back into the lake. The spray from its fall
struck Ch'êng Yün in the eyes. She swayed and
slipped, and must have fallen had not Chü-po caught
her in his arms. And they both rocked with laughter,
till she wiped her eyes on his sleeve, swayed back and
forth, laughing and scolding each other, and rocking
the boat till the boatmen had all their work to keep it
afloat.

The women and children in all the attendant boats,
a pretty flower-hung, silk-cushioned, carved fleet of
twenty, caught up the laughter, and echoed it shrilly.
The slave girls caught up their tiny instruments, and
laughing, sang to them. A slave boy clashed his tom-
tom, another beat his bells.

The blue kingfishers on the almond trees that fringed
the lake snatched up the music and the fun and
drenched the air with the sweetness of their song. A
great peacock, perched on the coping of the old stone
bridge, spread his indignant tail, and screamed a croak-
ing rebuke. And the little speckled trout, dived deep,
swam silently away.

CHAPTER III

C H'ÊNG CHÜ-PO knelt at Ch'êng Yün's feet.
"Motherling," he pleaded, fondling her girdle,
"not yet. It is too soon."

Yün frowned, and he continued more ceremoniously.

"O, honorable lady, jadelike and august, keep your
degraded slave with thy jasmine self."

"Fool," snapped his mother, "who speaks of sending
thee away? Or thinks of it? I do not propose to sell
or give thee to adoption. Dost think a Ch'êng, and a
Ch'êng of Shao blood," she added proudly, "will go to
his wife, or live in the house of her father? Your
bride comes to us—though she were the daughter of an
emperor, a descendant of the Two Holy Sage Ones,
or a daughter of the gods."

"Yes—lady—and mother, mistress and queen, thy
miserable slave knows that. But a new wife takes a
son from his mother, comes somewhat between their
hearts and the love they have held, especially if she be
fair and skilled in soft ways."

Ch'êng Yün drew in a breath sharply. "How do
you know that?" she said.

"I have seen my brothers wed. And you have
chosen fair maidens for their brides."

The woman sighed. "Yes. I know. The mother
loses her son when he weds happily—at least for a
time. I am loath to part with thee even so much.
And thou knowest it well. But our house has its
claims. We should have obeyed them ere now." She

15

laid her hand on his head, and tears came in her sharp eyes. "Listen, Chü-po. Of all I have borne, in thy own generation, and in that of my grandsons, thou art dearest to me. Thou wert our babe when thy most honorable father became a guest on high. Thou hast his look, and his way, as none other of them all has. Partly because I have so loved thee, boy, I have kept thee dangling here at my girdle, selfish, weak, reluctant to share thee with a wife, reluctant to share thee, my babe, even with a babe of thine own. Thou lovest me, boy?"

"Mother!" he cried, the wet in his eyes welling quick in answer to hers, "as the flowers love the sun, as the night loves the moon. Thou art my all. Drive me not away."

"Nay, never that," she said fiercely. "But only to loosen a little the grip of thy hand on my girdle, the grip of my hand on thine every hour. Another should serve thee at rice, another should sing thee to slumber, when the day beats hot on the red of the roses, and the birds seek the leafage that is thickest and coolest. Listen. I have left thee unwedded in selfishness—but, too, in a stern, self-restraint. Thou knowest how I have longed for a daughter. But thou knowest not why. In old age, and in illness a woman craves the companionship of a girl she has nursed on her breast, a woman younger and agile, of her own blood. There are days when the needle grows heavy, and the bright silks grow dull to the woman who bends to her embroidery frame with no daughters about her. A woman's sons' wives belong to her. The daughters she has borne are she—she herself—skin of her skin, touch of her hand, soul of her soul."

Chü-po nodded. He understood. It was rarely that he did not understand Ch'êng Yün.

"But no," she said, smiling gravely, "it was not for that, or but in a small way for that, that I have so besought the gods, have so heaped tribute on the altar of Kwang Yin. Still less was it to break an old curse —which reads well in a tale, and does for the babies to believe—but is but smoke in the estimate of the wise. Such old tales it is well to tell over and over. It is ill to let them die. But they are ill to believe. Fable and poetry trim life, and deck the fame of a house. But even a fool would not attempt to hew rock with them, or solve mathematical profound problems. No man comes to manhood's best development, no man knows the utmost of courage, until a daughter nestles on his knee. And for that I have prayed to Kwang Yin. But another reason has been beyond all sharpest and greatest. It is through its women—the women, not of its marriage, but the women of its blood—that a family gains power, augments and keeps it. The daughter we give a great noble in marriage, makes him as a child in her hands and, because her heart clings to the home and the blood of her birth, he becomes our friend and our ally. The sons she bears, carry his name, worship his ancestors. They eat his rice when their teeth have hardened their gums. But they suck our milk. They are his, but too they are ours, even though they never look into our eyes, or sit in our kô-tang. Our daughters leave us—and gain us ten score of allies. When we lift a girl into her flowery-chair, and send her out on the long way that ends at her bridegroom's door, we send an ambassador out across China—an ambassador who makes few mistakes—whose diplomacy rarely blunders or fails—and never betrays it-

self.   For one woman can persuade more than can ten
men.   The gossips and the babies praise the Manchu,
proclaim him generous, self-denying because he decreed, and has kept his plighting, that all Chinese girls
shall be inviolable against his desire."

"Yet," ventured the boy, "we have conquered the
Manchu far more truly than he conquered us."

Ch'êng Yün nodded.   "Of course, my own frogling—every race that has conquered our armies—and
these races have been many from long before the day
when Genghis Khan led his Tartar hordes here from
the Steppes of Russia—every such conquering race
has in turn been quietly influenced by us into a deeper
subjection than it had inflicted on us.   That is one of
life's greatest laws.   Perhaps its richest compensation.
And too—it is the inalienable heritage of China, the
birthright of the Chinese character, to subdue and con-
vert all that brashly break into her influence.   But for
all that same the dominance throned within the pink
palace walls at Pekin sleeps safer, sits firmer, because
neither wife nor concubine of Chinese blood sways on
her golden lilies across his carpets, to bestir and fer-
ment race feud and Mongol intrigue.   The witcheries
of Chinese women might have hurled him from his
throne even whilst he bent to caress her.   But the slow
alchemy of Chinese influence has but solidified the
throne and strengthened his tenure—Chinese thought,
Chinese art, Chinese custom—the great fructive cus-
toms of a wonderful race—have but refined, enriched
and more empowered the conquered and pupil."

She paused and studied her shoe proudly as it peeped
from under her wide trouser, a red jeweled shoe,
no larger than a   gigantic almond nut, and much the
same shape.

Then she went on—there is no end to the words of a Chinese woman, and never fatigue. "The Chinese can rule all their world—by its character alone, and can keep the blood in its veins unashamed, unimpured. Never shall the bird of paradise nuptial with dogs. But enough of the Manchu and of things from our point. Because it has been daughterless, the Ch'êng race has stood alone, unsupported by the stay-ropes of its women's alliances, unprotected by the outer guards of its women's devotion and influence. A man can adopt a son to celebrate his obsequies, to worship his wraith, but no adoption can gain him a daughter's subtle service. It was for the sake of your father's race, the augmenting of his prestige, that I have besought Kwang Yin to put girls in our cradles. It was for that that I hastened the marriages of thy brothers, wedding them to wives from daughter-full families, and have filled the courtyards with concubines till the whole place has tinkled with the sound of their stickpins."

"Alas!" laughed Chü-po.

"Alas! yes!" Ch'êng Yün echoed grimly. "And why have I not so hastened your marriage—now you shall know. It was not my selfishness nor my weakness."

"I know that," her boy interrupted proudly, fondling her hand. And he knew right well that neither selfishness nor weakness had part in Ch'êng Yün.

"The gods," she said gravely, "would be interceded with decorum—not importuned or hurried. It has been given to me that too many prayers may weary and then anger a god. And so I have learned to wait and be patient."

Chü-po dropped his eyes suddenly, and the hand on her hand trembled a little. He was her slave—he so

loved her, and she was so strong—almost he was her
dupe, and willingly so, but no drugging of fascination
or of love could for one moment delude him into the
faintest belief that Ch'êng Shao Yün had acquired
patience.

Perhaps she sensed it. For she added abruptly,
"But now the time has come."

"A little longer!" he caught her hand and pressed his
cheek upon its rings.

Yün laid her other hand on his head. "Well then,"
she said gently, "how long?"

"A year," he pleaded.

She shook her head. "Not nearly a year, my Chü-
po. Be more reasonable."

"Then, at least, until after the Feast of Lanterns."

"Until after the Feast of Lanterns," Yün conceded,
and her voice sounded to say it not unwillingly.

"And we will stay close together, every hour till
then? And we will walk and talk and play,—just you
and I—and till then let us forget—forget the marriage
that must come—I like it not—and the woman it will
bring."

"And we will stay close together," she answered
gravely. "And we will walk and talk and play, just
thou and I. But when the marriage comes you will
like it well enough—and I make little doubt that you
will like the woman it brings you better than I shall.
And in the meantime you shall forget it. I shall
remember it. A man," she added almost sadly, as she
rose, "rarely remembers; a woman never forgets.
Come, we will walk."

CHAPTER IV

THEY left the room, and crossed through the courtyard, past the devil-screen, to the outer door, and
into the outer grounds. Theoretically Ch'êng Shao Yün
passed all her hours within her own apartments and in
the "flowery" courtyard, as a Chinese woman of high
caste should. Actually she went daily here, there and
everywhere about her vast domain, her journeyings
limited only by her whim, and her face and voice as
familiar to every coolie on the place as the trees and
the red roofs of the houses were.

At first the house had been built about two courtyards, as a Chinese home should be built, but the many
marriages, and the lush influx of baby-life had first
crammed and cramped it, and then burst through it
quite; and that many of her children should not be
roofless, Yün had caused a grove of additional home-
quarters to jut out again and again from every wall,
and from them others, like red-topped mushrooms,
quarters leading all into the others, strung together by
doors and courtyards, and that were houses in themselves except in name, and independent homes but for
the vigorous over-ruling of Ch'êng Shao Yün, and that
in their irregular, straggling, sloping red-roofed mass
spread over several acres. But so wide were the gardens in which they lay, and so vast the fields and groves
and hilly vineyards and quarries circling the gardens
about, that the great congerie of linked buildings
looked snug and homelike.

They were all of but one story. In Pekin it was against the law—and in China law is obeyed—to erect a dwelling of more than one story—because Chinese ladies spend their lives within home-walls, and depend upon the courtyards of the "flowery" quarters for fresh air and sunshine. And so jealous is Chinese law and Chinese sentiment of the comfort and welfare of women that even an Emperor would not venture to evade the old custom which his subjects dare not disregard. In this, her Ho-nan stronghold, the woman tottering through a wilderness of flowers, leaning on her son's arm as she went, was supreme. She might, and she would, have built her home up to any height; but it never had occurred to her to heighten it by a foot beyond the one story allowed in the imperial capital. She approved the accredited regulation. And what Ch'êng Shao Yün approved that she did and obeyed.

All Chinese law is an expression of justness, and is built on sanity. Chinese law is omnipotent. Chinese laws are very few.

It is very difficult to say which is Chinese law, which Chinese fashion; they are so one in source and aim, sprung both from sentiment and tradition, whose only concern is to preserve and augment a people's health, happiness and peace. Chinese law has little machinery, and needs but scant personnel. Few formal administrators of law are needed where laws are few, and every law administered loyally by all, because sincerely respected and approved by all, and administered by cordial observance from the coolie in the wet paddy fields to the yellow-robed Emperor.

The most fantastic custom or rite in China has grown from some beneficent reason, is steeped in reasonableness. And the Chinese know it. They take their philosophies gayly, but the philosophies are sound and shrewd.

Of all made things, perhaps Chinese roofs are the most picturesque. The sun was just past its full when the woman and youth strolled together through the flowers to the bamboo groves on an Eastern hill. And in the slipping sun, the red-tiled, sloping roofs, curved and indented—the hundred roofs of the home of the Ch'êngs—glowed ruby warm.

The lovers, the woman and her son—gayer in satin, silk and jewels than any flower in all that flower-radiant place—planned how they'd make high holiday of every day left them before—before the Feast of Lanterns. She caught her youth back from his, and prattled to him as they went. Once she broke from him to chase a butterfly, and clapped her hands, applauding it, when it escaped and disappeared beyond a great forest of hollyhocks.

They passed a gardener asleep in the shade. They passed two sweepers throwing dice. They passed a mason setting a wall askew. Ch'êng Yün took no heed—except to shrug and laugh. Never had such a thing happened with her before. But this was carnival time—the play time of Chü-po, and the Suzerain of every fate within that domain's far-flung boundary walls would give no thought to aught but mirth and tenderness while he was at her side. She was bidding her boy good-by, and she would bid it, brave heart that she was, with laughter and with song, with jest and warm red wine.

CHAPTER V

THAT night she made him a feast and shared it.

As a rule she ate her rice alone, keeping her state in solitude, as Tze-Shi kept hers in Pekin. But now and again she commanded a son, or a favorite daughter-in-law to her table—and Chü-po oftenest of all.

Since he was a man, and she but a woman, she should have served him, or—for in China the precedence of motherhood often supersedes the precedence of manhood—he should have served her. But Ch'êng Shao Yün had never served any one in her life—not father nor husband; and she had no mind that Chü-po should serve her to-night.

They ate side by side. And for the first time Chü-po tasted monkeys' lips and torpedo's roe.

There are eight foods sacred to the Emperor. Unfortunately—for her conscience—Ch'êng Yün was inordinately fond of them all. For loyalty's sake she never let even the servants who prepared and served them see her touch one to her mouth. In priceless bowls they were laid on a side-table, in some vicarious ceremonial, or to be ready should the Son of Heaven unexpectedly appear and be a-hungered—and at the end of her own meal they were miraculously destroyed. When the servants had withdrawn, she swayed over to the malachite side-table, and swayed back to her own, carrying the forbidden bowls—scarcely perturbed by her own presumption, (since no one had it for example) and growing less so with each succulent mouthful.

But to-night she shared her imperial master's delicacies with Chü-po, while the song-girls shrilled through the casements, and the nightingale sang to the roses.

And when they had eaten and drunk from their tiny wine cups, and finished their pipes—she took up a samsien and sang to Chü-po while he lolled on the cushioned sandal-wood seat at her side.

And when they were tired of music, or she thought he was, she told him stories of his race—the endless stories of every great Chinese clan, gushing with sentiment, embroidered with poetry and fantasy, big with brave deeds, decently darkened here and there with crime, glittering with jade and amethysts, tinkling with laughter, grim and glad with the clash of arms—breathless stories of danger and conquest, whispered stories of exquisite women and of love. Some he had heard before, some were new. But Chü-po hung upon them all, playing with her girdle, fingering her rings.

Till nearly morning she kept him with her, and amused. Long after the household slept she told on and on the tales he loved to hear—the casement thrown wide to the sparkling, scented night.

Ch'êng Shao Yün, prompt at appointments, punctual in duty, had never been a slavish keeper of hours. Day and night were one to her. And for much she liked the night hours best. She worked by day, directing and prodding the many industries of her wide estate, but at night she read, and thought, resting her tireless limbs, and storing up strength and poise from the stillness and the dark for the strenuous, restless day with its intricate net-work of interests and activities. All that lay to her hand to do, this little Chinese woman did vigorously, eagerly and well. But she did all in her own way, and at her own time. She bowed to no un-

derling's convenience—and all were her underlings here
—and certainly to no time-table.   When she was hungry she ate.   When she was thirsty she drank.   Outside her apartments relays of wakeful servants squatted by night as well as by day, ready to rush to her
bidding at the first clap of her hands.   In the middle
of the night her stewards felt no surprise to be summoned to a saturnalia of farm accounts or sericultural
debate.   In the dead and middle of the night frequently
elaborate meals were cooked for her, and ceremoniously served.   A clanging of an outer bell roused the
boatman from sleep to man her skiff for a drifting on
the lake to an accompaniment of many musics, or that
she might fish by moonlight.   And that at midnight the
catch was small was neither here nor there.   It was not
to catch fish the woman loved, but to fish for them.
She loved the night, and to put into it all the exercises
and activities that she best liked.   Hours were for her
convenience, her servants, and not she theirs.

The instant Chü-po's laugh came a little slow, his
hand on her robe a little lax, she dismissed him.

When he had gone she lit her reading lamp, an antique, jeweled treasure fed on pungent, perfumed oil,
sharp as vinegar, sweet as attar, and drew a book of
poems to her knee.

Ch'êng Yün was too skilled, and she loved Chü-po
too well, to chain him too closely to her girdle in these
dear days of the last trysting of their closest intimacy
—the trysting whose close must mark some renuncia-
tion of her motherhood, and mark his childhood's
close.   His sex had thwarted and disappointed her beyond all her previous disappointments—for when the
sweet pains of his coming had throbbed their message

through her being she had known that her last of child-birth was at hand. If this were not a daughter, no daughter would ever come—to fulfill her paramount ambition, and in after years to wear her gems and don her robes. But she had loved him from the first with more than the sum of love she had given to his broth-ers, and when the woman had put him to her breast, and she drew her fingers across the down on his tender head, she would not for China and its wealth, not for China and its weal, have changed him for any girl. And as the full years passed he had been her one per-fect companion, her perfect joy, and her most unstinted pride.

She knew him too well, loved him too much, to keep him always with her now. And when his young eye roved across the peony beds to the dim outlines of the farther hills, she drove him from her to the chase—or bade him bring her from the distant river's bank some flower or fern that grew only there.

And if he had loved the freedom of his roamings be-fore, it was twice a pleasure now. So much it was his, the freedom, the zest of it, unwatched, undictated, uncensored, careless, irresponsible, that it seemed his very self, the ultimate expression of independence and self-suzerainty, that its curtailment or abandonment seemed not a remote catastrophe, but sheer impossibil-ity. He went where he would, how he would and while he would. Sometimes he dashed off on his sure-foot-ed Arab, all the bells of the high, carved saddle jing-ling a roundelay of speed and spirits, sometimes he went afoot, unattended, lingering in the lanes, bound-ing from rock to rock on a steep hill-side, eating fruits he tore from their stems, drinking at a bubbling, chattering brook, shouting aloud in his freedom and in the splendor of his youth, gathering flowers, gloating on their loveliness, and singing low snatches of some old love tune as he turned toward home.

And always he came back to her with an added love. And always she was waiting and watching for him, and welcomed him with a bowl of fragrant wine and with some new contrivance for his pleasuring: a prank planned for them to play, an old book found to read to him, a robe donned for him that he had never seen before, a priceless robe some ancestress had worn centuries ago, a troupe of strolling players summoned by runners from the nearest great city to enact a new play in her theater—a gilt and bamboo edifice spliced up by her carpenters in a day—or to reënact for him some chief favorite of his, a quail fight for him to watch such as even they had never had before, or a vase or bronze new-bought, or disemboweled from some old coffer—a troupe of boys from Foo-Chow to walk and dance for him on stilts, playing ball and juggling as they danced, a thousand birds of every throat and hue, released, at the clapping of her hands, from wicker prisons in the tangled grass, to take their eager brilliant flight above the pink almond trees up into the sky —far—farther—dim—dimmer—out of sight.

CHAPTER VI

BUT the Feast of Lanterns was at hand.
Once she spoke to him of what lay hot at her heart, and cold in both their fears—but only once.

"Have you any choice—any wish—my Chü-po?" she said.

"As to the girl?" he made no pretense not to understand her; it was not their way. Chü-po cheated no one, and she never cheated him.

She nodded.

"Choice? In what way?"

And then he laughed at her. "How is even a wish in the matter possible with me? I, who have never seen a girl!"

She could not contradict him in that. The peasant girls in their fields and in the cocoon sheds counted to neither of them. And to him the slave girls in his brothers' harems counted for less.

The mother nodded. "But from what province, from what family? With what traits?"

"No," he said simply, "why should I care?"

His mother sighed. She knew how much he might care—afterwards; care and regret, if her choice went awry.

"Will her feet be small as yours?" he added, however. "I like small feet—and hands like yours—the rest is little. But the hands and the feet——"

"Your bride's golden lilies will be small and well squeezed," she interrupted severely. "Small as mine will be hard to find—perhaps impossible. But they will be as they should, and her hands very beautiful. I promise you that."

Across one corner of the domain an old, old river lay like a broad band of silver. If it ran to the sea, it moved with such slow dignity, so silent and so calm, that no eye could catch its course, and no one make guess in which direction lay its source, in which its passing into the ocean's wide marriage bed. Sunshine and moonlight painted and jeweled it, but rarely rippled, and the fierce storm winds that blew now and then from the North far beyond the Hwang Ho and the Funiu Shan failed to ruffle its proud calm. And the great pink-throated cranes that came and mounted on the mossed pebbles at its bend seemed not to cut with the sharp scissors of their slender pointed beaks the imperturbable smoothness of its glass. The score of other waters that danced and foamed, laughed and rippled noisily through the wide-flung acres of Ch'êng Yün probably were as old as it, but they seemed babies, and it old as time. And perhaps nothing else gains so much reality from its seeming as does age—bubbling youth and quiet age. The little brooks and rills, with their churning and their frothing waterfalls, seemed of to-day, lusty but very young, reborn each day in ecstasy and glee—the infants of each sun, the urchins of each moon, with elves and water sprites for playmates, and sweet banked flowers and ferns for swaddling clothes. The river seemed very, very old because it was so motionless—so self-sufficient and so self-possessed. To Chü-po it had always seemed the oldest thing in China, and the wisest, and at once the most indifferent and the kindest. Its surface never moved. Its depth was veiled and screened by its thick calm.

When the lantern feast was very near—not four weeks off—and all China teemed and panted with excited preparations for her greatest festival, and with all the clatter of its New Year keeping, Chü-po, a little wearied of the incessant movement of his world—the cackle and the din—wandered away to the river's nearmost bank—ever from his babyhood a favorite haunt of his.

He had not come here to think. It was his wish and his mood to avoid thought. He had come here to be alone. He was fiercely tired of people, and harassed by the thought of a companionship to come, apprehensive of its claims and of its rasp. And the companionship of the old river, that he had loved longer than he could remember, was endurable only because it was so aloof and so still; saying nothing, irresponsive and apart.

Why he so shrank from the lot which was the honor of every Chinese, and the signia of manhood, he could not have told. Ch'êng Shao Yün had chosen maidens well through her reign, and each of Chü-po's brothers was happy *and comfortable* with his wife. There were no bickerings in the Kingdom of Ch'êng Yün—except when she chose to make them. And Chü-po, who had had the run of the flowery quarters far more, and years longer, than Chinese canons indicated, had found his sisters-in-law pleasant enough folk at all times, often amusing, if rarely restful, and sometimes well worth knowing. But he was younger than his years by nature; one of those whom the gods love and keep young till death, and, from the over-mothering of Ch'êng Yün, young—a little babyish—in a manly way. With all a Chinese's reverence for age in others, he was strangely ambitionless of age and the things of age for

himself.   He had no wish to wear a beard or to be
"nine thousand years old"—only an Emperor may be
called older than that.   The thought of the causal civil-
ities of marriage embarrassed him—to its more intimate amenities he had not given a thought—and he
wondered ruefully whether he'd have to talk to the girl
his mother gave him, and, if he did, what in all the
range of words should he find to say to her?   And
would she mind?

Probably she'd hate it even more than he.   Poor
little girl!   The new thought tinged his mind with a
new kindliness towards her—almost his heart with a
tender sense of comradeship.   It was the first feeling
of kindness that he had had toward his unknown, and,
as he believed, as yet unchosen bride.

Poor little girl!

What was that?

Sounds and movement came from beyond the wal-
nut grove—two drifts of each moving toward each
other, and bearing down on him.   One came from the
east, one from the west.   There were twenty ways into
the estate—but each puncture well guarded at its gate.
The pad, pad of straw-shod coolie feet.   The click of
palfreys' feet.   The ringing of horses' bells.   Who
was coming?   He could and would avoid them.   But
first he'd look.

Goat-nimble Chü-po left the bank, and climbed the
steep side of a rough ravine.   Half hidden in a belt of
firs on the low hill's crest—he had no notion to be seen
and perhaps interrupted of his solitude—he paused
and looked, then stood still and watched—a sumptuous
sight.

Two cavalcades were converging a few rods away.

In each bannermen, footmen, horsemen and insignia-carriers led the long retinue which ended behind its master and personage with a straggling herd of servants and slaves, so many that only a Chinese head could count them, and only a Chinese purse pay or feed them.

There was nothing to distinguish servants from slaves. Under the Manchu rule, the old system of Government slavery had long disappeared—as did so much of national ill—but the beneficent slavery of great men's personal ownership survived and throve. And among the hundreds of sleek, happy, well-fed retainers now pouring at their masters' wake into the Ch'êng domain, there was doubtless a goodly sum of legal slaves—happier than their freemen fellows, because more permanently attached to their lord's service, and more intimately of his acquaintance and care, and more secure of both—many of them bearing his name, all sharing in his pride of house and place.

The musicians were the most splendid in dress, mincing consequentially like gay human tulips along the paths. The dwarf-tree-bearers in one cavalcade, and in the other the cage-carriers, moved with even more strut and pride of gait than did the music-makers, for nothing else in all those twin throngs of mandarin display was of finer value, or cherished with more elaborate solicitude, than the tiny dwarf trees, each in a little tub of carved ivory or gemmed gold, and the little singing birds in jeweled plumage and jeweled cages of gilded bamboo or lacquer pierced-and-cut-lace. No man carried more than one tiny, jeweled tree, or one tiny, caged bird. And behind each such bearer walked an attendant with all the tree or bird might need while journeying—special food, special drink, careful contrivances for warmth and freshened air. Chinese birds are greatly loved. Chinese dwarf-trees are hardy as the race that rears and cherishes them, but like that virile race, are highly strung, and the trees must not be buffeted about, or moved with ruthless carelessness from place to place. And in this last the dwarf-trees are less persistent of life and character than the humans of the Chinese race.

Doubtless both birds and priceless trees were tributes of compliment to the Lady of Ch'êng—and doubtless many of the bamboo-corded bales, less easily and less carefully carried in the long processions' rears, held tribute too, to be laid at the preposterously small feet of Ch'êng Shao Yün.

Kites of every size and color, so like the bats and birds they aped that from a greater distance Chü-po must have thought them the living things they pretended, were carried in each procession. And when a light wind rose the æolian harps and the tiny bells tailed on some of them made soft music in the perfumed air.

Gong-bearers headed each procession and each was closed by an indescribable motley crew of umbrellas, banner carriers, tall-hat lictors, title-bearers, servants carrying changes of raiment, mounted guards, foot-guards, regalia-bearers, more gongs, fans, bastinadoes, swords, bludgeons, soldiers, incense bearers, executioners, more umbrellas, bludgeons, road-clearers carrying whips, jesters and acrobats.

The coming notables seemed of equal rank. As they met, one descended from his green chair, the other from his horse. And the near-by retainers of each ranged themselves at the sides of the path, standing stolid and incurious, as if with their backs to walls.

The officials greeted each other with elaborate ceremony—but too, Ch'êng Chü-po thought, with cordial-ity.

One Chü-po knew well, had often seen; the man who had left his chair to do his friend courtesy and stood blinking short-sighted eyes in the strong sunlight, his spectacles in his hand, for no Chinese could be so uncouth as to wear glasses when speaking to another. The Mandarin I—I Kung Moy—came from Pekin now and again to hold long and earnest conference with the lady of Ch'êng, and sometimes Chü-po had been called in to listen to their talk. And always I brought Ch'êng Yün dwarf-trees to enrich the "dwarf" forest already a pride of China.

Wherever, whenever, I Kung Moy came politics was afoot. He was in every sense a party man, and of ceaseless activities. And Ch'êng Shao Yün was a great politician—China had no keener. She rarely left her own domain, but almost daily her runners passed to and fro, up and down China and across, by path and river, carrying messages of serious political import, messages to Pekin and Annam, to Manchuria and Quelpart, and like messages in return to her.

She and I were of one mind on almost every affair of state, and that this was so, explained why he had not been stopped at the gate. Ch'êng Shao Yün was always at home to I Kung Moy, and no custodian at her gates but knew to kot'ow him instant admission. Chü-po was sure that his mother had not been expecting the mandarin, or any other guest, but I had come unexpectedly once or twice before, and could never come unwelcome.

Yün would receive him as a Chinese lady should, when such reception was necessary, with a heavy curtain hanging between them. And so they would talk and argue, and presently, when the talk grew hot, she would jerk the curtain aside, beckon him to a nearer seat, and they would speak low—in whisper now and then—for hours, as man to man. And when he passed from her presence, her sons would be called to do him hospitalities. But his visit and his confidences invariably were to Ch'êng Shao Yün.

But for the presence of the other mandarin Chü-po was at a loss to account. Him Ch'êng Chü-po had never seen before. But the stranger must have had some password sufficient for the eastern gate.

So determined were the two men each to give the other precedence that they seemed fated to remain where they were, bowing and gravely gesticulating forever, inextricably stuck in a bog of politeness. But at last the stranger with a gesture drew the other's attention to a closely shuttered palanquin withdrawn a little from his own retinue resting on the ground now, and guarded by armed eunuchs. At that I Kung Moy bowed quite to the ground, averted his eyes from the deposited litter, and after many more obeisances, backed up the path that led to the homestead of the Ch'êngs. And I's retinue followed I.

The stranger turned as if some one had called to him from the palanquin, and went towards it eagerly. All the others—except the eunuch guard—turned their backs to it—and moved a little farther off.

The litter's curtains parted, and a figure stepped out on to the path, a slender figure that as it walked reminded Ch'êng of some one—he could not remember whom. It was a woman, her garments told him that, tissues and brocades of jade green, dark blue embroideries flower-shaped, trousers of orange silk, a jade-green and silver veil quite hiding her face. It was a woman of rank. Her bearing told that. She was young, her carriage told him, and happy and well. And somewhere he had seen her walk before. He was sure of that; some one he knew well walked as she walked. Odd!

The golden-lilied women have as many individualities of gait as big-footed women have. This girl— Chü-po was sure it was a girl—scarcely swayed as she left the path and climbed the sun-drenched hillock beyond. Almost she scarcely seemed to move, but she did move—rather rapidly. And the old man moved smiling at her side.

It did not occur to Ch'êng Chü-po that this might be his bride—his dreaded wife.

Nothing occurred to him except a dull throbbing sense that he no longer wished to be alone.

But even had he been still lord of his wits, no such thought could have occurred to him. His mother had promised him no move towards his marriage until after the Feast of Lanterns—and though China fell, Ch'êng Shao Yün's promise held.

He had seen a girl.

And he no longer wished to be alone.

A girl veiled and shrouded. A girl in some distance, two hill slopes and the width of a narrow meadow between, but still a girl, living, breathing, moving —and a girl of his own patrician caste—patrician as Ch'êng Shao Yün herself—or Ye-Ho-Na-Lah—the empress-wife.

And now Chü-po saw that there were other, curtained chairs behind hers—plainer and less obsequiously guarded—her attendant women doubtless.

The low apex reached, the girl stood still and looked

about her through her veil. Then her hands shot out
from the jade-green draperies. They were very tiny
hands, but their shape and the loveliness—he knew that
it was there—were hidden by a crush of rings. With
an imperious, girlish gesture she lifted her arms, and
the loose sleeves fell back, leaving them and their exquisite loveliness all naked in the rose rays of the afternoon's waning sun. Ch'êng Chü-po caught his breath;
it stabbed him in his throat. He had never seen his
mother's arms. He had not seen the arms of any of
his brothers' wives—or, if he had, he had not noticed
them. He had not dreamed that flesh could be so fair,
or pull one so. Why did not that old man fall at her
feet?

The girl lifted her veil—she flung it back.

It was a girl!

All the gods, yes; it was a girl.

She wore no paint on this journeying. Her delicate
face was amber-cream and faint oleander pink. Her
little curved mouth was redder than the rubies on her
hand. The little teeth that just showed in dazzling
purity when she smiled up at the tasseled blossoms of
the flowering tree were whiter than Omi's snow. The
narrow brows were painted on her peachy amber skin
with a sharp velvet brush—a daring stroke of black
across the soft cream. Trembling jewels flashed and
dangled from the black gloss of her hair. Her eyes
sparkled in the light, but were soft as some young doe's
and deep-pansy-dark within their lashes' lace-soft
fringe.

The boy trembled as he watched. Was she real?
Could anything so beautiful be real?

She reached up and pulled a flower from the tree
that seemed to bend down to her as if proud and glad

to be torn by such delicate fingers—rifled of its loveliness by such greater loveliness.

But it was her arms that moved him most—round girlish arms, chinked with dimples, molded exquisitely, slender, soft and virile. He had often noticed how pretty the roly-poly babies' arms were in the courtyards of his brothers' wives. And he had thought dimples were the lovely livery of babyhood. Did girls have dimples too? And, if one touched them, would they feel as the baby dimples did?

He flushed.

She drew the blossom she had filched across her face, and for a moment held it there. Then, as she tucked it in her robe, at something the man beside her said, she laughed aloud, and the music of her little voice tinkled across to Ch'êng Chü-po and smote him to the soul—sent the quick, startled blood racing through his frightened veins, and surging up his throat. Again he asked the gods, was it real? Could such music be real? Could such sweetness sound in common air?

The old man held out his hand—and she put her palm in his, flung the veil back across her face—and they retraced their way. Tenderly the man stowed her, as something very precious, in her chair. The bearers lifted it shoulder high—and they moved slowly toward Ch'êng's home—the mandarin riding close beside her chair—for his jacket told him that, the button on his cap, the cornelian beads hanging from his neck, and the caparisons of his steed.

The boy—but now a man—watched them until they were out of sight—and then he stumbled back to the calm old river's edge—as best he could—not as he had come, but gropingly by the longer, twisting, circuitous path—an easy, even, gentle foot-way that sloped down imperceptibly—its gradient was so gradual—but Ch'êng Chü-po, the goat-footed, stumbled as he went, slipped, and once he almost fell.

He slid down beside the river, his face crushed into the ferns at its brink—and lay as still as it. But presently he groaned aloud—it was a birth cry—groaned because he was alone.

CHAPTER VII

THE stars were out when he went slowly home. Hours had passed.

They came hurrying to meet him, and brought him rice. He thrust it away—and waved them back.

When he had bathed and dressed, he went to his mother's room, the little carved and scented room where she kept her privacy, and went in without asking or leave.

Ah Söng was crouched outside the threshold. She knew his step. She knew the importance and the secrecy that were going on within. But she made no motion or word to stay him, and as he passed within, a shrewd, prophetic smile flitted across her sightless face.

The sole concern of Chinese diplomacy in those days was—and up till then had been—foreign affairs. So perfect was Chinese patriarchy, so beautifully it worked, that there was little chance of internal broil, and none of any so serious as to merit or need the cognizance of Pekin—no excuse for "party" clash or mouthings. Happy the country that has no politics. And China had none until priest and adventurer came bringing her the Cross and gun-boat. And even then, when the diplomatic hydra reared its gory head it found no chink or rent to stick its claws in, and so into Chinese home affairs. But already a miasmic shadow crept into China from the sea, threatening her with disruption and disease—the shadow of newer, rawer civilizations; civilizations less civilized, less humane, less tested, less honest and less dignified. The slow, rough influx of foreign interests was creeping slowly upon the Chinese rivers, past the forts. As yet it had but fastened on a treaty-port or two, and cankered slyly at Shanghai and Hankow, Hongkong and Tientsin, at Foochow and at its tiny stronghold of Shamien. But the plague was in the air, and threatened China to her core. And already a devoted band of Chinese men—and women—watching had taken alarm; men trained in observation and quick in thinking—serious, sober men, unmovable in their belief that to alter China were to poison and to maim. A resolute, resourceful band with whom to think was to act.

Chinese politics was born on the day that Hamel landed at Quelpart. And it had grown apace. And from it had formed such political "parties" as China knew or Chinese contentment brooked: the Anti-foreigners Party and the Indifferents—one hating and attacking all foreigners and foreign influence—the other ignoring both.

Ch'êng Shao Yün's father had been absorbed before her—as his father before him—in politics, an anti-foreign agitation that was as much a patriotism as politics, and that same politics—with the self-same one aim—had been from before her early marriage the obsession of her soul, the secret but most strenuous and vital industry of her life.

To drive the foreign villains out—out and back to whence they came, affrighted and cured of any desire or power to return—that was the great aim of her life, and she worked at it and for it ceaselessly with all her imperious might and main.

But still the missionaries and the traders came, and in their wake the credentialed envoys so uncouth and ill-born that they did not know how to behave at a court, or how to kot'ow in the presence of a liege.

To drive the foreign vermin out, and to be rid of it forever, was the fierce and tender ambition of her being—and of her judgment.

And it was of that that Ch'êng Shao Yün and I Kung Moy talked and planned as they sat together in her carved and scented room, the red curtain of her seclusion flung wide aside, sex forgotten, etiquette kicked contemptuously away.

They were conventionals, full of prejudice, the man and the woman—she even more than he—filled with a burning hatred of all foreigners, an unreasoning love of the past and of old established ways, a venomous loathing of new, untrod paths, and of the human sign-posts of those alien paths, the priests, the merchants, travelers, sailors, envoys from the inferior scum-lands of unknown and undesired peoples.

But there is something to be said for their self-opinionated point of view:

There is little insanity in China. There was none until *we* came. She never borrowed a yen until we induced her to—and she has always paid her debts scrupulously. The Chinese have been the making of every Christian colony in the eastern seas. A race without deformities, self-keeping and self-kept, living in comfort and content, ambitious for happiness and the sweet things of life, well-ordered, spending happily, saving sanely and gladly, revering books, unaffectedly worshiping nature, loyal and obedient, holding womanhood as high as it has ever been held anywhere, holding old age and childhood higher, and cherishing them more nobly than ever has any other race, kept ever-young by its universal bubbling sense of humor, greatly endowed by high ideals to which it hourly matched its daily life, and strong and straight from a truer, stricter sense of justice than any other race has ever reached, family rancor unknown, nepotism a fineness and a cult, but never a self-seeking or a vanity, the Chinese had little need of Potsdam, Whitechapel or Washington, and have reaped what advantage from European intrusion? Perhaps not one!

Usually at their many conferences it was Ch'êng Shao Yün who talked, I Kung Moy who listened, Ch'êng Yün who instigated, suggested and elaborated. This little woman, who had left her own estate but four times in twenty years, who for all corporal contact with the world beyond her gates, lived for the most as closely cloistered as any nun of Carmel, was the fire-brand of China's foreign policy, and its strongest dynamic force. And she had never seen a European or looked into their history or their creeds of life and conduct.

But to-day it was the mandarin who talked, while Ch'êng Yün listened and watched with flashing eyes, and gathering brow, picking her fan to bits, tap-tapping the floor with her scrap of jeweled shoe.

Until now, I Kung Moy had come to ask advice; to analyze and weigh it—and then, almost always, to follow it.

To-day he had come from Pekin to give advice and to press it.

A spoilt, tempestuous woman, life-used to rule and to decide—her veriest whim the edict of her little world—yet she was too big to resent being advised by one whom she so respected and admired—so liked. A tyrant, without hesitation or scruple, she knew that give-and-take was the solvent and lubricant of life, and constantly she used it so. It was not his advising, but the advice itself that he gave that galled and revolted, and wreaked her vengeance on the ivory and tissue of her fan—galled and infuriated her none the less because as he drove each unwelcome point home, she saw it clearly and recognized its merit. Her gorge rose and sickened—her judgment weighed and approved. For such was her clarity and balance that when infuriated most she could think calmly, decide justly and coldly. To no delinquent coolie in her lime kilns could Ch'êng Shao Yün show crueler tyranny than she could at need show herself—and at need did.

I Kung Moy had come to urge a change of tactics on the part of the ring leaders of the anti-foreigners policy. And hearing him Ch'êng Yün stiffened and fumed, loathed and approved.

He had come to ask her to send Ch'êng Chü-po to Europe—not for a year, or in the open service of their liege—that would have been hideous enough—and such debasing work was for Manchus, if it must be done— she could not admit the necessity—but to send her son, her youngest, best-loved son to England unobtrusively, to go to school with English boys—to live among them for a term of years—to mingle with them in such intimacy as he could achieve, and of his seeking—for a long term of years—to eat their food—*to eat with them*—if they would let him—to assimilate their ways, to become, at least for a time, as nearly like them as he could.

Ch'êng Shao Yün sickened at the thought.

To solve a problem it is first necessary to understand

it—so ran his argument.   The evil of foreign invasion
was growing day by day.   Whether it could be overcome by force—and, if not by force, by what—it was
impossible to say until a more intelligent understanding was reached of just what these foreigners were,
what their aim—their methods, their ways and depth
of thought.   "To circumvent them, we must know
them."   To defeat them by force might prove impossible.   Probably it would.   Chinese military power was
too scattered, too antiquated—and military prestige
was, among the Chinese, too low.   Whatever these
English were or were not—it was the English he chiefly
feared.   They were the persistent race—they were
mighty warriors.   Of so much he was convinced.   The
Chinese were not warriors.   They had been, of course,
and they would be again.   He did not forget the Prince
of Han, Ta'so Ta'so, Kublai Khan, Ch'ai Shao, Tsung-
ping, Wu Sankwei or any warrior out of all the long
warrior line of her illustrious ancestry—or of his less
valiant own.   But now China was out of tune for war,
and naked of equipment.   Whether this could be re-
trieved in time, he doubted.   If not, the foreigners must
be defeated in other ways—circumvented, or their
fangs drawn.   Neither of these things could they hope
to do until they knew them.   And to know men you
must live among them.   The best blood, the best young
brains in China must be banished, for a time, sent to
Europe, steeped and veneered in European ways.

Ch'êng slashed her knee angrily with her girdle.   But
she listened—and questioned him reasonably enough.

"At closer range, in their native land, the English
might even be less detestable.   The lads put forth to
exile and to school might not find it too unendurable."

Ch'êng Yün shrugged wearily with a quiet uplift of

shoulder that said more than any mere bitterness of
words.

Already a start had been made. He was sending
his own grandson to study in the home of an English
priest—the mandarin eyed Ch'êng Yün anxiously.
But she smiled a little indifferently. She had no fear
of Chü-po's apostasy, and, as for the contamination,
it was all contamination. That Chü-po might have to
listen to English prayers, enter English Joss houses,
was not worth a frown. To her mind religions were
made for man, not man for religions. She thought a
man as justified in changing his god and his temple as
in changing a coat, when it convenienced him. It
sounds a lax attitude for a woman, but it was characteristically Chinese. She worshiped her gods punctili-
ously, but she judged them shrewdly. She paid them
well—as she did her servants—but she expected them
to do their part. She had thrashed a too dilatory god
once, and she might do so again. I Kung Moy was a
native of southern China. He took his religion less
casually.

He hurried on, relieved. He was sending I Kow
to school with a learned man, and later, when he knew
the tongue and could pass the examination, to a place
called Ox-ford.

"It is terrible! I shall suffer—torture," Ch'êng
Shao Yün said slowly—interrupting him at last. "But
since it is needed, I will not grudge. For China—no
sacrifice is too great for China."

"Lady," the old man began, "Chuang Tzŭ told his
disciple——"

Ch'êng Chü-po burst into the room, and flung himself at his mother's feet—clasping her shoe in two eager
hands.

Ch'êng Shao Yün motioned with her shattered fan towards the mandarin.

But Ch'êng Chü-po spared no heed to I Kung Moy. "Mother," he cried, "I have seen a girl!"

"The place is full of girls," she said coldly. "There are a hundred in the north silkworm shed." She understood him perfectly and instantly. But she had no mind that I Kung Moy also should. "The place is full of girl things," she repeated with a tiny shrug.

Ch'êng Chü-po rose impatiently, stood before her straight and strong. His face was drawn and moved. But it glowed. And his eyes leapt into hers—imperious now as he rose.

"I have seen a girl," he told her again—proudly—"a lady girl."

I Kung Moy rose from his chair, passed quietly from the room, and left them alone: the mother and the boy that she knew that she had lost.

CHAPTER VIII

SELFISHLY—of course—Ch'êng Yün had been content that Chü-po should regard marriage with reluctance. The boy was very dear to her, and he was all she had—all that was quite her own. To her older sons she was more than their children or their wives. Every Chinese mother is that. No younger woman, no child that he has begotten, can oust a Chinese mother from the first place in the heart of the man that she has borne. That is the great security in every Chinese woman's life. No wonder that they long for sons. Let her but bear a son, and she is forever supreme with *one*. A Chinese father's influence is enormous, his authority unquestioned and autocratic, but a mother's are much more. Each son that Yün had borne was filial, and had remained so always. But the six elder she shared now with wives and children, with friends and quick interests of their own. But until this hour Chü-po—always, and always to be, the dearest of her sons—had been *all hers*. As a little child he had never had a toy he would not push away at her approach. He had a hunter's blood. But as a boy never he went hawking, but he looked back at her as he went. A word from her would call him back—and gladly back— the hawk forgotten and dismissed. He had liked the books that she had bid him like. He had seen pictures and porcelains with her eyes—and the very flowers that grew beside their paths, the wonderful panorama of the Chinese outer world. He had thought her

49

thoughts, breathed with her breath. The pulsing of her heart had been his. And all the love-light in his eyes had been hers—his unsoiled young passion hers. It was gone.

And in one hour she was called upon to sacrifice him to an absence that tore her to contemplate, an absence of long wearying years in an environment she abhorred and feared, called upon to yield Chü-po to that, to read in his altered face, his crisper voice, that she had been struck from her foremost place, thrust beyond a barrier—sent into the outer cold.

The gods forbid, and all her womanliness forbade, that she should wish him unhappiness, or in the marriage she decreed less than content. She would see to it that he was content, satisfied with his wife, shielded in quiet and in peace by a quiet, docile girl—a wife she'd choose so well that no scratching of his ease could come. But she had wished the gift to be from her— all that blessed, all that stirred him, from her; as much her sole giving as her milk had been.

Fate had stolen a dastardly march on her.

Not that Ting Tzŭ—she knew whom he must have seen, though he did not—could hold him from her long; his mother would be first and warmest with Chü-po when the marriage glamor had passed—*if* she let it come to that.

But he had begged her to hold her hand until the Feast of Lanterns had come and gone; and she had been well pleased to have him beg, well pleased to keep her dreams with his, to match his will with hers; and she had thought to keep him *all* her own, all for her loving, all loving of her, until the Lanterns had swung and blazed, and burned out.

Ah well—what was, was.

"Sit," she said gently, "and tell me."

"Yes, I'll try," he said eagerly.

It had been the habit of his fearless lifetime to answer her always readily, frankly and without embarrassment. Not so to-day. The words halted, and when they lagging came, came stupidly.

Ch'êng Shao Yün did not help him out.

She had always helped him before when any intricate telling had seemed to baffle his younger grasp of fact and use of words. All confidence between them till now had been mere dialogue and gossip interchanged, friendliest conference, rather than soliloquy, recital or confession. When he had knelt beside her as a boy to tell her of his first offense —the ruin of a priceless dwarf oak-tree, a century old and less than six inches high, against which his ball had dashed, he had played with her fan as he spoke, and she had heard him with her hand on his arm.

And—"Well, what of it?" she had said. "A sweeper will sweep it up. One priceless tree will not be missed from the thousanded forest of the Ch'êngs."

And he had nodded happily, and begged some treat for the morrow. And they had gone together laughing to their rice.

Not so to-day. Ch'êng Chü-po did not touch any garment of hers, or she of his. She heard him silently —that was ominous—and watched him grimly through half-shut, brooding eyes.

He told it lamely, but told it all. Her lips curled a little at his description of the girl. Ch'êng Shao Yün had seen many girls.

When he had done, the woman said dryly, "How do you know that she is one of us?"

Ch'êng Chü-po laughed. It was answer enough—
the proud quality of that laugh.

"Did she see you?" Yün asked him sharply.

"No," he said, "no one saw me." The woman's face
cleared a little.

"No one must know but you and me."

"Of course," the boy replied.

Ch'êng Yün sat deep in rapid thought. The girl
was damaged—in that a marriageable man had looked
upon her unveiled face. But the girl herself was innocent of the catastrophe. And the damage was slight,
even in Ch'êng Shao's exigent judgment. Such
chance preëncounters were not unknown in Chinese
life. And in Chinese romances they were a commonplace—the pivot of half the novels written from Lo
Kuan-Chung and Shih Nai-an to Wang Shih Ch'êng
—from P'u Sungling till to-day.

Ch'êng Chü-po came nearer, and knelt down again
beside her.

"Mother! You will give her to me? I was born
for her."

Ch'êng Yün rose angrily. So! She had borne her
man-child for an unknown girl chit! Indeed! She
paced the room hotly. But she controlled herself, and
said presently, speaking dryly from the casement side,
looking at him again, not too kindly, "How? We do
not know even who she is."

"I do not," Chü-po retorted quietly. "But they
came here."

"Oh!" Yün conceded grudgingly. "Then it must
have been Ting Lo that you saw."

"The mandarin Ting?"

His mother nodded. "They brought me word that
he was here. I did not expect him. But I was willing

that he should visit Ch'êng Ping-yang, and sent your
brother word to welcome him and give him tendence,
and entrance to Ch'êng Ping-yang."

So—it was the father of his eldest brother's wife that
he had seen—the old man on the bedizened palfrey.

"He was welcome to welcome," Ch'êng Yün went on.
"But I did not know that he had brought a woman in
his train!"

"He seemed more like in hers."

The mother made an impatient gesture with her
hands.

"Chut!" she said.

"And the lady?" he asked, "Tell me her name."

"I do not know," she said sullenly. But in her heart
she knew.

"The daughter," he began, "is——"

"Daughter!" his mother scoffed. "More probably a
new young wife!"

"No," Ch'êng Chü-po said, "she is no wife. It was
father and maid I saw."

"So ho! precocity! You are very shrewd. His wife,
I say!" It was a jealous lie. "Old men are fools."
That was not a Chinese theory. But Ch'êng Shao Yün
was always independent in her words, and sometimes
in her thoughts. And she was angry with the gods.

But Ch'êng Chü-po shook his head. She could not
frighten him so. And nothing could frighten him
to-day.

Then he went towards her where she stood by the
open casement, and held out his hands, his face quivering with tenderness—and, too, with understanding.
For a moment she kept him at bay. Then she smiled—
a little—and took his face in her hands.

"My little boy!" She whispered it. And her eyes filled with tears.

"My mother!" His eyes brimmed too.

"You will always love me, Chü-po?" It was the old prayer of universal motherhood. It choked her as she spoke.

"Always," he said stoutly.

He linked her arm in his, and they leaned together looking out at the stars.

"The night is very still, Chü-po! . . . . And how sweet our garden smells. . . . . Our country is very beautiful, my son."

They held their tryst a little so—and it was reconciliation too: his atonement, her conceding—her relinquishment.

"Wait," she told him presently. "You must wait, Chü-po."

"But not long!"

She smiled. But she neither promised nor refused. And she sent him from her then, and forbade him to come again until she sent.

In all his eighteen years Ch'êng Chü-po had always gone to his sleeping mat at his mother's bidding. So complete had been her dominance of him that almost invariably he had not only lain down, but had actually slept when she told him to.

To-night he did not even go in the direction of his apartments. He passed out into the night, paced the garden paths from bed to bed, from lake to little water-fall, beyond the lotus pond on the terrace—telling his story to the drowsy flowers and to the night.

This was his betrothal night. In his heart he vowed it so.

A serving woman passed near him going to the house. Chü-po knew her for an attendant of Ping-yang, his eldest brother's wife. And he ran after her and called her to him. She came readily enough—she had nothing to hide or fear. Her mistress had sent her on her late errand.

"You have visitors in your courtyard?" Ch'êng Chü-po began.

"Yes, honorable lord."

"Your honorable lady's honorable father—and—her honorable sister."

"Before evening rice they came, thrice honorable sir."

"Can you tell me the most honorable maiden's name?"

Nan Tung shot him a shrewd glance. But she answered in a moment in a steady voice—her eyes subserviently cast down.

"Ting Tzŭ, my honorable lord," she said, "Ting Tzŭ."

Ch'êng Chü-po turned and walked away—no longer knowing that the serving woman was there—or lived. And Nan Tung scuttled off, laughing softly, to the house.

"Ting Tzŭ," Ch'êng Chü-po breathed it twice.

"Ting Tzŭ," he told the moon. And then he told the little flowers. He told the tiny twisted trees in the forest of dwarf oaks, and the passion flowers. He told the lotus cups sleeping fragrant on the burnished bosom of the lake. And his heart was beating very fast.

Far into the night Ch'êng Shao Yün sat where he had left her—gazing broodingly into space.

When she had gone into her sleeping room, disrobed, and lain down on her mat, Ah Söng, lying, as was her service, just outside her mistress's door, heard Ch'êng Shao Yün sobbing piteously—hard, bitter, racking sobs.   Ah Söng had not heard Ch'êng Yün sob before since the night Ch'êng Yün's lord had died.

CHAPTER IX

CH'ÊNG PING-YANG leaned giggling against the sundial in her own courtyard and Nan Tung squatted giggling at her feet.

"Get up," Ping-yang said, pushing the maid with her shoe, "and go now. Tell him to come at once—that I bid him haste—that Ch'êng Ko is crying for him, and will not be comforted."

Nan Tung jerked herself up with alacrity. "Oh, he'll make haste," she cried, as she ran.

"And so must I," Ping-yang said turning to the house.

The wife of Ch'êng Hsu was the mischief-maker of the place. But her practical jokes were harmless, friendly even, as a rule, and she was more liked than disliked by them all. A plump little creature with wicked eyes and nimble wits, she had considerable strength of will, well-cloaked by a careless manner, and an ever ready laugh. Her will and her mother-in-law's never clashed. Their lives ran on lines that rarely met and never crossed; and Yün, somewhat underestimating the other's mentality, as intellectual women so often do that of those whose mental tastes differ from their own, little thought how often Ping-yang took her own way, or how persistently she pursued it. Still less did the dowager suspect how much Ch'êng Ping-yang influenced not only her husband, somewhat phlegmatic and easily led, but all the courtyard lives, and many of the retinue without. Ch'êng Yün thought Ping-yang the least interesting of all her daughters-in-law, but liked her for being a contented, sunny little thing, lazy at her needle, but a capital nurse, skilled at the zither, a devoted mother, and, best of all, a peace-maker in that crowded place—a little dull—but, some of us must be dull. It was a blemish, but not a crime. And Yün thanked the gods that in the matter of wives, Ch'êng Hsu was so easily satisfied. It would have humiliated her to have had a marriage she had negotiated turn out unpleasantly.

Ch'êng Ping-yang was far from dull. But she was essentially a woman's woman. She cared little for men —which was perhaps as well; for with her kitten-purring ways, her skill at making menus, and her gluttony for fun, and expertness in getting her own way, she might have brought domestic water to the boil, and her husband to some annoyance, if nothing worse, had she had a mind for coquetry.

For women's women Ch'êng Yün had little flair. She herself was a man's woman—the friend and liker of men—and from her birth men had been within her thrall. Virtuous always, living, until the limited emancipation of her widowhood, hidden within the courtyard and the "flowery" quarters of her home, yet she had been loved by many men. Her father had been her serf. Her brothers had adored her. Her sons, only less than her husband had been, were all her lovers. There was not a man—from the poorest coolie—on the place that had not some feeling of affection for her. They liked to see her come—even though she came to berate and tyrannize—and the bigger men that came to see her from Pekin and from Söul and Nanking, came eagerly—and more than one made excuses to come. She had the qualities that lure men, and the qualities that hold them too: a rarer gift. She had much beauty, sparkle, a quick wit, and that indescribable greatest quality of all: Charm—the quality that lasts longest, and survives most—lasts through the disfigurements of age and pain and poverty, lasts till death— lasts and persists as only one other quality does, the quality of high breeding.

It is the woman's woman that is a matchmaker. The man's woman rarely is. If men care quickly for her, she as quickly cares for men. And she has no special delight in any man's absorption in any woman other than herself.

Ch'êng Yün had married her sons from duty, and being her duty she had done it well. But she had done it somewhat coldly. And now that the time had come —and almost passed—for the marriage of Ch'êng Chü- po, in her heart she had disliked it more than he.

Ch'êng Ping-yang was match-maker to her curled and shielded fingernails. She had ached and itched for years to make a match—and curtailed as the opportunities of a guarded, patrician Chinese woman, locked within her manless courtyard, are, she had encompassed it now and then. Several marriages between the retainers on the estate had been made by her. And at least two of her brothers-in-law had fallen deeply in love—after marriage—with their wives, under the direct impulsion of her machinations. But she had longed with all her merry soul to be the dea ex machina of a true romance—a love affair of quality. And now she thought she saw her way. No wonder that she bubbled happily as she ran off—and the very pearls hanging from her hair glowed and clattered merrily and were glad.

When Ting Ping-yang had left her early home for

the long journey in her flowery chair she had felt one keen grief, the deepest sorrow of her life, and through all her placid, contented married life it had lived on in her jolly little heart, an active gnawing sorrow still. The leaving of a baby sister had wrung her heart.

And now that sister, a slender, soft-eyed girl with amber rose-petal hands, who had just reached the marriage years, had come with their father to visit her.

Ting Tzŭ had not seen Ch'êng Chü-po the day before, but Sun Fuh, one of her waiting women, had— and had gossiped of it to Nan Tung, wondering who the slender young lordling was, all dressed in gold-wrought satin and brocade, but with a hunter's pointed face, who had stood and gazed and gazed with hungry eyes on the unveiled features of Ting Tzŭ. And Nan Tung—knowing well enough who it must have been, had regossiped it all to Ch'êng Ping-yang when she had tied her hair, and Ch'êng Ping-yang had chuckled and hatched a plan, and had given Nan Tung a tinseled scarf on which Tung had often thrown a lustful eye.

How good the gods! She must try to remember to burn them an hundred extra joss sticks. She really must, the dear, good gods! Her heart had sung to them yesterday when her father, in answer to her imploring of years, had brought to her Ting Tzŭ. That surprise had suffused her with happiness. But now! now she saw a way to secure Tzŭ's return again, and always stay. O, gods! O, gods! That very night for evening rice, she would make for their father a compote of apricots such as he loved best.

"Ch'êng Ko," she called, as she ran through her rooms, "Where are you, my fat frogling? I want you, Ch'êng Ko!"

When Nan Tung gave her message to Ch'êng Chü-po he followed her, as she had foreseen, readily enough—and without surprise. Ch'êng Ping-yang often sent for him. They were special friends. And when spoilt Ch'êng Ko was ill or very bad, nothing else could heal or reform him so surely as a visit from his playmate and uncle, Ch'êng Chü-po. Ch'êng Chü-po came with Nan Tung at once, and no less willingly because the summons had come from the sister of Ting Tzŭ.

When Nan Tung brought Chü-po into the courtyard, and left him there, Ch'êng Ping-yang was waiting impatiently just inside her own door-way, Ch'êng Ko in her arms. When she saw Chü-po she set the baby sharply down on his yellow feet, and as she pushed him through the open doorway she gave the sturdy plumpness below his spine a sounding spank. It did not hurt him unendurably, but it offended and outraged him intensely. And the angry baby ran bleating to Chü-po —which was just what his mother had intended him to do.

Chü-po caught up and cuddled him, and Ping-yang dashed back into the house.

Ping-yang was almost crying when she burst into the room where her young sister sat sorting skeins of silk.

"Go—go find it for me, Tzŭ, go quickly. Ch'êng Hsu will kill me, if he learns I've lost it!"

Ting Tzŭ rose slowly. Naturally she had not seen much of the brother-in-law, and was supposed not to have seen him at all. But the gossip of the flowery quarters is detailed and shrewd. The idea of harmless Ch'êng Hsu killing a fly was absurd, let alone his slaughter of the wife that under his mother ruled him.

"Go where? Lost what?" the girl said lazily, more amused than interested.

"The little dragon of jade he gave me when Ch'êng Ko was born, and swore me always to wear, but never to lose. Go, girl, go and find it quickly, or I shall go mad." And Ping-yang sank down on her heels in a frenzy of weeping that seemed to indicate prompt fulfillment of the prediction of Ch'êng Hsu's wife-slaughter.

"Where do you think the bauble is?" Ting Tzŭ said coolly.

"Bauble!" screamed Ping-yang. "Oh! my jade dragon. Oh! I tell you find it, Ting Tzŭ."

"Where?"

"I must have dropped it near the sun-dial in the courtyard, near the Hoang Ko tree when Ko was tugging at my chains."

Ting Tzŭ sauntered towards the door.

"Hurry," Ping-yang begged.

"It is too hot to hurry." But she sauntered a little less provokingly slowly.

But Ping-yang sprang up vehemently, and rushing to her, clutched her back. "Not like that," she said in a sharp, business-like voice, pulling a stick pin from Ting Tzŭ's hair and thrusting it in again at what she considered a more seductive slant. "Wait! Wait, I say, you need more paint!"

But that was too much. Ting Tzŭ thrust her off. "You *have* gone mad," the younger sister mocked. "More paint to go look for an old stick pin in the courtyard. Was it a stick pin though?" she added from the doorway, "or a dangle of your chain?"

"Yes—yes. I mean both!"

"Indeed! And what kind of jade?"

"Yes, yes. Any kind."

Ting Tzŭ's lazy suspicion was convinced and scoffing

skepticism now. But she threw her sister a scornful glance, and went off, laughing to herself, to see what was at the sun-dial near the Hoang Ko tree—to see what hoax Ch'êng Ping-yang was playing now.

Ch'êng Chü-po was at the sun-dial near the Hoang Ko tree, playing with Ch'êng Ko.

Ting Tzŭ saw him before he saw her. She gave a little smothered breath, and went a step nearer him. If he had never seen a girl, she had seen many men young and comely. She had many brothers, and more than once at home and from the curtains of her palanquin had peeped. A tiny smile curved her pretty painted lips. She knew now why Ping-yang had cried out for more rouge, and told her idiotic lies about a bit of jade that was stick pin, neck dangle and both. She took another step, a very cautious step, gave a tiny musical scream, dropped her eyes in great confusion, and stood stock still—one hand clutching her robe above her heart —a terrified girl too overcome to retreat or move.

Ch'êng Chü-po looked up, and Ko fell thump upon the ground—too angry even to cry out. But he might have cried the courtyard down, for all the help he could have wrung from aunt or uncle now.

Their hour had come.

There was neither question nor entreaty in Ch'êng Chü-po's blazing eyes. They worshiped, but they claimed her. And as he gazed she lifted her jeweled head and looked at him.

It was betrothal.

Neither spoke, or yet thought to speak. There was no need.

Ch'êng Ko sucked his thumb amazed—too interested now to wail, or assert his outraged dignity.

Ch'êng Chü-po held out a hand.

Ting Tzŭ went toward him a step.   Birds have gone to snakes so, and sunflowers turned toward the sun.

Ch'êng Chü-po reached out both arms.

"My lord!" she whispered to him.

"Ting Tzŭ!" he cried at that, and moved on her, but not far—with all the passion of his sex and years in face and voice—and all the passion of his passionate race, all the passion of inviolate manhood patrician born.

Ko wriggled fatly afoot, to get a fuller view.

"Ting Tzŭ," whispered Chü-po tenderly, as her mother might have done.

The dark-eyed girl gave a little joyful sob.   Then, at a thought, she clapped sudden palms to her face, and ran like a lap-wing into the house.   It was genuine.   She had remembered how little paint she wore, and was shocked and appalled at the indecency of his having seen her so.   And Ch'êng Chü-po understood, and loved her better for her modesty.

She brushed by Ping-yang, inside the door, and would not be caught; but she called over her shoulder as she fled, "Ch'êng Ko has swallowed your jade dragon."

CHAPTER X

BALKED of her sister, Ch'êng Ping-yang betook her to her son. But Ch'êng Ko had found his anger again, and his voice and finger-nails. Twice outraged within an hour! It infuriated him to the proud baby soul of him. He would have none of her. He spat naughty names at her, and toddled off to find Nan Tung.

Ping-yang crept out to the courtyard.

Ch'êng Chü-po was standing very still. And when she saw his face, Ping-yang, sex-wise, did not speak to him, but turned and went slowly back.

She was well pleased at her success.

At last, she'd made a match. And such a match!

There might be trouble with Ch'êng Shao Yün. Probably there would. It was quite impossible to say. Good luck to it, if there were! It would be her next game to play—her next trick to win.

All that day Ch'êng Shao Yün, after she had made time to send for Ting Lo, and welcome him, sat in conference with I Kung Moy.

Toward sunset they sent for the older mandarin, and late into the night the three sat together, deep in earnest talk—talk of China and her perils, and no word of marriage crept into it.

A dozen international encroachments shadowed in the air even then, and one or two were well afoot. Japan longed and schemed for some excuse to seize

Korea, that pointed like a dagger at her throat.   Shantung and Liatung were marked for pawns in the game
that Russia and Germany played, and were only too
ready to play bloodily.   And in that game, even then,
Japan dreamed to take a hand, sharpening deadly
weapons stealthily beneath her pretty robes of flower-
and-butterfly embroidered silk.   England held Hong
Kong, and held it arrogantly, newly naming its city
and port after England's own queen, and telling decent
Chinese at what hour they must scurry from the freedom of the streets.

Strict sense of time is not a Chinese trait.   And
among the wealthy there is almost none.   When they
are drowsy or weary they lie down.   When they are
hungry they eat.   And when they talk interminably
tossing a subject back and fro—tearing it to tatters,
leaving the main issue for ten hundred by-paths—
harking back to it again and again—stripping it naked,
dressing it in every elaborate garnishment of quota-
tion, simile, historical allusion, metaphor, poetical quo-
tations, every other sentence loaded with epigram—
time ceases to move for them.   The cliché has great
pride of place on every Chinese tongue.   Statesmen,
little children, fine ladies and beggar men use common tags of speech, bits of old fable and countless
epigrams as surely as they talk.   Only Chinese memories could hold the store of common lore, of national
philosophy and classic tags of thought and speech
that pack the Chinese mind high and low.   And only
a Chinese mind could have followed the intricacies
and digressions of the long converse of Ch'êng Shao
Yün, I Kung Moy and Ting Lo.   But for all its seeming disjointment, it was succinct to them—a variegated

expression of one crisp axiom: The Foreigner must go—and a careful canvass of how to enforce it.

At its close—for to-day at least—it had been agreed that each should contribute a son or grandson—one or more—and much taels to the immediate furtherance of the Cause.

It was characteristic of Ch'êng Yün that having accepted the necessity of banishing to Europe much of China's best youth, risking and subjecting them to all that might befall them there, a necessity bitterly repugnant to her, she should push hotly to its accomplishment. I Moy had come to urge her: she urged him now.

But when there seemed little more to say for the moment on these things, and she clapped her hands for guest-tea to be brought, and the mandarins were about to take the hint—as they must—and go, she turned to the father of her daughter-in-law, and expressed her pleasure that he had brought with him his younger girl.

And the pleasure she spoke in courtesy might have been sincere enough had but Chü-po kept his chance view to himself. If Ping-yang had not been Ch'êng Shao's favorite daughter-in-law, she had been her least troublesome one, and a marriage between Chü-po and Ting Tzŭ would fit in rarely with his mother's plans. The girl's dower would be enormous. The girl's ancestry could not have been bettered. And here was an unforced opportunity at hand to see the girl's person, and study her character for herself before initiating a proposal from which it might be awkward to withdraw. But Chü-po's ill-advised display of willingness made Ch'êng Shao Yün strangely unwilling for the match. However, the girl was here, and she might as well have a look at her. Indeed, hospitality and the merest politeness demanded that and more. So when Ting left Ch'êng Shao Yün he took a gracious message, saying that on the morrow they should meet.

Ting Tzŭ had been surprised that the message had not come before, and Ping-yang was affronted by the delay, and for that all the more determined to circumvent the opposition from Ch'êng Yün, which she foresaw, to the consummation of the match she had so successfully made.

Ch'êng Shao Yün would have preferred to take Ting Tzŭ unaware, by running across her at some unusual hour in Ping-yang's quarters. But she concluded to begin with no such flagrant breach of etiquette her acquaintance with a girl so high born and who might become the first wife of her favorite son—though she had practically determined that the girl should not.

She knew that this was weakness on her part; and she despised it. But Ch'êng Shao Yün had taken her own way too long to be thwarted of it even by herself. She had determined to send Chü-po to England because she loved him less than she loved China, and to part with him, to lose him even, would hurt her less than it would to refrain from any possible service to China. And, if China were to be benefited by this new hideous means, the house of Ch'êng must not be left out of the priesthood of the sacrificial movement. And, if a Ch'êng were sent, it must be the best of all the Ch'êngs. But in the selection of a bride she felt no such compulsion to scourge herself. It was for her to select, and for Chü-po to accept. And she intended that it should be so.

Chü-po had made no attempt to see Ting Tzŭ again. The sisters had expected it, and Nan Tung had hovered near his door and across his path, ready to take a token or a word. Chü-po understood why he ran across the handmaid so often in one day, but he gave no sign. And, fortunately, it did not occur to him that her mistress had given her the cue—still less that Ting Tzŭ was party to the ruse. Nor was Ting Tzŭ. Chü-po's name had not passed her pretty painted lips, nor any hint of him.

The Chinese boy was finer than his women-folk. He had been glad of the encounter that had confirmed his infatuation of the previous day. But he had no wish to press farther a clandestine suit. He had her promise, and she had accepted his. That was fixed and firm, although no word had passed beyond his whisper of her name, her whisper of "My lord." It was ecstasy to know that they were bound—indissolubly bound, and that they mutually acknowledged it, and mutually rejoiced. But all the rest should be done in propriety, as his ancestors and hers had been wedded for three thousand years. He had no wish to see Ting Tzŭ again, or hear her voice, until he lifted the red veil from her face on their marriage hour. If another meeting now had been offered him in plainer terms, he would have avoided it. And had her shadow fallen upon the grass when he walked by the tulip beds, he would have turned his eyes aside, and strode away. While they lived he would not yield her or his right in her. Nothing should move him from that. But he would not approach her until marriage—scarcely with a thought—or suffer her to be cheapened. But when he learned that she and Ping-yang were going at noon to the temple in the bamboo grove, he hurried to the path beside the flamingoes' house where she must pass, and strewed it with jessamine flowers—not ostentatiously, but here and there a spray that might all have fallen from some careless hand—that he might go there again and find perhaps some spray her foot had crushed.

Nan Tung, watching, saw him do it. But she told no one but Ah Söng, not even Ch'êng Ping-yang, and Ah Söng told no one.

And when passing by the yellow oleanders Ch'êng Ping-yang exclaimed and bent down to lift up a spray of jessamine—Nan Tung stayed her with a cry. The lady must not, it was ill-luck. And Ping-yang, as superstitious as any living woman, obeyed. But Ting Tzŭ said, "What nonsense. Where is it written? Nowhere, I think. We have no such warning in Chihli," and bent down and lifted up the spray, and smelling it drew it across her face, and tucked it at her throat. And another spray, that she did not see, she trod upon and crushed a little with her light foot.

And Nan Tung fell behind giggling.

CHAPTER XI

IT was the same day that the three—Ch'êng Yün and her guests—sat in such long conclave, that Ping-yang and her sister went to the temple to pray, to deck it with a lotus flower at the old god's feet, and to fume it with joss-sticks. The old year had but two days to run, and on New Year's Day all must be in order for the gods, and all slight earth enmities forsworn, all earth debts paid. And still more must temples be swept and decked, and gods appeased when the Feast of Lanterns—but seventeen days off now—dawned.

The old joss sat on a pedestal, and Ting Tzŭ tiptoed up to stare him in the face. It was wonderful how the little mutilated feet—just one toe each—could do it. But they did. And Ting Tzŭ swayed in perfect balance leisurely, and took a good, long look.

"He needs a new coat of paint," she said disgustedly, tottering down on to her heels, "and lots of gilt."

"Our gods all do," Ping-yang answered with a shrug. "They are all a shabby sight. I wouldn't keep a coolie so. But Ch'êng Shao Yün is angry with the gods, and keeps them so for punishment."

Ting Tzŭ was a pious little thing, but she was in no humor to join in criticism of the lady mother of Ch'êng Chü-po. "The gods must do their part," she said.

"They have to here," Ch'êng Ping-yang laughed, "or go like poor Wealth God, and worse. See," and she touched a deep welt in the lacquer shoulder of the god, "Ch'êng Yün thrashed him well one day. And I have heard her threaten to burn him."

Ting Tzǔ was plainly shocked. But she only said gently, "I shouldn't like to burn a god." But she tiptoed up again and dusted the Wealth God's grimy nose with her scarf, and touched his long, ugly scar compassionately. "Never mind," she whispered as she lit another bundle of incense, and stuck it where the slightest breeze must puff its delicious sweetness up to the worn and paintless nose, "you shall have a new coat, a very bright new coat of paint, and lots of finest gilt some day." And then blushing furiously at what the promise implied of her future power in the temples of the Ch'êngs, she plumped down on her heels and was lost in prayer.

"Trusting a foreigner is 'like climbing a tree to catch a fish,' " Ch'êng Yün was saying, when Ting Tzǔ had bent down and picked up a yellow jessamine spray, and she was saying the self-same thing two hours later when Ch'êng Chü-po slipped through the oleander trees, and caught up a spray of jessamine from the grass.

It was early next day when Ch'êng Shao Yün sent for Ting Tzǔ. The girl was glad to go, and rose, shy but eager, when the message came. She had grown a little impatient waiting for the courtesy. Ch'êng Yün bade Ping-yang to her presence too, but Ping-yang was seized with a sudden cramp, pressed her hands to her head, and toddled moaning to her own room, sending a humble message to her husband's mother by Ch'êng Hsu. Then she clapped her hands

for Nan Tung to let down all the blinds, all but half
of one nearest her mat, then bring her a novel and a
gorge of rich sweetmeats. And Ting Tzŭ went in to
Ch'êng Yün alone.

The stricken Ping-yang dearly would have liked to
have gone too, and listen and watch. But as the elder
and married sister etiquette would have obliged Yün
to address to her most of her remarks and attention,
and Ping-yang contentedly secure of the impression
the child would make, and divining too that Ting Tzŭ
would be less embarrassed so, resigned herself to solitude—which she hated—to cramp and to sweetmeats.

And so Ting Tzŭ went in alone.

The girl was frightened and very shy. But she
was happy.

Ting Tzŭ was prepared to love.

Ch'êng Shao Yün was prepared to hate.

Sometimes love conquers hate. Sometimes hate conquers love.

Ch'êng Yün had made but little toilet. Why should
she? Even to herself she would not acknowledge that
the visitor she had sent for was, in any sense, a rival.
Ch'êng Yün dressed with care and splendidly for guests
of importance, for Chü-po always, and for the gods,
when they were good, but by no chance for a little girl
who came but for an hour.

She sat on a low dais at the carved and cushioned
divan's farther side—alone but for blind Ah Söng,
who sat in the shadow of the divan tatting noiselessly.

Yes—the girl was beautiful. Ch'êng Yün could but
see it at a glance. The robe of violet satin embroidered
with lemon chrysanthemum flowers and gray-green
leaves, slashed open above a vest and trousers of bright,

delicate green, turquoise-sewn and tied with silver cords, each end a pearl, and the jewels that she wore —rings, nail protectors, buttons sparkling on her coat, and all the gems pendant from her hair were rich and beautiful, even in China. But they were little to the girl. And with all her Chinese worship of beauty speaking in her veins, Ch'êng Yün found the friendly, lovely eyes a little hard to hate. And the child's carriage was as faultless as her face. Even in dingy, soiled sackcloth she must have looked unmistakably what Chü-po had proudly called her: a lady girl. The jessamine in her hair was no sweeter than her timid smile. And when Ch'êng Yün looked down sharply at the other's feet, she almost smiled, her face grew a little more amiable, and Ah Söng knew that her sigh was one of relief. The feet of Ting Tzŭ were just a shade larger than the feet of Ch'êng Shao Yün.

That they had been well bound the woman knew the instant she saw her move. Ting Tzŭ swayed like a zephyr-buffeted lily as she came, but she neither staggered nor splodged. Ting Tzŭ was mistress of her feet. And when Yün spoke to her, she answered in a voice that was startlingly sweet. No wonder Chü-po had lost his silly head. What must he not have done, if he had heard that scented, silver voice?

Ch'êng Yün bade Ting Tzŭ to a seat, and when all the needed ceremonial things had been said, she questioned her, "How do you like Ho-nan?"

"Here," Ting Tzŭ told her, "and for leagues before we reached your honorable gates, it is more beautiful even than my own home. But my honorable father, who has traveled much, tells me that all China is very beautiful."

"In which province would you wish to live when you are wedded?" Yün said graciously.

Ting Tzŭ reddened a little beneath her paint—she was well painted to-day—but the eyes lifted to the shrewder woman's eyes did not flinch. "That," she answered quietly, "is as my honorable father pleases."

"But have you had no dream—of a province?"

"Of a province, honorable lady, oh, yes. I have dreamed always of Shantung."

"Why?" Ch'êng Yün said sharply.

"That I might live in the province of the holy crystal tree," the girl said softly.

Ah Söng laid her tatting on the checkered floor, and rose and stood near Ting Tzŭ.

"Shantung!" exclaimed Ch'êng Yün, "there are devils dicing for Shantung—devils that live on a river called the Rhine, devils from Nippo, and for all I know from France and England too."

"They must be killed, then," Ting Tzŭ said proudly. And hatred had had a blow—beneath the belt perhaps. But often it is so that women hit.

Ah Söng sat down on the floor, and touched with her hand Ting Tzŭ's little padded shoe. And the girl looked down, and knowing her history, she laid her finger tips just a moment on the blind woman's face. Ch'êng Shao Yün liked the girl for that. Oh! her blood told—there was no denying that.

Presently Ti-tô-ti left his mistress's side, and came and looked up at the visitor with a little yelped request.

"May I?" Ting Tzŭ asked Ch'êng Yün prettily.

Yün nodded pleasantly. She began to like the girl, in spite of herself—and to like her very much.

Ting Tzŭ hesitated to caress or lift the tiny plead-

ing creature because of the fineness of her breeding
—and from a natural instinct of deference to a woman
older than herself, and her hostess. The little Chinese girl was but a child and worldly green. This
visit was more of a social function than had fallen
to her before. But her ancestors had been gentle for
hundreds of years. But her little natural courtesy had
an especial appeal to Ch'êng Yün, among whose sharp
traits was a violent resentment of any touching of a
personal belonging of her own—above all a living
belonging.

The girl lifted the tiny wriggling creature, and cuddled his soft curly head under her chin. And Ti-tô-ti's
big bulging beads of eyes almost bulged out of their
sockets with gratification, and his tiny tail beat a violent ecstasy against her breast. And Ch'êng Shao
Yün could but read it for an augury, for Ti-tô-ti rarely
made friends, and he was very psychic.

She kept the girl with her more than an hour, and
questioned her mercilessly. What had she read? Could
she write the grass characters rapidly and exactly?
What were her accomplishments? Did her feet ever
hurt? Did she like jewels best, or birds and flowers?
The one ornament in the room was a porcelain ewer
of thin, crisp Ming ware of the L'ung Ch'ing period,
with a long rustic spout, and the characteristic faint
green glaze over its white surface, and silvery-blue
panels of figure subjects; a graceful, priceless thing
the Ch'êngs had owned for more than three hundred
years. Ch'êng Yün bade Ting Tzŭ take it up and feel
its glaze—and say what she thought of it.

All this would have been a rudeness, and perhaps
a cruelty, from an Occidental woman—and an embarrassment, if not an angering to an English girl. But

Ting Tzŭ took it in the best of all good part. She approved it cordially, conscious that just so carefully would she catechize a girl she thought to ask in marriage for her son, should the gods bless her to have a son to her lord Ch'êng Chü-po—as no doubt they would. For she had learned his name from lisping Ch'êng Ko.

She took the porcelain gravely, and chatted happily of ceramics, and of the greater arts which they but reflected. And when Ch'êng Yün bade her play and sing, she rose instantly and selected a lute from the instruments lying on a window ledge, and to its accompaniment sang a silvery staccato song.

And again, in spite of Ch'êng Yün, she pleased Ch'êng Yün. For it was not the amorous love song that the woman had half expected—and that most Chinese girls would have sung, knowing few else—that Ting Tzŭ sang, but an old classic thing, vestal simple and sweet, about the stars and trees.

Ch'êng Yün nodded approval. Then, testing her taste once more—and liking her voice, bade Tzŭ sing again.

And Ting Tzŭ sang a little song of Spring that Wei Ying-wu had written twenty-seven centuries before :—

"When freshets cease in early spring and the river dwindles
   low
I take my staff and wander by the banks where wild flowers
   grow.
I watch the willow catkins wildly whirled on every side;
I watch the falling peachbloom lightly floating down the
   tide."

Then Ch'êng Shao Yün called for the guest-tea, which bade the girl go. And she went happily and happy—delighted with the mother of lord Ch'êng Chü-po. And when she slept that night she dreamed that the room was full of wild ducks, circling o'er her head, and that beneath them Ch'êng Chü-po bent over her with eyes aflame, smiling at her through a mist of crimson gauze.

But Ch'êng Shao Yün, when the door panel had closed in again, rested her face in covering hands, and sat a long, long time lost in thought and jealousy.

CHAPTER XII

NO other people work at once so hard and so sanely as the Chinese do. Almost every month has its holiday-break, and, if the lives of the hardworking populace were not so punctuated and their tremendous toil so punctured, it seems improbable that even Chinese grit could stand the enormous strain to which Chinese industry subjects it.

New Year's Day is the great obligatory day of feast and fuss. Debts must be paid before the New Year dawns. And every one must eat and play. No one may toil. Women in labor and silk worms about to hatch must have some tendance. But nothing industrial that is avoidable may be performed. China halts for the day, and stands at attention before her history and her gods.

To commit suicide during the great month of New Year festival would be too heinous a selfishness, and, far worse, it would be bad form. And to no people is bad form so impossible as to the Chinese. Even to die is scarcely pardonable—to be avoided, or put off, by every possible device of ingenuity. In 1875 the Emperor died on the fifteenth day of the Chinese year, and the entailed omission of the Lantern observances was as heavy a national calamity, as acute a grief, as the death of the imperial boy itself. No profusion of lamps might be outhung on street or building, from the inn's pretty balconies, in private park or on country path. None might wear best robes.

Indeed not one mark of the sacred feast might be taken except an inordinate, and almost private gorging of the traditional sugared mince-meat balls. And for months the national temper and stout tranquillity suffered from having lacked the tonic stimulant of the accustomed relaxation and inspiration.

The Chinese are supposed to like noise because they make it so intensely. But this, as almost everything else said of China in our generous Christendom—is ignorant and libel. The unutterable noise made at every Chinese festival is but a loud precaution to scare the devils away. Devils are great cowards and brainless too, as every Chinese knows. The screen set before the dwelling's outer entrance, or just within it, serves to keep the demons out, only because they lack the wit to swerve a little to the left or right, and pass it so. The youngest Chinese babe that has learned to toddle, the dullest Chinese dolt, is never thwarted for a moment by the devil-screen, but navigates serenely past it without an instant's loss of time. And the most devilish devil of all the black art dares not face the incredible, hideous noise of a Chinese festival, but picks up his wicked tail and horns and claws, and runs and runs and runs from the onslaught of such terrific din. Small boys and tender girls in America fire off fiendish fire-crackers, fearsome torpedoes and sizzing rockets in honor of sacred liberty. Children in England do it in vindication of young misrule and in imitation of older drolls. But, in China, gray beards, priests and princes do it to drive the evil spirits cowed away.

New Year is the national carnival of noise. Even the more elaborate fireworks, that scream and paint the New Year's night, spattering the Chinese sky with ten thousand cascades of noisy stars and lurid flaming caricatures of a thousand familiar things, are let loose to the dark more in rebuke of evil spirit things than for pleasuring of the gaping, living populace.

New Year festivities begin at the rising of the year's first moon. No debt must be still unpaid when that slender crescent breaks palely through the night. And then the month-long orgie of gift-giving begins, and the noisy and furious keepings of the New Year reek and reel on to end in the Feast of Lanterns.

The Feast of Lanterns is the beauty-keeping time of the Chinese, and every item of its observance is full of significance and of soul. It had its birth two thousand years ago when the Hun dynasty ruled over China. At first it was a formal ceremonial rite of worship performed in the temple of the First Cause. It lasted three days then. Now it lasts six, and has grown from its strict religious beginning to what it is now, the home festival, the most elaborate expression of Chinese art and artifice, of Chinese observance and belief, of Chinese spirit and hope—of Chinese brotherhood, peace and good will. It had no lanterns and no name of Lanterns on its old first day—for China then was lanternless. It began on the thirteenth of the first moon and ended on the sixteenth, bringing to an end then, as now, all the explosive festivities of the New Year's festival; visits, feasts and shrill uproar. The moon at its full round was the light by which the devout sacrificed and prayed to the great First Cause, with an excess of ritual which even Egypt never surpassed. For eight hundred years they kept it as at first, and then the lanterns came—the lovely, eloquent lanterns that are now as characteristic of China as is any inanimate thing, specking with quaint beauty, drenching with fantastic shapes of light, her every night, her palace parks, her lonely mountain paths, the banks of her heaving Yellow Sorrow, her precipices, her barnyards and her glens, and with their pretty parti-colored outlining make every Chinese street of night-merchandise a votive grotto and a fair. Another three hundred years and the beloved festival— the Chinese love it best of all—was stretched by some days, and so—as now—when Ting Tzŭ and her father kept it in the home of the Ch'êngs—it lasted full six days and nights. The third day of the Feast of Lanterns is its great day of all, and on the nineteenth of the moon, at dawn, China bends again her strong yellow back and takes up the heavy workaday burdens of common daily life.

I Kung Moy had gone on the second day of the year. On New Year's Day itself he could not travel —and his business with the lady Ch'êng had kept him in Ho-nan till then—but Ting Lo and his girl lingered still—the mandarin nothing loath, and urged by Ch'êng Shao Yün. She was not ill-pleased to show him how the House of Ch'êng kept holiday, and he was glad to be the longer with Ping-yang, and glad to keep from home, because of a new young wife who was a shrew, and had made of the Lanterns' last feast a penance and a scourge. December and June mate more happily in China than elsewhere, because Chinese age is virile and well-knit, and Chinese youth is deft and content. But even in China such union is but makeshift at best, and a desperate gamble always. It had worked badly in the yamên and in the home of Ting Lo. And this, his absence from home at the Feast of Lanterns, was almost without precedent. It is the one time in the year when every Chinese wills and tries to be at home.

And it is the Chinese time of woman's public license. Within her "flowery quarters" she has extraordinary license all the time. But during the Lantern Feast she may mingle freely in the crowds of men—even unveiled, if she will, unless herself a stickler and of highest rank—going on foot, or carried in her litter, to see and swell the laughing, chattering throng, and all the sumptuous show, and masque of light.

All was in readiness. The cakes were baked, and the lanterns hung. The cakes were piled in mountains, heaped in thousands on lacquer trays: the flat round moon-cakes, crisp, wafer-thin, honey sweetened disks —and the small white globes of sugar-covered mince-meat that are sacred to the feast. These are cere-monial balls and are made with the greatest care and exactitude, of one perfect snowy white, round as a billiard ball and about two-thirds its size. For days the Ch'êng kitchens had been busied with their pretty manufacture, and in every home in China some at least were made. And the greedy kitchen gods licked their fat lips in hungry anticipation, for to the kitchen gods always are given the first batch of the Lantern cakes else would they be tough and bring cramp. They are the one item of the Lantern feasting never omitted. Even if an Emperor lies newly dead—as in 1875— and every other detail of the great play-time is fore-gone, the cakes are made and are eaten in incredible quantities. The lower class and middle class Chinese, and many of those in purple born, eat melon seeds all the time. But once a year, all China to a tooth, de-

vours the round, white lantern cakes. The day before
Ch'êng Ko and his mother already had devoured some
pounds of them—she had helped to make them, with
her sleeves tucked away from her arms—from dimpled
wrist to dimpled elbow—from elbow to dimpled shoulder; and before the festival was as many hours old
as his years, Ko had crunched and swallowed so many
of the sick-sweet things that his little yellow belly
stuck out from him as round and hard as they.

The decorating of the grounds and of the houses,
Ch'êng Shao Yün supervised herself. A Chinese in-
terior must be sparsely adorned, lest beauty jostle
beauty, and jostling clash. One flower in one fine vase,
and the finest room in China is adorned enough. But
at festival time every tree, every shrub and bridge,
every point from which anything will hang, to which
anything can be fastened out of doors, is begilt and
bespattered with streamers, artificial flowers, strips of
gilt and festoons of lanterns.

Many Chinese lanterns are costly and veritable works
of art. Some hanging gayly now, roped and garlanded
from tree to tree, coolies had brought in hundreds
from K'ai-fêng Fu and Ch'ên-Chow Fu but the other
day. Others were heirlooms kept with the family jades
and bronze, and almost as valuable.

Those not reserved for the procession of the great
night, she had festooned about the place for criss-
crossed miles. It was important that the pretty,
painted, pendent baubles should be so arranged as to
give the greatest pleasure to the onlooking spirits of
the dead, who at this time at least moved and lived
again with their kindred. And so Ch'êng Yün arranged and rearranged till, of the hundred helpers
who worked with her, every back and arm ached but

her indefatigable own. Nor was this work alone for
hireling hands. Taste was as essential as strength.
Her sons worked with her, and even their wives. And
for this one festival the women of the harems darted
busily here and there on their tiny, nimble feet—veiled,
of course, but not so thickly that they could not see
to do all the intricacies of her bidding. And many a
veil slipped off; and no one cared—least of all Ch'êng
Shao Yün, a tyrannous stickler for decorum and tradition where neither interfered with the common sense
and business of the hour, but as ruthless on occasion
in her disregard of etiquette and others' opinion, as of
the disinfavored gods. Ting Tzŭ tripped beside her,
silent, a little in her wake. Ting Tzŭ was closely
veiled—for she was not at home here, and would
take no license of her maiden state. But the veil
thinned a little across her eyes—and as she walked
she smoked. It was easy enough to slip the slender
stem of her tiny-bowled pipe between the edges of
her pearl sewn veil. She held it decorously together
with one little gem-heavy hand, and with the other she
managed her jeweled pipe, emptying it with a quick
twist of her wrist, and filling it again, from the embroidered pouch hanging at her girdle, every few moments; for the diminutive bowl held but a pinch of
the silky, scented tobacco. And she took no part in
the work—that was a family toil, for Ch'êng hands,
and liegemen of the Ch'êng. Perhaps she'd help next
year. And at the thought she sighed a little, remembering that she might never keep the feast again in
her childhood's home, or hang her silken lanterns on
the tulip trees that sentineled her father's doors. It
had been such a happy, happy home until her father's
new young wife had come. And even so her father,

for her sake, defied the pretty shrew now and then, as he had in coming here and bringing Tzǔ with him.

Chü-po held aloof. He had never cared to work with his hands. He sat for the most part on the fantastic stone railing of a bridge or on some carved stone seat, and tweaked his lute. And when they were near enough, his mother called to him for comment or advice, and he called them gayly back. But he never looked at Ting Tzǔ, or she toward him. And at last he went away—and they saw him no more that day.

On the roofs and crevices of the silkworm houses, Ch'êng Yün suffered no lanterns to be hung, lest the light and the myriad candles' heat should creep in and harm the delicate brooding worms. But festoons of rich scented flowers, orange blossoms, arbutus, sweet laurel-like tung ch'ing holly, and the perfumed blossoms and lovely tinted foliage of the tallow tree, she had hung there instead. For the silkworms love every sweet fragrance, and it nourishes them.

When your feet have taken silk, and they are happier than they have ever been before, do you ever give a thought to the nun-like girls in China that were foster-mothers to the delicate wormlings that spun your stockings' super-silk?

The story of silk is the story of a woman's movement, and a womanly movement—not always quite the same thing. Men are interlopers in sericulture, and somewhat recent ones. They have been useful along the line of its commercial development; but the honor and the history belong to women.

Silk was born in China. A little Chinese girl probably discovered it a few thousands of years ago when she, under a mulberry tree, sat playing jackstones with a handful of cocoons. And a Chinese queen gave the infant industry her patronage and her labor, cherished and cultivated the silkworms, planted the mulberry groves, invented the loom. And for centuries the royal women of China tended and developed the cult in all its branches—silkworm farms, dyeing, weaving—until the sericulture that began in one royal woman's interest and patriotism became, as it still is, the imperial art of an imperial people.

China may play at a Republic, may masquerade as a democracy; but she can no more slough her ancestry, or permanently betray it, than she can roughen and coarsen the imperial fabric of her silk looms by calling it "cottons made in Manchester." China is an Empire, and her workmanship and her silks are imperial.

No other silks approach them. To the silks of China, the silks of Japan are as cheap glass is to jade.

From its dawn, women have been as potent in China's history as men have. And, as a rule, the greater the Emperor the greater in personality and in influence have been his mother and his wife.

The Lady of Si-Ling—probably one of the three most celebrated Chinese women, the wife of Huang-Ti, the Emperor who reigned in China twenty-six centuries before Christ, and who was the arch-patron, and in many ways the father, of Chinese agriculture—gave the first great impetus to the silk industry of China. She grew mulberry trees, and encouraged the people high and low to do so. She studied and improved the rearing of the worms, and the reeling of the silk. She herself invented the loom and perfected it for the patterned weaving of the beautiful silken webs, which were sold for more than their weight in gold, not only in Persia and in India, but in distant luxury-loving Greece. She gave her personal time and the work of her own hands to the lovely industry, as has almost every Chinese Empress since. Even the famous Dowager Empress of our day—the most libeled woman in history—found time to tend her worms and use her loom. And it has been the invariable practice of the ladies of the Chinese Court, the women of the nobility, and the peasant women of the far-off, far-scattered countrysides, to ply regularly some part of the exacting industry.

Chinese girls, scantily clad that they may be exquisitely sensitive to the slightest change of temperature, watch over and time all the stages of the silk-worm's life. From the time the first worm is hatched until the last has spun its cocoon they require skillful and absolutely unremitting attention. The shed must be well ventilated, weatherproof, and in every particular scrupulously clean. The attendant girls must be quiet, cheerful, gentle and even in their movements, clean in person and sweet of breath. They must live on simple, unscented food. One strong whiff of garlic will ruin, if it does not kill, the finer silkworms, and injure the coarsest. The silk girls may live on honey and rose leaves if they like, but they must never eat onions or ginger.

In some silkworm houses—in Sze-Chuen, for instance—for greater warmth, the best cocoons are sheltered in her own bosom by the attendant girl, and after that she must be quiet indeed. There are nuns in China, holy women for the most part, leading cloistered lives, but their daily life is worldly and vibrant compared to that of the silk-girls.

For centuries the Chinese guarded all the secrets of
their sericulture well.   Even yet some of them are
closely kept.   And the perfection of Chinese manipu-
lation cannot be approached.

A Chinese Princess, marrying an Indian Prince, carried in the lining of her head-dress silkworm eggs and
mulberry tree seed to India, and, from that, silk and
silk industries spread over the world.

Ho-nan is not a province of the richest silks.   It is
the province of wild silk.   But the indefatigability of
Ch'êng Yün had wrought miracle in the sericulture of
the estate.   Her silks were noted now, and not even
for the pleasuring of the sainted dead would she risk
the welfare of her pregnant worms.   Besides the
flower-hung break in the wilderness of lamps would
give relief and variety to the eyes of the spirits, as
to their nostrils; and it would make an oasis and a
fragrant sanctuary for the outshone fire-flies, the
"lamps-of-mercy" that lit so many a poor pilgrim on
his perilous, candleless path across the steep hillsides
to the copper-roofed temples in the north, and the fire-
flies would hang their own festoons of jeweled lights
about the matted roofs of the thatched palace of the
worms.

At dusk she ordered all to rice and sleep.   And most
of her servitors did sleep—dog-tired from her cap-
taining.

The day broke clear, but for that season and place,
cold.   And many a woman shivered as she hurried at
that cold moment just before the dawn to the temple
where she chose to pray.   The temples were the
women's until the dials and the water-clocks warned

the approach of eight, and then any man that would,
could seek a god without risk of brushing some close-
veiled figure as it flitted back from prayer to rice.

When Ping-yang and Ting Tzŭ came into Ping's
own court-yard, just as the delicate first outriders of
the sun were opaling all the sky with molten wisps of
rose and green, they saw it as if fairy hands had
decked it in the night. The grass was widely lozenged
with strips of silken carpeting. A thousand tiny lanterns hung—not yet lit, of course—about its house-
enclosed sides. A great Ch'ien Lung vase nearly as
tall as Ping-yang and chin-high to Ting Tzŭ stood
near the Hoang Ko tree. The big vase was full to
its brim with attar, wasting in pungent, cloyed sweetness a fortune in the air. A mat of woven jessamine
flowers, pink, lemon and white, and their bright gray-
green leaves lay before the vase. An open book and
a gemmed and silver lute lay on the fragrant mat.
And the old sundial was an altar with a throng of
worshiping flowers. For unlit tapers, tiny ivory bells
hung circled on the dial's upmost rim making soft
music ripples of tinkling love and prayer at every
slightest pulsing of the day's fresh breath. And on
the dial's old flat face, a red rose, still wet with dew,
pointed the hour when the great glittering procession
would form and pass with music across the estate
from gate to gate, circling twice the lotus lake.

Ting Tzŭ bent above the dial, and drank the roses'
breathed-out wine. But Nan Tung, sitting stolid a
pace away, mending a shoe of Ch'êng Ko's—though
none should work to-day—neither looked up nor spoke
—and neither sister questioned her, "Who has done
this thing?"—but when they had gone out through the
doorway that led presently to the dwelling's door, and

Nan Tung saw that Ting Tzŭ had dropped a bit of honey-suckle, she went and picked it up—and hid it in the baby's shoe, and hurried through another door.

By seven the whole domain was in a hum of merriment and ecstasy. Even in the open, great bundles of joss sticks burned down to their light stems, to be replaced by others before they went out, and heaping all the grass and paths with little hills of white ash.

Pageant followed sports, and sports followed pageant, all day long. Every one munched white sugared mincemeat balls, and every one was glad and gay— and there was no silence in all the place except in the acres where the cocoon sheds stood. But it was decorous merriment, with an added courtesy beyond the quiet courtesy which is the garment and the nerve of Chinese daily life—for the dead were here to-day, threading their kindly, silent way among the teeming human things, watching and enjoying all. It was for these spirit guests, ancestral and honored, that the incense burned, that no grosser man-smells should by any chance offend the nostrils of the gracious ghosts. Fire-crackers crackled out in fearsome burst, and drums threatened rattlingly—not for the coarse amusement of living ears, but to affright and drive every evil, prowling entity away, lest they profane the presence of the beloved dead, or injure or annoy them.

Even the silkworm girls were here, in glad-eyed relays. Ah Söng was in charge of the worms to-day, with only now and then a handful of girls slipping in noiselessly to see if all was well, and watch with her for an hour. Ah Söng cared nothing for festivities.

Chü-po was very brave in crimson silk and pink flowered brocade, a pouch with all its dangle of ac-

companiments swinging from his girdle. Ch'êng Shao
Yün had made and embroidered it, and had contrived
herself the dozen pretty nicknacks bunched with it.
Every Chinese dandy wears such a pouch and pretties,
and many a grave graybeard. And always it is the
token and the handwork, of mother, sister or wife.
In his tunic a great green diamond blazed, fastened
across the stem of a little honeysuckle spray. And
behind him walked upright Zo Min-yü, his favorite
bear, halting at every third step to beg, catching for
his pains one of the sugared mincemeat balls. It
seemed he ate a thousand, and then begged for one
more. But even a Ho-nan bear can have enough, and
after some hours of gorging he heaved a gigantic sigh,
and lay down on the path, and went to sleep, for coolness on his back, all his shaggy paws stretched up
like ill-shaped steeples, and his great sugar-packed
stomach between them like a great brown onion bulb.
And all day long, feasting and procession, juggling
and wrestling, swerved aside from where he lay, yielding him pride of place with a good-natured laugh.

And Ch'êng Shao Yün, her daughters and her guest,
sat in a great pavilion of sandalwood and jasper, and
watched the fun—with the handmaidens and the concubines sitting at their feet. And when the ladies
wearied of the sport, or of the heat, they slipped away
into one of a group of tents to lie and rest, sip iced
cups, or sweet hot wine, gamble a little, or gossip and
eat.

Every woman in that festal multitude carried and
plied a fan—as did most of the children and many of
the men—in the surging humbler folk as well as the
"sash-wearers" gathered at the pavilion, and strolling
more leisurely about the park-like place. All Chinese

garments have their story and their significance, as well as their beauty and their use. But the fan has become almost a part sentient and actual of the Chinese human body—another hand, a necessary organ. It has written Chinese history, and has marked it. It has illuminated Chinese literature for centuries. It illustrates Chinese daily life—the eloquent, time-honored Chinese fan, in eloquent, supple conservative Chinese hands. And every woman there wore in her hair at least one stickpin, blue-enameled and azure—encrusted with the precious feathers of the kingfisher—the jewel-bird of China.

A quick side-light may be thrown on a phase of Chinese life not always accurately understood in Europe, by one small incident that came just before the great hour of the processional.

"Who was that girl who hurt her hand on Ch'êng To-jung's wife's stick-pin?" Ch'êng Hsu said to his wife, as they met a moment near the pavilion. "I saw you bind her finger with a corner of your scarf."

"Oh, that is Ma-wung, your number three concubine," she told him carelessly. "I like the girl."

And Ch'êng Hsu looked as little interested as he was.

With the dark came the great throbbing hour of all the festival: the procession of lanterns, and the carnival of fireworks.

Ch'êng Yün and the younger ladies watched it all from a little fleet of lacquered boats floating on the bosom of the lotus lake. The men, and the women and children not of Yün's party, watched from every coign of vantage on the shore. Even in the darker evening time the sky looked velvet blue, speckled with its radiant powdering of brilliant stars. From every bough of every tree lanterns hung, lit now, that the ancestral spirits gathered here, moving lovingly about their old earth-ways, might have light to see. A Chinese coolie will half starve himself for months rather than risk the spirits of his ancestors stumbling in the night-time dark of the Lanterns' long festival. The tree-hung lanterns here were beautiful and odd, no two alike, but they were the merest utilitarian attendants of the hundreds of masterpieces of the procession.

No English words could half describe the beauty of that festal sight—probably no eyes or hearts not Chinese and centuries-trained see it quite. The night was very still. The stars looked very far and pale— and now and then one shot across the sky in a little rush of flame. The lantern bearers were all bravely clad, happy but grave, selfless but important in the meaning of their task. And the incense smoking up almost imperceptibly from the burning sandalwood rose like a warm mist in the quiet evening air. Twenty little boys came first, each carrying two swaying censers of gauzy lanterns. Then a long, slow moving stream of older, sturdier youths. Here one walked alone to better show the beauty of some special paper lamp. Others came abreast in twos, in threes—and wider ranks. No flower grows in all great China that was not mimicked by lanterns of gauze or silk. Every lantern was hand-painted by a master's hand—except here and there one wonderfully embroidered. Many of the lovely, swaying lights were so heavy—for all their fragile surfacing—that they must be slung on long, stout bamboo poles resting on the shoulders of two men or more. Some were fashioned of tissue so delicate that it scarcely was visible, showing the candles within clearly cut, and the paintings on the gauze seemed to ride unsupported through the air. Some were built of thick, clear silk and the hidden candles gave out a soft blurred, opalescent glow as if a swarm of fire-flies burned within alabaster prisoning. Every fruit of Chinese fact and fancy had its lantern picturing. Birds, fish, peacocks, eagles with wide tigerish eyes, beasts from the jungle, tamed animals of farmyard and barn, spinning wheels, all the lovely leafage of long bamboo stems—and the East has nothing lovelier than its bamboos—squirrels, cranes, wolves and pretty parti-colored ducks, inexpressibly beautiful clusters of wistaria in bud and fuller bloom, oranges and orange buds and flowers swinging from one sweep of green-leaved twisted stems, melons, pineapples, cacti in flower, great grape clusters, the very sight of which might have made a Bacchus reel, boats, caravans, old warships, state barges, snow-topped mountains in red eruption, every jewel of the wide world's wealth cut into some exquisite shape, temples, gods, warriors and dancing girls, babies in their tall cradles, stern old men with flowing beards of snow-white flame—perhaps the tulips were loveliest, or the peonies, perhaps the chrysanthemums or the begonias, or blue and rose larkspurs, or perhaps the little humming birds. Many of the lanterns were vase-shaped, picturing for the people China's wealth of porcelain art—the lovely but least of her fine arts. Of the more intricate and fantastic lanterns, many were made with such extraordinary mastery and skill, and of texture so delicate and marvelously balanced, that at the slightest touch of wind they shifted into other shapes; the rose became a rose-pink gull, the green-leaved red

tulip a green-leaved cluster of dangling cherries, the
gentian flower a blue swallow in proud flight. A school
of kittens seemed to play at ball. Bears pranced and
begged, persistent as spoiled children. Great fat turtles
sprawled, and green lizards crawled. And yet the
procession had but begun.

On and on it passed, wending its slow illumined
way, the watchers breathless, silent for the most part,
but now and then, when something of special beauty
or of deeper meaning passed, the people gave a great
sigh of pleasure or of sympathy—once or twice a
woman sobbed—and when the great dragon came, a
gust of feeling swept and swayed the onlooking ranks,
as a wind of summer hits and swings the swelling
tassels of the ripening corn, and they broke into a
happy whispering of song. An impassive people! A
cruel bestial people! And inferior to the Japanese!

Hail to the missionary! And to the incrawling, in-
breaking European throng! China needs them so, to
bring her civilization, to teach her the art of living,
of which all other arts are but handmaids, and to
give her soul!

And this was not a sudden spurt of excess, sump-
tuousness and riot expenditure to dazzle a visiting mandarin, but just the annual home festival of the Ch'êngs,
in welcome of the home-coming of their dead. They
had kept it here and so for hundreds of years. Not
a coolie or a slave girl here but from birth or purchase had watched it every year.

The dragon—the Great Dragon, for many others
had gone before among the great waxen lilies and the
flaming trumpet-flowers—was the apex but not the
end of the long spectacle of beauty and of feeling.

All day long little balloons had floated in the noise-torn air, some released and free, hundreds tethered to the glass bracelets on almost every childish wrist, or string-held by little yellow hands. From many of the chubby gas-filled balls dangled little delicate chimes of bells, making soft music as they went—just a whisper of elfin sound, tinkling down sweetly between the pauses in the fireworks' holocaust of sound. And when the darkness grew each released balloon was radiant with an increased light, or with a coating of phosphorus. And all day long occasionally aircraft had skimmed through the ether. For airships were invented in China centuries before fanatic inventors or obsessed patriotism thought of them in Christendom. What we invent and acclaim to-day, China did centuries before Britain was mapped or Europe known, and when our ancestors waded through the weed-thick marshes of Thorny, wearing woad and greasy blue paint or less, Chinese science mastered the air, and refined the daily life of China's far-flung, puissant peoples. When the night came, the aircraft gliding overhead showed lights of rose and silver, riding like dolphin-birds through the ocean of the sky.

A thousand illuminated balloons proclaimed the Dragon's approach, and a great air-bat, flying like a winged snake of green diamonds, heralded it.

But when the Dragon came, the children forgot their balloons and their kites—the daylight had been thick with kites, free and held—and the pretty, shining toys dragged gas-spent and neglected on the ground.

A hundred men—inconspicuously clad in gray, that the splendid monster might the more seem independent of them—carried above them the gorgeous leviathan that seemed to sprawl slowly through the air its scaly, horned and corrugated sides.

It wriggled like a fat, supple demon as it went, satanic contortions quivered its painted, caved and hillocked sides. Every few yards it turned its awful head, oped wide its terrible jaws, and belched out on the delighted people a soft mist of warm perfume. The people squirmed and grinned with happiness as the fine musk-scented rain showered and drenched them with sprays so fine that it caressed them gently, and scarcely seemed the wet it was. And many a good gift fell with the rain of scent. Of all those gifts the *ruyie* were most prized—precious little emblems of twisted jade, mascots of good luck, just such as the Son of Heaven himself accepted and gave on his birthdays in imperial Pekin. And the youngsters clutched joyously the sweetmeats that the huge writhing monster spat them as it went—sweetmeats they were too happy and too already-fed to eat, each sweetmeat inscribed or embossed with a beneficent character meaning "Peace," "Felicity," "Good Luck," "Fidelity," "Great Learning," "Health," "Longevity," or "Gifted in Art."

Before the shining Dragon swung—tantalizing, just out of his reach—a great sheeny pearl, modeled out of tight-stretched changeable white, rose and silver silk: and emblem of "The Unattainable." He followed it. He snapped at it. But never he reached it. When he hurried, it hurried. When he almost mouthed it, it just escaped. He nearly contrived, it just evaded.

When the great Dragon had gone, passing out of sight on its long, fiery way, a troup of children—but old enough for the long walk—came carrying armfuls of fresh flowers. Then youths intoning classic poems.

Then actors, dressed for their parts, reminded all that, though the greatest day of the great festival was spent, the morrow held great treasure in her womb—more games, and the great theatrical event. Last of all came a shy band of vestal girls, delicately clad, singing a good-night hymn of sweet repose.

Each succeeding day of the feast dwindled a little from its day before; that the inevitable and salutary homespun end might not seem abrupt or harsh. But each day was packed with pleasure and kindliness. And the Feast of Lanterns slipped away to the last observance and the last indulgence of its last night's last hour.

And almost as the day broke and the chill wind of coming morning whispered them "To bed" and then "To work," and plucked the little love songs from the instruments hanging in half the trees, the happy people (the ill-used Chinese people) went—singing softly as they went—weary with gladness and delight —contented to their homes, to rest a few hours on their mats, sleep if they could, then to spring up at the first clap of the "get-up" cymbals, refreshed and inspired, to the strenuous daily toil which is the backbone of Chinese life, and is half of Chinese happiness.

Ye little gods of Europe, will not the greater Heaven itself peep through the blanket of your petty dark, and bid you cease your busy-bodying in Asia, and heal the sorrows and the souls of your own peasantry and cultured working class? If but some Power would give you the gift to see yourselves as Asia sees you!

CHAPTER XIII

IT was raining ominously when the train moved away towards the outer gates. Great angry clouds were swooping down from cold Manchuria like angry beast-birds of prey. The flowers were shivering on trembling stalks, and the fruit shook frightened on the quivering trees. The coolies, moving busily about the place, wore their ragged rain-coats of long, coarse grass—as did the humbler servants of the departing Tings.

But Ch'êng Chü-po wore still a gala dress—robes almost as rich and gay as a bridegroom might have worn. He stood with his brothers just outside the outer door, and did homage with them as the mandarin's long cavalcade moved away; it would have been a rudeness to his mother's guest had he not been there. But when the Tings had disappeared behind a winding of the path, and his brothers turned to the shelter of the house, he sped, by a shorter way he knew, through the rain, to where he had stood almost a moon before —to where he had first seen the face of Ting Tzŭ. But now when the train passed by on the road below, he stood boldly forth, his red and green and rose robes shining clearly through the rain. The mandarin, not minded to dismount, though indeed that extreme of courtesy was not his obligation to one so much younger and of lesser rank—(the old man was riding on his palfrey, defiant of the storm)—but highly pleased, pretended not to see the boy. But the curtaining of a girl's palanquin parted an inch—perhaps in answer to the wind, perhaps in scorn of the rain —and Ch'êng Chü-po knew that she had seen and understood.

And when he no longer could see her chair, he gathered up his long heavy robes, and ran like the boy he was, taking again steep, narrow, short cuts he knew, running sometimes where there was no path, and scarcely foothold, until he reached the outer gate, and stood waiting there when the long cortège came.

And this time Ting Lo dismounted and greeted young Ch'êng as an equal. But Chü-po would have none of that, and kot'owed to the very ground, saying, "I am thy slave." And Ting raised him up, and embraced him lingeringly. And again the sun came out, the storm drew back, and again, as Chü-po held the mandarin's stirrup and served him at his mounting, Ting Tzŭ's curtains parted a narrow breadth.

Then they went.

And in a pepul tree a bird, leaf-sheltered, began to sing.

Ch'êng Chü-po sought admittance to Ch'êng Shao Yün, and she gave it him.

And when he had made obeisance to her three times thrice, and had said to her all the due ceremonial things, saying them with an added ceremony, as befitted the grave importance of his errand, and too, because he had come to force her august hand, and, as he sensed, perhaps to hurt the older heart he loved, he knelt down and clasped his hands upon her knee.

"When?" he said.

"When? When what, Chü-po?"

"When shall she come?"

"She shall not come," his mother told him slowly Chü-po rose, and stood before her smiling, but deferential still. "What fault have you to find, my honorable Mother?" he began.

"With the girl? None."

"I meant not to ask that," Ch'êng Chü-po said quietly, "for you could have none. The honorable maiden has not one. But with the marriage?"

"Fault enough," she replied briefly. "And I have other plans. To-morrow I send to ask the hand of——"

"Listen, my Mother," he interrupted her—almost as hideous an outrage from a Chinese son as if he had struck his mother's face. Ch'êng Yün bit her lip, and the hot blood painted all her face.

"You forget yourself, worm! It is for me to order, and for you to obey."

"In all but this. And I do not forget. In all but this I will obey you while we live. I do not forget my duty or your years, the birth you gave me, or my long happiness at your dear side. But I remember my love."

"Your love! Your bastard indecency, you mean," she raved. She beat the air. She screamed and tore her robe. She called him many a foul name. She would have heaped abuse upon Ting Tzŭ, had she dared. But even in her insane rage she dared not— as yet. She threatened him with her clenched fists, as if she'd strike him to the ground.

And Chü-po stood steadily still and smiled.

"Speak! Answer me!" she panted, gasping for her spent breath.

"I will die unmarried, or wed Ting Tzŭ," he said. Then she forgot everything but her jealous fury, and she hissed out a foul opprobrious term, and linked it to Ting Tzŭ.

Ch'êng Chü-po went proudly to the door.

"Come back," she screamed.

He paid no heed.

Shao Yün rushed after him, and caught him roughly. "Stay till I bid you go, thou base reptile."

"Not to hear one rudeness of her." And he flung Ch'êng Yün gently off.

"I will have thy life," she stormed, and the tears were pelting down her cheek.

"That you can indeed do, lady," the boy said gently. "Command my death, and I will instantly obey. But I think, O Mother, you will not do that."

"I will have you tortured, vermin."

"It is within your power, great Ch'êng Shao Yün. And I, whom you bore and gave your breast, am helpless to resist—as helpless as when you suckled me."

"Out of my sight," she hissed.

"Lady, yes. But hear me first. You must."

Ch'êng Shao Yün sank speechless to her seat. "Must!" from a son to a mother! Did China live! Was Ho-nan real?

"I think you will neither kill nor torture me. You are angry——"

She found her voice at that, and laughed, "Angry —oh! no, I—I am thy——" (Her anger hissed and choked her.)

—"But I think you could not live to know the sentence carried out, even if you summoned the slaves, and gave them order for it. But—oh, listen, Mother —this I swear to you, by the sacred presence within the pink walls of the vermilion palace at Pekin, and by the crystal tree that grows above the holy grave in

Shantung, by all the honorable ancestors of our great house, and by the love you bore me, lady, by every time of all the thousands that you have laid your hand on me in kindness, unless I lift the red veil from the face of Ting Tzŭ, I, with my own hand, will take my life."

This was their hour of mutual torture and of mutual trial; so strained that neither had noticed that he had spoken her name—something a Chinese son may not do.

Again he turned to go. And he thought that Ch'êng Shao Yün would not yield. He had never known her yield.

She sat and watched him through inscrutable eyes. She knew that he would keep his word.

"Go, then," she said, speaking quietly again. "Go. I have other sons and grandsons, too. My grave will not miss thy unfilial worship."

But when he put his hand upon the sliding panel, which was the room's outer door—"Chü-po!" she sobbed, "come back to me, varmint!"

He ran and caught his mother in his strong young arms. She threw her head down on his breast, sobbing wildly now, and he sheltered her in his arms, and comforted her, and held her very close.

Ting Tzŭ had won.

CHAPTER XIV

DWARF trees grow in China, but not dwarf souls.
Having yielded—even though it had been because she must—Ch'êng Shao Yün did it magnificently.
She was not petty. Venomous in anger, revengeful
even, full of prejudice and arrogance as a monkey is
full of mischief, a tyrant from her cradle to her grave
—and why not—daughter of tyrants, and mother of
tyrants?—except in the immediate eruption of her
rage, or under the lasting bitterness—cold and merciless—of the conviction of justice outraged or trust
betrayed—for all her pranks of temper and airs of
sex, she was not petty, and would no more condone
a meanness of her own than one of friend or foe.
Chü-po had beaten her, or rather Ting's chit of a girl-
child had, and after her first—and last—shrill out-
break, she took her first defeat like the true queen
thing she was; regally, smilingly and graciously. And,
if for it she loved Ting Tzŭ none the more, she did
love Chü-po for it with some added love, for it fed
further her great pride in him.

He had cowed her with his threat of suicide. There
is nothing a Chinese fears or deplores more than a
kinsman's suicide. Self-slaughter dismays them not at
all. Suicide honors the self-slayer, but lays an ever-
lasting ban on those who cause it. To send Chü-po
to the execution ground would have been simple and
stainless—could she have done it—even to have sent
him the cord of dispatch, bidding him use it, was think-

able, for that would have made the slaughter hers,
not his, his hand but her instrument conceded to his
pride by her charity, conceded for his blood's sake.
But his voluntary suicide would have heaped a shame
upon her which nothing could cleanse or redeem.

The very threat of it defeated her. And her defeat
was complete. Well, now to turn it into triumph—
like the great lady she was—greatness and strength
the very marrow of her. Or, at least, if she could
not trick herself to feel that it was her own triumph,
to so deck it—her sacrifice—that she should trick her
world and following into thinking it so: *her* act, *her*
wish, *her* triumph.

And Chü-po's terrible, stern threat had told her
something else, had convinced her of more than her
own defeat. It told her that he indeed belonged to
Ting Tzŭ—that his soul was mingled inseparably in
the soul of the girl, his heart pulsing in Ting Tzŭ's,
and that, for the time at least, they were wedded already. For Ch'êng Shao Yün had loved Ch'êng O,
and had been loved by Ch'êng O, and she knew
what the big love was, knew its purple signs, and
that when it mantled so, in most chance, it had come
to stay.

But again Ah Söng, lying on the mat without her
door, heard her sobbing through the night.

On the morrow she met Chü-po with a smile. And
she dealt with him then, and on all the days that followed, with a tender gayness and a brave gracious-
ness that rang hollow only to blind Ah Söng, whose
pathos only Ah Söng knew, and of all others none—
but Chü-po suspected, and he himself but half suspected.

Chü-po was grateful, and he clung to her even as he had never clung before with a tenderness and a deference and a leaning on her that were like a little child's, and too, manly with a new-come manliness.

And she set all her strength and all her exquisite wit to pleasure him.

Having yielded to him in the one thing supreme, a smaller woman might have thwarted and girded him in a thousand little things, finding so, or seeking to find, outlet and relief for a sour spleen of disappointment. And Chü-po would have accepted it with splendid gentleness. But Ch'êng Shao Yün was not petty, and she scorned to smirch her yielding with any seeming pettiness.

She caressed her boy, deferred to him, invited his caress and accepted it lovingly. And they clung together through all the days, and each hour tied and bound them together with some new tendril of devotion and gratitude. She thwarted him in nothing. And he waited her pleasure with perfect and sunny patience.

Each of their old mutual pastimes they took up together again, if only for an hour. And he was very gentle with his mother, for he knew that she was saying good-by—the mother's terrible farewell to her boy.

What she felt, he sensed. But she showed it not at all.

As a little boy it had been his chiefest pleasure to watch and hear her call the birds. And for him she called the birds almost daily now. Many Chinese are gifted so—especially women. The Great Dowager could call the wild birds to her in all the leafy stretches of the Summer Palace grounds. And Ch'êng Shao Yün called the Ho-nan wild birds to her when she would. Holding up a long wand new-cut from some

young tree, and fresh-peeled of its tender bark, all wet
and fragrant with its sap, she would call out a bird-
note in her voice of utmost music, and presently the
little wild bird would answer. The woman called
again, and presently the bird came down and perched
shyly on the wand. Yün called again. The bird answered. And after a time it fluttered down to her
hand, and let her hold it to her face. In part this
was her personal magnetism. In part it was the ac-
cumulated magic of a race that has obeyed for countless generations Confucius' commandment to "hurt no
living thing." Ch'êng Chü-po never tired of watching
Ch'êng Yün call the wild birds—not even now when
half of his soul slept from his mother, dreaming of
Ting Tzŭ.

She thwarted him in nothing. And so she did not
delay beyond the pause that Chinese decency and the
dignity of their great house demanded and enforced
—to send her marriage tenders to Ting Lo.

And when at last—for life's greatest function takes
long in China, moves slow—Ting Tzŭ came with clash
of gongs and panorama of cortège to her bridegroom,
Ch'êng Shao Yün received her with tender kindness.

Even in China marriage was not often so splendidly
performed. Picture followed picture—pomp crowded
pomp. A thousand perfumes reeked among a thousand glittering lights. Ten thousand flowers nodded
rosy welcome to the red-veiled girl, twice ten thousand blossoms heaped before her binded feet. Jest
followed ceremonial, song followed prayer. No one
on all the vast estate did any work except in service
of the bride. Ch'êng Ko ran unregarded riot unrebuked. Almost the silkworms were forgotten.

They carried Ting Tzŭ to him in a procession that

stretched in color and gorgeousness more than a mile.

She sat alone in her bridal chair, trembling a little within the gauze shelter of her red wedding veil; eager but frightened to reach her long journey's end, and to reach the very presence of Chü-po. Motherless, she grieved to have left her first home, and grieved bitterly to part from the father who had both fathered and mothered her through all her tender, cherished years. Happier than most Chinese girls so carried in their "flowery" chairs, in knowing that her red veil would not be lifted from her pretty, painted face by a to-be-hated bridegroom—still she felt a little cheated by that very surety and the absence of suspense. Like all her race a gambler-born, life's biggest gamble was robbed for her of some of its palpitating zest by her knowing something of the man to whom they were carrying her, and too she felt some social damage—slight but acute and real, in having been seen, even though through no fault of her own, before their marriage by the man upon whose favor all her future happiness must depend. Would he ever in all the long years to come hold her less dear, even a little less worthy for it? She shuddered miserably at the thought, and lifted her veil to study yet once more her face in the jewel-circled mirror of polished steel into which she had already gazed anxiously a thousand times since they had carried her—sobbing and struggling—through her father's door, and packed her like some very precious bundle into her red and gilded palanquin—sobbing and struggling, but doing it carefully not to crack her nuptial paint, or disarrange the dangling beadings of her crown, or crush or tear any atom of all her splendid yards of bridal finery. It had been her duty to sob, protest and struggle. And she had done it well—for she was dutiful and very proud of all the traditions of her race and caste, as proud and careful as Ch'êng Yün herself. But it had been her privilege to keep herself looking nice—and she had done it to a miracle.

The mirror was reassuring, and the face reflected in it cleared.

It was not a light disc to hold, and her little fingers were almost crippled with a barbarous weight of rings and nail protectors. Reluctantly she laid the clear steel down, and leaned back again, sighing a little, in her chair—and fell to dreaming of Chü-po—and the hour to come.

The looking-steel had reassured her, and her thinking of Chü-po was reassuring too. It was a catastrophe to have looked into his eyes already, and a damage too of her; she did not blink that—could not. But the eyes had been kind. And she had seen love in them: such ardor and petition of love that no girl, even any one of all the denser races, could have failed to read it or to recognize it. Chü-po loved her. She knew it. Could she hold that young love, making it the flower and perfume even of her old age? She sighed quickly, but not too unhappily—for her father had told her that Ch'êng Chü-po came of a loyal, constant clan, Ping-yang had said it too—and surely she knew, for she lived among them, and they had an aunt whom Tzŭ much resembled, who was lovely still at the great age of fifty, and probably she—Tzŭ— would bear him sons, *and* within her crimson robes she wore an amulet the old witch woman had given her at home, a charm to chain forever a husband's love.

She wished she had not been seen by her lord—so unfortunately preseen—that was far more calamity than that she had seen him. It would have been a delightful, heartbeating business to be going to him knowing nothing of him or of his features. But what she already knew was reassuring. And probably she would find still some surprise in marriage and in her years of wifehood—where happier girls found nothing else.

She had seen Ch'êng Chü-po. She had read his heart. He had laved her with his desire. And to its demand her own heart had gone quick and warm. And of all the smaller things, that, as she knew, made up so much more of daily life and rice-side felicity, she had learned of him from the courtyard gossip and from busy-tongued Ping-yang all that could be told.

Ting Tzŭ leaned back against her perfumed cushions smiling to herself and dreaming rosy, quivering dreams.

"Ch'êng Tzŭ," she whispered to herself, and then beneath her paint she blushed redder than her veil.

Then bells clanged. Ten thousand crackers spluttered out their sharp poppings. Incense puffed in through the curtains of her litter. Tom-toms clashed and tore the silence to a thousand shreds of noise. Wild music—wild and wilder—bleated beside the paths. They were carrying her more slowly and more proudly now. And she must, she knew, have reached the outer gate.

She clutched the talisman within her robe. Kwang Yin grant that she should keep, while she lived, her lord's love!

Ting Tzŭ was trembling newly now, and her heart beat wild and sick.

It seemed an endless way now—and yet too short.
They set her down.

She heard her father's voice. She thought he spoke her name.

Then silence came.

A quick foot pressed to her chair.

A man's hands parted her curtains, and lifted her up into a man's arms.

She was trembling violently now—no need to pretend reluctance—and as Ch'êng Chü-po carried her reverently across the threshold, lifting her athwart the marriage-fire burning on the door-step, not speaking to her—yet, but for all that sending her a message and a comforting as he bent his head to hers, she thought her heart had lost a beat.

And Ch'êng Chü-po thought so too, and he felt her cold within her robes, and felt the fluttering of her sweet girl-flesh—and it ran racing through his veins.

At last they were alone.

She was his wife.

The interminable ceremonies were done.

The night was coming near.

They stood alone—life's greatest sacrament at their lips—together and alone in the garnished room that was to be the inner sanctuary of all their wedded life.

The husband lifted his wife's crimson veil and threw it from her face.

For a time they stood so—she swaying a little on her tiny feet—he clenching his hands in a desperate, generous attempt at self-control.

Of the two he was trembling the more now.

But, when at last, she looked piteously up to him, he

smiled down at her with tender gentleness. But the trembling of his young lips betrayed the tumult within —but his voice was very quiet—when presently he spoke to her.

"Ch'êng Tzŭ," he said slowly, "Chêng Tzŭ!"

"My lord," she whispered—when she could.

He took her hand in his—scarcely touching it—at first.

Her little hand was icy cold. But it warmed quickly in his clasp—and then Chü-po's tender touch grew bolder—not less kind, not less considerate, and grasped Tzŭ's little fingers in a joyous vice.

The room was garnished for this hour. New mats of silky rice-straw strewed the lacquered floor. One —just one—great branch of sweet flowering jessamine leaned from an ivory bowl. One picture hung on a wall. One sentence of good import was written on one wall-hung scroll. And near the window through which the fragrant garden stretched stood a great vase of flambé Ch'ien Lung ware. It was the same vase that had stood till now in the courtyard of Ch'êng Ting Ping-yang. And even in her new confusion Ch'êng Ting Tzŭ knew it, and knew too why it was here—why her lord had wished, willed and contrived it.

She smiled at it. She could not smile at him—yet.

Ch'êng Chü-po caught Tzŭ to him with fumbling hands, and poured out to her an ecstasy of halting, pelting and compelling words.

It is not so that Chinese girls expect to be wooed. Ch'êng Chü-po knelt at her feet. He laid his hand in entreaty on her shoe. She looked down and giggled shyly. He half rose and clasped her knee, and drew her down to him, and held her so.   And they sat together, his arms about her, so leaning against the great Ch'ien Lung vase—happy and shy as two children in a new-found, sudden intimacy that was very sweet.

CHAPTER XV

THE marriage throve.

For they had gone unspoiled to it, the boy and the girl, and both were true and lovable: two children growing up together in harmony and trust.

And such is Chinese marriage as a rule. The new ideal of marriage that Europe is finding to-day— urged by bishop and scientist, philosopher and race philanthropist, in desperate anxiety for our man-sex, and in hope for the future of our race—and a new wisdom that red-handed, sad-eyed, wide-eyed war has taught, and urges—China has held, and has held to, for centuries. When the marriage-need comes, the marriage is there. The marriage-opportunity heaps young lives with happiness, content and health, and makes of appetite a sacrament and not a nameless lust, a wholesomeness and not a disease, an innocence and not a sore—makes human birth as sweet, as natural and as welcome as the birth of the flowers that bud in the sheltered leafage of sunny spring.

Ch'êng Tzŭ thought her young husband more godlike and more manly than any other of all earth's men —because she had no knowing of any other man.

Ch'êng Chü-po gave his first passionate caress to the girl at whose feet he knelt on their marriage evening, and he adored his wife—because he had frittered away no part of love's outer garments.

Neither had had earlier loves—or even love-passages—with which to compare this anointed love of theirs (perhaps to find the new and lawful lacking in some phase or lure)—and so, were absorbed in it, and he in her as she in him.

And when they knew that a babe was to come, all the jealous bitterness went from Ch'êng Shao Yün's heart, and she loved Ch'êng Tzŭ as her own. And waiting for the baby's birth, they three were almost as one.

After the interruption of marriage negotiations and long ceremonial, Yün took up her own life again vigorously, and faced solitude grimly—hiding her jealousy beneath a feverish, imperious industry. But Ah Söng sensed how it rankled, and knew that beneath all her stern, driving rush and fuss of daily things, Ch'êng Yün was waiting scornful but tortured for Chü-po to come back to her.

Chü-po never did come back—in the old fullness. Ch'êng Tzŭ filled his being. But soon he sought his mother's companionship, claimed her advice about many things; and Tzŭ crept into the older woman's heart, slowly at first—but the girl won upon the woman day by day, the more easily and the more surely because from the first Tzŭ had loved Ch'êng Yün.

And all went well with them.

Scarcely a silkworm ailed that year. Scarcely a rice grain withered or mildewed. And the great birthhour raced with the Feast of Lanterns.

Tzŭ thought the Feast would outstrip the little child. Ch'êng Yün thought her grandchild would be there first. And the two women made a jeweled bet.

But neither won it.

It was so sweet to carry her child—her child and her lord's—beneath her girdled heart that Ch'êng Tzŭ was not impatient for its birth; even perhaps she was a little reluctant to share it just yet with any other love and hands but hers, reluctant even to share it with the wide-eyed flowers, or the sun and air of day.

But Ch'êng Shao Yün was all impatience. She could scarcely wait. For she knew that at last a girl child was to be born to them: the fabled daughter of the Ch'êngs—maiden-minister of China—sweetest flower of Han.

Every augury proclaimed it a girl. And so did every wise woman on the place.

But Ch'êng Shao Yün had little use for such prophecies. They had failed her too often. But in herself, with all her soul, she knew this was a girl. She had no smallest doubt of it.

Just as the first lantern was lit the child was born.

It was a boy.

Ch'êng Ting Tzŭ tried not to be glad.

And Ch'êng Shao Yün fell into a frenzy that threatened her arrogant life. When ¡Ti-tô-ti came fawning to her for a sweetmeat she kicked the little loving thing away. And scarcely any dared approach or speak to her save only Ah Söng. Ah Söng watched her shrewdly through the sightless eyes that saw so much more than others' eyes could see, and when Ch'êng Yün's enraged disappointment had a little worn its fury out, spent and dashed itself to pieces against the hard rock of the proud woman's splendid spirit, blind Ah Söng told her that lord Chü-po's lady was very ill of body—dying perhaps, and tormented and soul-crushed because instead of the so-hoped-for girl, a mere man child had come to her swelling breast.

At that Ch'êng Shao Yün tidied her disheveled hair, shook out her twisted garments, loaded herself with

gems, and hurried to congratulate and to console
Ch'êng Ting Tzǔ. And she carried with her an arm-
ful of red roses and great scarlet hibiscus flowers.

It was a very tender face the woman bent over the
pale young mother thing, lying with the wee, new-
come, red and buff manling crooked in one dimpled
arm—for Yün remembered her own chagrin and suffering in such self-same hours, and forgot her own
selfish disappointment as all her big womanly heart
went out in sympathy to the girl who had borne the
Ch'êngs another boy.

Ch'êng Tzǔ—coached by Ah Söng—lay very still,
and tried to look miserable.

"It is only a boy," she whispered with a sob.

"Chut," Yün told her sharply, but proudly too,
"forget all the folly I talked. I was mad. Thank all
the gods it is a man." And she kot'owed to the
unconscious babe. When had that proud thing
kot'owed before? "See!" holding out her flowers.
And moving about the room, she decked it with the
red roses and the great crimson hibiscus flowers—
chamber of birth and triumph!

And Ch'êng Chü-po breathed softly a sigh of secret,
great relief. He had greatly feared that for the bearing of a boy, his mother would hate Ch'êng Tzǔ. But
he need not have feared it. Dwarf trees grow in
China but not dwarf souls.

Ch'êng Shao Yün pretended to be delighted with
her grandson, to think him more precious than any
jade, the flower of all the jades, and to love him as
she had never loved before.

And before Ch'êng Lo Yuet—for so they named
him—was a week old, she did. And the Wealth God
was lifted up from the ignominious dust, repedestaled

and given yet another coat of finest gold-leaf from shoe to shaven poll, given a big blazing sapphire of price to dangle in his tinsel crown. And often Yuet's grandame would fight his mother for the holding of him, nursing him for hours, and crooning to him old lullabies she had not sung since Ch'êng O had died— and had thought not to sing again.

CHAPTER XVI

ALL this time Ch'êng Shao Yün's purpose to banish Chü-po, to sacrifice him and her own heart to China, had neither slept nor sagged.

And when the Feast of Lanterns was passed his mother sent Ch'êng Chü-po to England—sorrowing but obedient. Nor was he altogether unwilling; for he, too, saw now the peril gathering over China— sensed the big white bear that lumbered on her from the Russ land, heard the swords sharpening in every garden in Japan, treachery boiling up in Korea, rapacity and avarice scheming in half the chancelleries of Europe.

And when the time came to go, he went with an unmoved, if a mask-like, face. And the two women who loved him most drew close together—a new friendship linking them, and Ch'êng Lo Yuet cradled in their arms.

The years passed slowly for the women waiting for his return in the teeming Ho-nan home.

Ch'êng Shao Yün bore it best—partly because it was her temper to bear all heavy things so—little frets she never bore—partly because of a daily growing infatuation for little Yuet—a lovely child with Ch'êng O's eyes and her own splendid indomitable temper, delicately cloaked with the pretty silken manners of Ch'êng Ting Tzŭ.

Several sorrows fell upon Yün in those slow years of Chü-po's long absence.

Each year she grew more anxious for her country.

Smallpox—always China's scourge—swept down across the Fu-niu Shan range, and devastated half a village.

Again it came—and left Ping-yang a childless widow.

Yün's second son, journeying at her command with a message to Pekin, was caught in the whirling rapids of the Hwang Ho, and China's turgid yellow sorrow had robbed Ch'êng Shao Yün of another son and of that son's sons, for at her wish they had gone with him to see something of the old capital, and to make first obeisance at the footstool of their Liege.

One by one death reaped her golden grain of life and hope till none of her bearing were left her but those that she had given away into adoption, and Chü-po in England, and Chü-po's son clinging to her hand now as once Chü-po had done. Such family-out-wiping is scarcely rare in China.

She bore it all with proud quiet—holding Yuet's hand the closer, scarcely letting him out of her sight, and sending long letters more and more often to Ch'êng Chü-po.

He would have returned to her now; and craved it, but she forbade it, commanding him to stay until his task in England was done.

Only a woman, and a Chinese woman, and passing rich at that, could have outplanned the elaborate festivities that had marked the marriage of Ch'êng Chü-po and Ting Tzŭ.

Ch'êng Shao Yün did it for the home-coming of Chü-po.

And he came at last—slowly—in state—carried in an endless cortège of grief.

Cholera had caught him at Hong Kong, and he had died there.

It killed Ch'êng Ting Tzǔ—snapped her radiant life off as some sudden gust of storm might have snapped the slender stem upon which a lovely blossom grew. And Ch'êng Shao Yün and Yuet were left alone.

Waiting to be newly wooed, and newly a bride, the black news cut through Tzǔ like a knife. She caught her hand to her heart, gave her child a look, and heaped down on the ko'tang floor at Yün's feet.

If her pain had been intense, its torture was brief. She died as she fell.

They buried her with him—buried them on the very spot where he had seen her first.

The family burying ground lay farther north. But on the day that he had left them, Chü-po had told his mother that it was there he'd pray to be laid when his time came to be a guest on high. And his wish—remembered now—weighed with Ch'êng Yün far more than any command of Feng-shui, had Feng-shui ordered it otherwise. But Ah Sông wailing about the courtyard—wailing in a human grief, but seeming too, half in trance—cried out that the hillock near the stream was gods-decreed for the burial of lord Ch'êng Chü-po; and then the necromancers hurriedly found it so.

Ch'êng Shao Yün showed no grief. And only blind Ah Sông understood—and knew Ch'êng Yün's grief was too great to be shown or seen. Only the sightless eyes of the old seer and slave had sight to see that agony. And only Ch'êng Shao Yün and Ah Sông knew—or suspected—that Chü-po's mother was newly jealous of Chü-po's wife—jealous because Ch'êng Tzŭ lay coffined at Ch'êng Chü-po's feet.

Yün built a paifang, in honor of Ch'êng Ting Tzŭ, across the path between the still river and the new graves, holding—and admitting—so, to all, that being slain by the mere word of her lord's death proved the devotion of Ch'êng Tzŭ as clearly as if the girl had hung herself beside his corpse.

Yün gave little Ch'êng Lo Yuet two loves now—the love that she had borne him already and with it all her love that had been Chü-po's.

Yün lived and had her being for Lo Yuet—and for China: always for China. China first of all!

And what had been a sacrificial purpose before became an obsession now. And she would not be balked of it. The more her love of her grandson the sterner her resolve to send him from her. Ch'êng Lo Yuet should go to England, as his father had gone —and should return and live, as that father had not, to work and win for China.

She had promised a son to China. And no accident so small as death should rob China of the gift, or her herself of the completed sacrifice.

And surely China's need grew sore. Already war threatened concerning Korea. The big white bear stretched out its taloned paws. Theft dared to turn its covetous Christian eyes even on the sacred grave where the crystal-tree grew in Shantung.

Ch'êng Lo Yuet should go to England, to learn of Europe—Europe's rank nefarious wiles—to return home to hoist the impertinent invaders with their own hot petard.

But he should marry first—and beget a child—for China must not be left Ch'êngless—or the Ch'êngs gone-on-high without earth-living worshipers.

Ch'êng Lo Yuet should beget a son, here where his father had begotten him, and then he should go.

He should beget a son.   She gave the old hope up —almost the wish.   That, too, she sacrificed.

And when Lo Yuet's age came ripe for it she found him a wife, and gave her to him without a pang.   Her capacity for personal suffering was dead—buried in the coffin of Chü-po, Ah Söng thought—but not her capacity for loving—since she still loved Lo Yuet even more than she had loved Chü-po.

No pre-romance prefaced the marriage of Ch'êng Lo Yuet.

Ch'êng Shao Yün left him with his tutors, and made a great journey—an almost royal progress—across China, visiting a score of great families, studying their daughters well.

She selected Hua Foh T'ien, a maiden of a clan older than her own, and as great.

And when Ch'êng T'ien was big with child, Shao Yün sent Yuet to England.

The child was born—when the painted lanterns swung red and rose and gold in the radiant processional of the glowing feast, and the great twisted dragon belched its fiery challenge to the stars—again a boy.

The years passed—quick busy years for all on the old Ho-nan estate.   And the reports that came, from Oxford now, of the progress of Ch'êng Yuet, could but satisfy the all-demanding heart of his grandmother.

But fate had not yet buffeted Ch'êng Shao Yün enough.

When Yuet's absence had less than two years to run, his young son died.

Ch'êng recalled her grandson home.

Again when the line of Ch'êng seemed secured she sent him back to complete his European days as at first planned: a few months more in Oxford, then a final year of travel.

But fate was not yet done with Ch'êng Shao Yün.

The young Chinese—the foremost student of his college, and easily its most brilliant, died at Oxford a few weeks before taking his degree.

Shao Yün heard it with a bitter smile, and bade them give great tending to Ch'êng T'ien.

For, if fate were or were not done with Ch'êng Shao Yün, Ch'êng Shao Yün was not yet done with fate.

Her purpose held.

CHAPTER XVII

AH SÖNG came from the chamber of Ch'êng T'ien and hurried through the garden. She carried no stick or staff, but she sensed her way with a double second-sight. She breasted the bridge, skirted the lotus pond, found the terrace, and left it, threaded the twisted paths and the molten quivering tulip maze, without a hesitation or one mis-step. She knew every inch of the vast, scattered estate, Ch'êng Yün's only rival, in sure, intimate mastery of its every path and nook.

A carrier pigeon winged from its cote, and followed her, flying low, circling her head again and again with a curling waste of time and a wanton indirectness of flight that told its flying a dallying and no execution of message-business—calling down to her now and then, and watching her expectantly through its hard glittering beads of crimson eyes. Always Ah SÖng had a word for every bird. She had none to-day. On the terrace the peacocks strutted to her screaming, and tweaked her skirt for grain. But she thrust them off, tearing her garments roughly from their clamorous beaks, and pushed through them on towards the silkworm sheds. Ah SÖng had no time for peacocks now.

The Lady Ch'êng sat brooding—lost in thought—on a bench near the worms' largest shed, and did not even look up as Ah SÖng came.

"Honorable mistress, thy slave brings news!"

"So——" was Yün's scant reply, nor did she lift her eyes.

"The honorable Ch'êng T'ien's time has come."

"Her women are with her—and the midwives?" But Shao Yün scarcely seemed interested.

"All that, jade-like. It was very quick."

"Nay—it was high time."

"It is not that thy slave means, O honorable."

Ch'êng Shao Yün did not trouble to ask what it was than that Söng had meant.

"Her hour has come—and gone."

Ch'êng Yün looked up at that. "You mean—the child has come?—Speak to the point!"

"O, mistress," Söng stammered brokenly.

"The child?" Yün demanded fiercely. She rose slowly—and saw that tears were tumbling from the sightless eyes, down Ah Söng's withered face.

"The child has driven Ch'êng T'ien on high," Söng retorted—almost as fiercely as Shao Yün had spoken —and then the slave whimpered, then sobbed; for she had loved the young mother of Lo Yuet's child.

"That!" Ch'êng said contemptuously. For what of it? Lo Yuet was dead. His wife could bear no other child. Ch'êng Yün thrust out an angry arm and clutched Ah Söng's wrist. "The child?" she hissed at the other, stamping a foot—and a sob broke through the hiss.

"The child lives, lady. It will live. It is well with the honorable great-grandchild."

"So——" Ch'êng Yün said more gently. "I will see it presently," and she turned and went a pace towards the cocoons' shed.

Ah Söng followed her, and caught at her robe.

Yün looked back at her with cold astonishment. The old blind servant was privileged—loved even— but not privileged to such license as this.

But Ah Söng held tightly to the garment she had caught. "Stay!" she implored. And she kot'owed till her old knees creaked. "My honorable mistress, it—it is a girl."

CHAPTER XVIII

"THOU liest? Thou darest to lie?" Ch'êng Shao
Yün was stammering now. A painful red crept
into her paintless cheeks.

"The honorable babe is strong and well," Söng said
proudly. "And it *is*—a girl."

Ch'êng Shao Yün hid her face behind her hands.
They twitched a little too.

"The gods are good," she whispered presently.
Then she turned, and moved slowly towards the house
—the dwelling house where she had borne her sons,
where now the girl dead in child-birth lay, and a
daughter of the Ch'êngs lived—lived to lift a curse,
lived to service China.

The child throve.

When the time came to name her, she was named
T'ien Tzŭ.

They named her T'ien Tzŭ, but not, of course, to
call her that for years. On the third day, when her
tiny ears were pierced, and the soft thread of strong
red silk left in, she would be given a milk-name—she
who could never know her natural milk—and she
would gain a cradle-name, and presently a pet-name,
Jade, Moonlight, Jessamine, Lotus, Rose, Violet or
any other lovely flower. Though probably milk-name,
cradle-name and pet-name would be the same. She
would be spoken of, as every new-come girl in China
(where girl babes are murdered, so 'tis said) she would

be spoken of commonly as "my thousand ounces of gold." Later she would have a school-name, though girls of such high birth do not go to school. But her name was Ch'êng T'ien Tzŭ, recorded so for ever on the scroll of the Ch'êngs.

And if Ch'êng Shao Yün had loved Chü-po, as she almost madly had, if Shao Yün had loved Lo Yuet even more, it grew to worship, the love she gave Ch'êng T'ien Tzŭ.

Never an hour they spent apart. And when T'ien Tzŭ was old enough to notice and crave, the very foods she might not have Ch'êng Yün eschewed, living again on the pap things and savorless simplicities that children thrive on best.

From the first Yün taught the little girl herself. All that a Chinese girl of high birth should know was instilled and drilled day by day into this young daughter of the Ch'êngs—accomplishments and learning of sterner stuff. And she too, was taught much that many maidens of her own caste are not often troubled or privileged to master. Above all Ch'êng Shao Yün taught her history—the history of China as Pan Chao —the famous historian of the first century (a woman, by the way)—had known and written it. All other history seemed of small account to Yün—as did the peoples whose past it recorded. For herself she scorned to waste an hour upon it—her hours grew few now—but because she destined her great-granddaughter to fight and worst those inferior peoples, and knew the fight would need much equipment of understanding them, as well as supersubtlety, Yün judged it right that Tzŭ should know something of the unworthy histories of unworthy Christendom, and especially of the English whom Yün held China's foremost menace.

And for that purpose Yün procured and employed a tutor from the University at Pekin, a learned Chinese who had spent some years in Europe, and was credited with speaking English well, and with having studied diligently at Oxford. He came when Tzŭ was only six. And Ch'êng Yün paid him richly to teach Tzŭ English, a smattering of English ways, all he could of English history and of its inner meaning, and, above all, to teach his pupil to hold China ever higher than the barbarians among whom she already knew she was soon to live.

But the child's Chinese education Ch'êng Shao Yün gave her herself, and was well able to do. The teeming literature, the splendid arts, the kind philosophies, the unsurpassed cultures and the pretty graces of China, the doyen lady of the Ch'êngs knew well. She had taught her sons, and her sons' sons, and was as able as she was willing to teach Ch'êng Tzŭ.

So ambitious was Yün for the child that she stinted her of play and of playmates—but did not quite deprive her of either.

Mung Panü, a slave girl a little older than Tzŭ, shared some of the lessons and the scant hours of play. Ch'êng Shao Yün had no mind that Tzŭ should forget, while in banishment, either the language or the thoughts of China, and so purposed that Mung Panü should go to England with Tzŭ, that they might speak together for an hour each day—speak Chinese. And for this it was important that the maid should speak the purest Chinese, and know something of the finer things.

On warm spring-time days sometimes lessons were relaxed for an hour, and Yün would take Tzŭ by the hand, and wander with her among the trees, and call the wild birds down. And little Tzŭ would flute and

chirrup to them too, and once a katydid came and
perched upon her tiny wrist, and poised a moment
there, happy so.   And always at the New Year festivities, all Tzŭ's tasks were laid aside, to be neglected,
forgotten, if she would, until after the Feast of Lanterns.

Of all the mighty race of Ch'êng only they two were
left to watch the Feast of Lanterns now—Ch'êng Shao
Yün, growing old at last, and little Ch'êng T'ien Tzŭ
clinging to her skirts.   But each year Yün decreed that
the Feast should be richer and lovelier than it had been
before.   That seemed impossible.   But the indomitable woman wrought it.   She had boundless wealth,
and at her aid the incomparable arts of an imperial
people which, if not as immeasurably superior to all
others as Ch'êng Shao Yün thought, must be conceded
by any sane and intelligent judgment, second to none.

Ch'êng Shao Yün had always loved the Feast of Lanterns, and she had always loved to display her wealth.
And she suspected—there were hints of it—that in the
flesh she should not see the feast for many more years
now.   The grief of her life had strained her, and
strained her all the more because she had willed to show
no sign of it, to meet and greet it with an unmoved
face.   And the shock of Tzŭ's birth, a girl come to
them at last, had strained her even more.

And she chose to make for Ch'êng Tzŭ out of the
Feast of Lanterns a picture book that should epitomize
all the great panorama of Chinese art and life—China's
history, China's tenets, all that was spiritual, all that
was bed-rock of glorious fact: China's very soul.   She
sought to give the child a picture and an imprint deep-
bitten, a memory and a sense, that could not fade, go
where she would, do what she might.

Ch'êng T'ien Tzŭ was a still child. For a Chinese of her sex she was almost tongue-tied. Her hates and loves were hidden deep—if she had them. They rarely showed. But she took a passionate delight from the first in the Feast of Lanterns. It gave her her first vivid impression, and her most lasting—an impression that each year deepened, to which each year added glow, detail and significance. In it she sensed the soul of China, and through it learned her glory imperial and imperishable. Through it she grasped the dual religion of her race, and made it her own, as through nothing else she could have done— the pulsing, living religion that is half ancestor worship, half worship of the beauty of nature. For the Feast of Lanterns, as Yün taught her from the first, is China's yearly offering to the quick spirits of her dead; and each jeweled, embroidered lantern, swinging and lurching pendant to the less radiant night, reflects and records some flower or other gem of nature or some jewel of China's story, as Chinese porcelain reflects and records the treasures of her greater arts.

The Feast of Lanterns came to be a sacrament to little Ch'êng T'ien Tzŭ. It is that to most Chinese.

Tzŭ knew how long and how arduous was its preparation each year, what skill and industry went to the making of it. And the knowing made of Chinese ceaseless industry a rite and a dignity. For always Ch'êng Shao Yün—leaning now a little on her ivory staff—was at her side to speak the illuminating word, to wake the burning Chinese thought. Yün intended that Tzŭ should go to Europe, but Yün intended that Europe should leave Ch'êng Tzŭ cold.

The first thing Tzŭ could remember was the Feast of Lanterns. And when her time came to become a guest on high, her last earth-lingering thought would be of the Feast of Lanterns.

When Tzŭ was ten the festival was kept with such extravagance of splendor, such ingenuity of new device, that Ch'êng Shao Yün knew that even she could never hope to surpass it in all the years to come. She was satisfied that it should be so. For years would pass before Ch'êng Tzŭ should see the great home feast again.

They watched it hand in hand. But they watched it silently. Even Yün had nothing more to tell the child, and the woman's throat was stiff and choked.

On the morrow the little Chinese girl of ten began her long journeying. She went wondering but placid and obedient, neither anxious nor depressed. She went with many obeisances, but scarcely with regret. Her young sheltered life had been so free from pain or doubt that she could not conceive that either could ever come to her, or indeed conceive of them at all. And, too, she came of a race whose women for thousands of years had, when little older than she, been sent from home never to return, lifted into their "floweries" and given to a new home, an unknown husband and to other mothering.

Ch'êng Shao Yün felt the parting more—felt it so sharply that almost she showed it.

She felt that she might not see Tzŭ again. She knew that ill-health and break-up threatened her. Even if she lived many years, this was her parting from Ch'êng T'ien Tzŭ. For the girl would return to China of marriageable age—and more. To be sure, Yün had no thought to give her in marriage—but rather to adopt the younger son of some great house, both that the ancestors of the Ch'êngs might be duly worshiped, and that Ch'êng Tzŭ might live her life out in the stronghold of the Ch'êngs—still a Ch'êng and the mother of Ch'êngs: doubly Ch'êng—Ch'eng by marriage as Ch'êng by birth.   But even so the English years would change the girl.   The child that she was giving up would never come back to her again. In giving Tzŭ she was giving her all—more than her life, because the music and the sunshine of her life, the one companionship left to her now from all her long life's wealth of love.   But never for one heart-beat did Ch'êng Shao Yün waver—or even think of it—from the purpose that I Kong Moy had stirred in her on the day that Tzŭ's grandfather Chü-po had first seen Tzŭ's grandmother, Ting Tzŭ.   For the imperious old woman was abjectly and devotedly the servant of great imperial China.

CHAPTER XIX

ENGLAND was very kind to the little Chinese stranger within its fog-hung gates. The child's sweetness was unmistakable, her dainty high-breeding told instantly on all who met her—on those who were precluded from realising just what the strong charm was almost as much as on those whose caste-sympathy recognized it as a fine something in which they themselves had their own lesser share, and her personal beauty was irresistible. For when the oddness had worn off a little, even the dullest English eyes, and the most isle-bound British taste, could not fail to see that Ch'êng Tzŭ was very lovely.

Ch'êng Shao Yün had known from the first that her great granddaughter was strangely like the girl with whom Chü-po had fallen so madly in love—and, as it proved, so irrevocably. And year by year, Ch'êng T'ien Tzŭ grew more and more like her father's mother when the elder Tzŭ had been loveliest, and had just come to Ho-nan and to love. Critical and familiar eyes could scarcely have told Ch'êng T'ien Tzŭ from Ting Tzŭ at the same age, had it not been for one difference slight but marked—a difference that was the granddaughter's one visible inheritance from her mother.

Ch'êng T'ien Tzŭ had the characteristically Chinese lovely and luminous eyes, but they were set straight in her head, as Manchu eyes so often are, and as Ch'êng Hua Foh T'ien's had been. And more than once

Ch'êng Shao Yün had wondered if there were any truth in a scandal centuries old that had discredited a lady of the Huas with a Manchu lover of imperial rank. It had never been proved. And Hua Foh T'ien's dowery had been fabulous, and her feet almost smaller than Yün's tiny own. But every few generations some babe of descent from the impeccable Chinese house of Hua came into life with its new eyes straight set.

Tzǔ liked England from the first. And from the first she won her way into the English hearts about her. After the first brief, sharp homesickness all the lines of her English sojourn fell in pleasant, kindly places.

Ch'êng Shao Yün was obsessed and imperious, but she was sane.

She had made no attempt to select herself the house of Tzǔ's European stay—appreciating that she, Chinese and in far off Ho-nan, could have no wiseness concerning the child's English environment or entourage. So she put its determining into Shêng Liu's hands, and into those of a Chinese official in London. Neither man blundered.

Ch'êng Yün's sanity had exacted of her one other concession concerning Tzǔ—a concession that cost Yün considerably more self-control and sacrifice. She had made no attempt to instil her own acrid hatred of the English into the tender, sunny soul of little Tzǔ. She had taught her that with every decent Chinese China came first—that the Chinese *was* first of all the peoples —and that a Chinese of high birth, any Ch'êng, could give China nothing short of worship and selfless fealty. But beyond these broad lines she neither went nor tried to go. For she realized that a pre-prejudice must cramp the young plastic mind, and incapacitate it to understand best, and best learn from, the English. And she trusted the girl's own Chinese instinct and acuteness to draw their own conclusions—always to China's favor—and to harden into just enmity when the time for enmity and action should come. For she had seen her own intellect, her own force, her own indomitable persistence beneath the gentleness and the exquisite loveliness that Ch'êng T'ien Tzŭ had inherited from Chü-po's wife. And she was well assured that in her child's scarce conscious heart throbbed a patriotism and a loyalty as deep and as uncompromising as her own. She trusted Tzŭ, for Tzŭ was Chinese and a Ch'êng—descended from half the greatest clans in China—descended, best of all perhaps, from the house of Shao. She sensed herself within the child; and perhaps trusted her most, as certainly she loved her most, for that—and she felt secure that when she left the earth-land she loved, and to her utmost served, her own soul would live on in Ho-nan in the bosom of the girl with the perfect eyebrows and deep, jade-like eyes, set Manchu-level in a peach-like face.

To this second concession—so difficult that only a great soul could have made it, or a great will enforced, little Tzŭ owed even more than she did to the first of her happiness in England.

Ch'êng T'ien Tzŭ was very happy in England.

And while she grew there, and grew not a little into English ways and thinking, the bereft grandmother lived on in China, growing strangely older, but busier and more busied than before—she grieved, but it was not in her to repine or be idle. And she saw each day China's peril, and China's need of loyal service and action, growing more and more.

Each year the Feast of Lanterns kept its solemn,

sparkling festival. But Ch'êng Shao Yün never watched it now—scarcely turned her head from book or document when the crackers cannonaded through the paths, much less went to her casement to watch the great illuminated dragon as it passed. She would watch the Feast of Lanterns next when she watched it hand-in-hand with home-come Ch'êng T'ien Tzŭ, or— more, probably, she thought—when she came back to it a guest from on high.

She leaned heavily on her ivory stave now when she walked, but she went, even more ceaselessly than before, about her great domain where the coal mines belched up a rich daily harvest of black gold, and the silkworms—though Ho-nan is a province of wild and inferior silks—because Ch'êng Yün willed and planned and watched it, and her servants obeyed, spun her a sheened, supple wealth that fed upon the fabric markets of the world. A Tzarina wore coronation silk that had been the Lady Ch'êng's, and a cardinal wore it in the Vatican, and the very by-products of the place wove and piled her fortune a Rothschild might strain to match.

And in every village and hillside home there was peace and plenty, and at least one woman who carried cocoons in her yellow breast, and when their time had come—her day's housewifery done—lit her oil-fed light, or her resined torch, scalded the cocoons, and her own patient heroic hands, spun the cocoons' gleaming off-flux, and wove it on a homemade bamboo loom. And to every humble home that was her people's, the Lady came and served and ruled it as tenderly and ruthlessly as she did the gigantic industries of the place —the great silkworm sheds, the dark coal mines, the teeming acres of cotton fields, the busy factories, the

art works and the great store-houses opulent with grain
—tottering sometimes on her own tiny, indefatigable
feet, carried sometimes in her palanquin.

Too Ch'êng Shao Yün often went from Ho-nan in
these later years of her loneliness. Probably she
would have done so in any case, since she wished it, and
thought it best—for, however subservient to custom
such imperious women may seem or hope to be, they
never are in fact subservient when subservience would
entail an unwilling and not self-willed abnegation of
self and of personal conviction. The Ch'êng Shao
Yüns of earth rule their own daily destinies everywhere. But even in China—perhaps more in China
than anywhere else—a woman as old as Ch'êng Yün
was now, as rich and as strong of character and poise,
may do, and even go, much as she will.

Again she had a son, a boy adopted by her that the
ancestor-worship of the Ch'êngs need not lapse or fail,
that the Ch'êng name might not die, but live in the sons
of Tzŭ, and that Tzŭ herself should neither be hus-
bandless nor dwell permanently elsewhere than on their
own estate. The boy was being educated in Pekin,
strictly in accordance with the judgment and wish of
Ch'êng Shao Yün and under her strict supervision.

But it was not to see him—Ch'êng Wên—that the
woman journeyed to Pekin, as she often did. He was
but a passive pawn in her game of life, in no way, and
in no way to become, of her affection—just a necessity
bought and paid for, a chattel necessary to her scheme
of life for Ch'êng T'ien Tzŭ. And it was Tzŭ—not he
—that Yün intended to rule, when Tzŭ had come
home, and she herself had joined their ancestors.

Ch'êng Shao Yün pilgrimaged to Pekin to hold conference with the great Dowager. They had been

friends for years, the Manchu Empress and the Chinese chieftainess, close-knit in their one love of China—their burning patriotism—and in their hatred, and growing fear, of the encroaching foreigners.

The Chinese peril grew near and acute—not the "Yellow Peril" of which the papers of Christendom prate glibly when copy's scarce, and which may yet strike Europe harder than any one of Fleet Street thinks (but in its nastiest, most merciless scourge to come from a smaller, younger, less honest people than the Chinese) but a dual peril threatening China from within, and from the prying aliens without.

War menaced, international war. And the secret societies festered and cankered at home.

The two women, great enthroned Manchu and great Chinese, were troubled and anxious. Anxiety grew to alarm. Tze-Shi and Ch'êng Yün were almost somewhat distraught.

But in England, the girl Tzŭ—almost as blind as British statesmanship—took no heed of such things.

She grew in the cool English green like some happily transplanted exotic flower in the quiet garden of her simple country rectory home.

Ch'êng T'ien Tzŭ was well content in England.

Mung Panü was not.

CHAPTER XX

MUNG PANÜ disliked everything in England, and Ch'êng Tzŭ disliked some few things very much.

She missed the sun. Even in summer the sun seemed far-off to her and cold, as it had never seemed in China. And in the long, sunless stretches of the English winter she suffered an agony of spirit that was even worse than the withering shrinking of body. She wore furs in the house, and Mrs. Ford, tenderly anxious for the Chinese children's comfort, piled up the Rectory fires until the servants feared she'd burn the Rectory down, and the Rector said so, and often in the night rose from his comfortable bed to prowl and peer about the house unhappily, sniffing and looking for smoldering disaster. But in that first winter of her English stay little Ch'êng Tzŭ was never once really warm. "Does the sun never shine in England?" she cried more than once to the fog when it blanketed the Rectory and the village in impenetrable gloom. But summer came again, and brought her flowers. And when the next winter came Chinese Tzŭ had grown a little acclimated; if not reconciled. But she never ceased to miss the sun, the hot, downpouring Chinese sun, and to long and even sicken for it, as the drunkard, denied, craves for wine.

Often the Rectory food revolted the child. Mrs. Ford kept a generous table and had an excellent cook. But the best English cooking is so inferior to the everyday fare of well-to-do Chinese that it is surprising that Ch'êng Yün's great-grandchild contrived to eat enough to keep her well during those first savorless months at the Rectory. Beef is a positive offense to most Chinese palates; it was to Tzŭ's. And the knives and forks frightened her. And Mrs. Ford made culinarily the greatest mistake of all, and made it, as such mistakes are so often made, out of the veriest kindness—in attempting to tempt little Miss Ch'êng with Chinese dishes. She questioned Mung Panü and ransacked books of Chinese travel for food hints. The preparing of the resultant dishes first made the placid Rectory cook sullen and then quarrelsome, and set before Ch'êng Tzŭ she found them even nastier than she had found their predecessors. That they were Chinese she never even suspected. Then Tzŭ's Rectory menu settled down to a long deluge of rice. Such rice! Ch'êng Tzŭ hardly recognized it at first.

But she was young and strong, and determined to be pleased, if she could. And, if she never learned to relish beef and roast potatoes, she grew used to much that was set before her, and throve and kept bonnie on chicken and tomatoes, pancakes, bread and milk, fruit and the Rectory eggs and fish.

Cold baths she would not endure. Indeed Mrs. Ford never tried that but once. Once was quite enough. Tzŭ never succeeded in getting in England a bath that she considered hot, until she had an English house of her own, but she did get them—after that first memorable cold one—of a temperature that she admitted endurable. Mrs. Ford called them boiling.

Her new English clothes troubled the Chinese child not a little. She felt them uncomfortable, and saw them hideous. But she was obedient—Ch'êng Yün had

enjoined it—and Beatrice Ford was lenient. She let
the child select the colors she was to wear, and wear
English cuts and trimmings somewhat modified
towards Chinese modes. Tzŭ insisted upon tying her
blue-black hair with crimson ribbons—the signal color
of Chinese maidenhood, and Mrs. Ford made no ob-
jection. And twice a year a box of clothing came
from China, and in her own room often, and in the
general house sometimes, Ch'êng Tzŭ was allowed to
wear her lovely native dress. Why "Madame Ch'êng"
sent Tzŭ the Chinese garments greatly puzzled the
English lady. For Chêng Liu told her that the venerable lady in Ho-nan imperatively wished that Tzŭ
should in all possible ways conform to English cus-
toms. But Ch'êng Shao Yün as little wished Tzŭ to
forget what Chinese clothes were, or how to wear them,
as she wished her to forget how to read, write and
speak Chinese. The Chinese clothes were sent, as
Mung Panü had been sent—to remind Ch'êng T'ien
Tzŭ of home, and to keep her accustomed to things
Chinese.

Long Chinese letters came to the child, and went
from her. She had Chinese books with her, and musical instruments, and quite a horde of Chinese toys
—clay and wooden figures and animals—gayly painted,
a score of games and half a score of costly Chinese
dolls—all treasures of her younger days. Tzŭ at ten
was quite too old for toys. But she loved them all.
But Mrs. Ford soon found that Tzŭ preferred not
to show her Chinese toys, and liked nothing less than
visiting or being visited by English children. And
nothing would induce her to bring her lute or her
guitar out of her own room, or to play her Chinese
music except there.

At first Shêng Liu came to the Rectory often, and stayed always several days. Then—as the girl grew more accustomed to her new surroundings—he came less frequently and stayed more briefly. But he never ceased to come, and he wrote to Tzŭ, and she to him.

The Rector liked to teach. Tzŭ loved to learn. And they two got on famously together. She was appalled at his ignorance—of China, and despised him for it not a little. But she soon learned that most English folk knew even less of China than he did: he knew that there were eighteen provinces in China, he knew that white poppies yielded the better crop, and he had heard of Marco Polo and of the great observatory at Pekin. Most English people, she discovered, had not.

She had no playmates here. The Ford boys were away at school in Germany—all three of them, and would probably not come home until she had gone to school in London, which she was to do as soon as it could be arranged, and she had learned enough English, and enough of English ways. And she learned both rapidly. She had no playmates, but she had had but few in Ho-nan. And, when she found how Tzŭ disliked it, Mrs. Ford soon gave up inviting English children to the Rectory over often. But Tzŭ had Mung Panü with her always, and Shêng Liu to come to her, if she wished him, and to come as fast as English steam would bring him.

And so the child led her little dual life—English-seeming, Chinese at core.

Mrs. Ford wondered how soon the English part would get the upper hand, and drive the old Chinese thought and feeling into obscurity, and banishment. And sometimes Shêng Liu grimly wondered it too.

Mung Panü feared it. And Panü combated it with all her might and with all her Chinese skill. Of all her great devoted retinue none had ever served Ch'êng Shao Yün more ardently than the homesick slave girl Mung Panü did—none unless blind Ah Söng.

Beatrice Ford taught Tzŭ to skate and to ride. The Rector taught her golf and chess, and the lessons that seemed to Shêng Liu most desirable.

Tzŭ liked Mrs. Ford. She liked the Rector better —until he began to press his faith upon her a little unwisely. Possibly like her great-grandmother, Tzŭ had more flair for men than for women. Certainly she liked Shêng more warmly than she did Mung Panü, and preferred his company to Panü's, liked the Rector—at first—a little better than she did his wife, though Mrs. Ford was destined to wear better in the child's regard. And the greatest friend she made in her Rectory years was a man, and her capture of him was something of a triumph. Gibbs the old gardener was sour and gnarled. He worked well. But he was never known to speak unless spoken to, and rarely to answer with decent civility then. And he hated all she-things—two-footed or four—with a deadly, venomous hatred. Tzŭ made him hers within a month. They spent long hours together, trowels and watering cans in hand, and he told the Rector that the "little yellow heathen" made the flowers grow. Perhaps she did. For she loved them. And she warmed one churlish old English heart.

A sincere churchman, it was not to be expected that Philip Ford would refrain from trying to show Ch'êng Tzŭ the error of Chinese theologies. How could he? It would not have been to his credit. But his cau-

tious attempt at proselytizing only served to lose him
his first place in Tzŭ's regard.

He went to work very subtly, as he thought. But
the Chinese girl instantly discovered his intention, and
her Chinese soul took offense,—not fright—and its
wings beat back to the painted gods of China. She
had one with her, in a box of camphorwood. She
had forgotten it—but now she took it out, and put
it beside her picture of Ch'êng Shao Yün. And Mrs.
Ford and the maids thought it quite the ugliest of
her dolls.

If the English cleric had been less profoundly ignorant of the belief he aimed to annihilate, his chance
of success might have been more. But probably not,
for irreligion is fairly invincible. And in any European sense the Chinese mind is essentially irreligious.
Confucianism, Taoism and Buddhism are accredited
the three religions of China. But the statement is lax.
Confucianism is not a religion. It is a philosophy, a
code of ethics, and of conduct. Taoism, more spiritual—and to-day more debased—is scarcely more. Buddhism has little hold in China—except upon the sim-
plest minds here and there in the remote North. The
religion of China is a mingling of common sense,
reverence for ancestors, and adoration of nature. And,
because it satisfies its adherents, it will not easily be
undermined. The Rev. Philip Ford never got one
word of his message through to Tzŭ—nor would he
have done so, if she had spent as many years at the
Rectory as she spent months. He was a good teacher.
He knew his theme. But he did not know Tzŭ's.

She had seen the kitchen gods abused and left sup-
perless at home when her rice had displeased Ch'êng

Yün, and regularly as the dinner hour came around
Ch'êng Tzŭ regretted that Mrs. Ford had no kitchen
gods, and longed to procure her a pair—to supervise
the Rectory cooking.

But the Rector made an admirable English scholar
of Ch'êng Tzŭ and quickly taught her how to beat
him at billiards every time.

Tzŭ loved no one, except her great-grandmother
across the world in Ho-nan. But they all loved her,
and were tenderly good to her. Beatrice Ford cried
herself to sleep the first time she saw Ch'êng Tzŭ's
naked feet. Mung Panü was furious. Tzŭ was
greatly offended. But from that hour the English
woman devoted herself to the Chinese child almost
fanatically. And the busy days passed fairly happily
for the exiled little Ch'êng.

Of course, she was home-sick sometimes—and except for her own companionship, and the companionship of the flowers, and the animals about the place,
she was very lonely.

Beatrice Ford's heart bled hourly for the child. She
was sorry too for Mung Panü. But Panü was older
—and, as Mrs. Ford told her husband, Panü had her
feet. But Tzŭ was such a baby—barely ten—and her
feet so cruelly maimed. Beatrice Ford thought that
the old Ch'êng woman in China must be insane—or
else a monster—to send such a child so far, to live
among entire strangers—strangers alien to her in every
way.

And there was something little short of tragedy in
it, truly enough! A child of ten, a girl child delicately
reared, exquisitely sheltered till now. Born in riotous
sunshine, brought up in sunshine, living all her little
life in a land throbbing with color and with festival,

ringing with laughter and song; steeped in glowing traditions and in picture, the very devils picturesque and amusing, suddenly sent across the world tossed on the great, seemingly-shoreless ocean, in a monster ship, no woman of her own race near her, only a slave girl more frightened and homesick than herself for companionship, thrust into the English fog and mist and cold, given strange foods to eat, with strange utensils, told to speak a language she did not know, stared at if she went outside the gate as if she'd been a circus or an unbelievable sleight of hand performance or some abnormal growth or a "freak" of nature—to live her girlhood out among people who could not possibly understand her, and whom she could not possibly understand! Beatrice Ford wondered that such an experience did not kill or craze her.

Oh! she was very good to Tzŭ—and scarcely less good to Mung Panü.

And indeed to meet the experience as little Tzŭ did told her very callous, or very brave.

Tzŭ was wonderfully brave. Her race had been brave for many centuries. And she had boundless confidence in Ch'êng Shao Yün. She knew that whatever her great-grandmother had done was kindest— and deserved her burning gratitude. And her love and loyalty never wavered.

And in Ho-nan Ch'êng Yün sickened for her child.

And Tzŭ was very busy. Her great-grandmother had told her to work. She worked! And there was so much to learn. And she wished to learn it all. And she had dreams for comforters, warm day-dreams of her going home, of the time to come when her hand would lie close and safe again in Ch'êng Yün's hand. The lilies in the courtyard would make her garments sweet, and the fireflies at the night time would turn the garden into fairyland.

But sometimes her face quivered a little in the darkness of the night, when the winter rain beat upon her window-pane, and the wind whistled down her bedroom chimney. Sometimes, when she was sure that Mung Panü slept, she crept out of bed, and caught up a doll, or a spotted wooden tiger, and took it back to sleep with her—and once she took her god.

CHAPTER XXI

WHEN the Earl died, and his income followed his title to a distant kinsman, the Ladies Worthing looked about them hurriedly for something to do.

They were penniless and plain. But they were sensible and full of pluck. They had no stomach for charity, and no appetite for permanent penury.

And, realizing how scant other capital they had, and somewhat undervaluing their sterling capital of personality and character, they cast about them for avocations in which their titles would best count as capital.

Joan and Lucy decided on a bonnet shop. They began modestly enough—they had to begin modestly—in Putney, but by dint of sheer hard work they achieved Kensington and a solid bank account *via* Bayswater, and after ten strenuous, anxious years. Mary thought the titled milliner stunt overdone—she said—and besides, it needed heaps of talent, which no Worthing had ever had, and, she added, she was too passionately fond of clothes, above all bonnets and hats, to be willing to make her living botching them—or, if she learned to turn out successful ones, to part with them to other women. She disliked most women, almost as much as men seemed to dislike her, although she had some flair for growing girls. The pretty ones intrigued her, and the plain ones pulled her sympathy.

Lady Mary Worthing decided to open a girls' school.

Her sisters cried out shrilly, her acquaintance mocked, the family solicitors argued.

And moreover, however could she? That was the final, clinching dissuasion of them all.

And it did seem rather final.

Lady Mary hadn't the haziest idea how to accomplish it, or even of how to begin trying to do so. She had very clear-cut ideas of just what manner of school she wished hers to be. No modest Putney beginnings for her. Hers was to be a fashionable finishing school near Belgrave Square, very expensive and very successful. Lady Mary wished to make a great deal of money.

Lucy tittered, and the Lady Joan screamed with mirth. Thorndyke, Hall and Thorndyke shrugged relieved blackclad shoulders, and smiled indulgently. It was a harmless ambition, and perfectly safe, since quite impossible of fulfillment. Fashionable finishing schools just off Belgrave Square require lavish monetary capital; Lady Mary had none and no means of getting any.

Quite. But Mary Worthing did it.

How she did it is a not uninteresting story. But it is her story, not ours. And one passing hint must suffice. Lady Mary Worthing had had a Scots mother.

She not only did it, but she made it pay, long before her scoffing sisters' bonnet shop did.

It was the starting at all that smacked of modern miracle. Once started the rest was easy and simple, and success a foregone conclusion.

Lady Mary had no educational fads—scarcely an educational theory, and none too much education of her own. She played a fairish game of bridge, but the tradesmen's books beat her every time. But she dressed exquisitely—as soon as she could—her man-

ners were both patrician and charming. She flattered
the parents, and she made her girl pupils happy, and
"turned them out" highly creditable both to herself
and to the Court of St. James. And it was perhaps
her best asset of all that she knew to a nicety whom
and what to exclude from her teaching staff, and from
her list of pupils, and did it rigorously.

And to the surprise of every one—and to the frank
and open envy of her sisters—she married. But,
though her husband was no kinsman, his name was
Worthing too, and she felt it an added advantage that
she need not change her name to achieve the coveted
prefix of "Mrs."—though "Mrs." understood. James
Worthing was a gentleman and a decent, friendly soul.
And the tradesmen's arithmetic held no alarms for
him. He could boast little more education than his
wife, but he could do shillings and pence and even
pounds and ounces. Lack of sufficient means had
driven him from the army—but his brief soldiering
had been creditable, and was an advantage to him still,
and an advantage to his wife's school—an advantage
of which she made the quiet most— which was a useful
something which no one living could do better or with
more perfect breeding than Lady Mary could. Captain James Worthing had been very honorably wounded
in the Boer War, and had not only deserved, but, what
is rarer, had received the D.S.O.

Captain Worthing had secretarial work at the Chinese Legation. He was no sponger on his wife. And
he made her a good husband. And she rewarded
him after five years of steady matrimonial good conduct on his part—hers goes without saying—by making him a proud parent. The welcome offspring proved
—a little to the dulling of his pride, and to Lady

Mary's frank disgust, not only carrot-haired, but twins.

But the boarders were as delighted as amused when the mother and her daughter and son returned to Belgrave Square, and the Chinese Minister sent two priceless christening cups of opalescent jade.

No other babies came to the school near Belgrave Square—and Lady Mary bore it placidly, having learned incidentally that for more than a century twins had been very prevalent among the Trulls. James Worthing had had a grandmother whose maiden name was Trull. But these two babies soon made the school a home. They did not have the run of the classrooms, of course, but they soon had wide freedom of crawl at recreation hours, and many a girl there then owed a sweetness and a womanliness, that was her lifelong wealth and charm, to the fact that two red-headed babies had crept into her heart, and clung there, gurgling, contented and at home, when she was at boarding school.

It was a nice school. Captain Worthing neither kept unduly in the background, nor over obtruded—was a thoroughly nice fellow, and Lady Mary was a nice woman and exceptionally sane.

She ruled well. And she was growing rich.

CHAPTER XXII

DONALD—he was almost five now, and naturally Edith was too—made a fat dash for the toasting fork, but Lady Mary made a quicker grab for his pinafore, caught it, and wrenched him back and up into her lap.

Elenore Selwyn was toasting crumpets—none too easy a task even on the wide grate's glowing coals, for at its other end Justine du Bret was popping corn.

This was the girls' own hour, their time of complete freedom. This was their sitting room and sanctum. Here no teacher might come, be her errand what it might. "Home from home" the girls called it. And at this, their hour of twilight sanctuary, even Lady Mary never came without special and explicit invitation. She was popular with her charges, and careful to keep her popularity and her welcome unworn and cordial—so careful that not always would she come even when urged.

It was winter, crisp and clear, the sun just down, and the logs piled ready to lay on the ruddy coals when the schoolgirl cookery should be done.

"My, how good!" the mistress said, as she munched the first crumpet, sizzling hot and buttered thick.

Baby Edith stood behind Justine with chubby arms about the French girl's neck, red curls cuddled on the black. Edie meant to have the first taste of the popcorn.

Dorothy Fielding was pouring the fragrant tea.

And a dozen or more other girls lounged prettily about the cheerful room. They were all licensed here. Even moderate slang came and went unrebuked. Lady Mary herself had been known to drop a sly word of it here now and then. And here she never spoiled sport. She rarely spoiled it anywhere needlessly. Her policy was far different.

When the meal was nearly done, and a pause came in the chattering, Lady Mary said suddenly,

"Shall I tell you a story, girls, before I tote the babies off to bed?"

They turned to her expectant, and surprised. She did many companionable things for them, and often. But she had never told them a story before. They had not suspected story telling to be among her comfortable, straight-cut gifts. And they were most of them rather old for story telling.

"Please," the Infanta Mercedes said, the first, as always, to remember her manners even here.

"We have a new pupil coming to-morrow," the Head began. "It is very interesting—quite like a story in a book, I think. I am peculiarly anxious to make her one of my successes—and that she should be happy here—and learn a great deal. And I want you all to help me."

The tense interest of the girls grouped about her laxed almost noticeably. New girls were no great rarity. And they had chill sympathy with any girl who could be unhappy here. And there was little thrill in Lady Mary's beginning—and no promise of anything novel. She always was anxious to make you one of her very special successes, and to have you work tremendously, and learn lots. Story, indeed!

Then she told them Ch'êng Tzŭ's story—as much

of it as she knew. Its vital core, the real reason of the girl's banishment, Lady Mary knew nothing of, nor suspected.

A little Chinese girl, a Princess or more in her own country, fabulously rich, an orphan without one near relative living, even in China—(the fall of Port Arthur had killed Ch'êng Shao Yün—though she had lived more than a year after it, dying but a year ago) was joining them to-morrow, to learn all that their teachers, Lady Mary and the girls themselves, could teach her. And Lady Mary begged for her not only the sufferance, but the friendship of the girls.

"She is very young, the youngest girl I have ever taken—not quite thirteen—precocious, my cousin writes me, lovable when you come really to know her. She may feel very strange among us—I suppose she will—but perhaps less strange than we'd expect, for she has been living for two years, a little more than two, with my cousin, Mrs. Ford, at the Rectory, and so she already knows something of quiet English country ways—but nothing of London. She has never been in a city—or even a large town—in her life—not even in China—except that she must have passed through Hong Kong and Liverpool, when she sailed and landed. She has never been to a function in her life, more exciting than a rectory croquet party."

"Does she speak English, Lady Mary?"

"After two years in an English rectory? Of course she does, Elenore. But she has not forgotten her own language—for she has a friend with her, an older girl, with whom she has spoken Chinese, for at least an hour every day."

"They boze come, Madame?"

"Try to say your 'th,' Justine," Lady Mary reminded kindly. "No, Miss Ch'êng comes alone. Miss Mung is ill, nothing much, and is to stay with the Fords, for the present. Be good to her, girls. Remember she is very far from home—a stranger here, perhaps a stranger there too, when she goes back, since none of her family is living. Be good to her." The last words were a plea, and a little anxious. Mary Worthing knew how hard girls could be. And on her own account she had hesitated seriously before consenting to receive little Miss Ch'êng. She had no great liking for Orientals—not that she knew any well, or many at all. But it had seemed an exceptional opportunity to show what she could do. And her ambition as an artist in "turning out" girls admirably had pricked her on to this somewhat unwelcome, and certainly difficult, attempt. Lady Mary was deeply in love with her work.

"Do your best—I know you will," she said, with just a tiny sigh, as she rose to separate Donald and Edith, who were squabbling lustily with each other for sole possession of the pop-corn popper. And when she had taken it from both of them, and "toted" them off to bed—a protested process always—an uncordial, smoldering silence fell upon the room.

Justine broke it. "Mon dieu. I zink it time I go back to France."

"A Chink!" one English girl said bitterly.

"Don't you think we'd better wait until we see her?" Elenore Selwyn suggested. But there was more British love of fair play than conviction in her voice. She did not say it warmly.

None of them liked it.

Several of them were far from home, exiled from their own homes and kindred—the French and Spanish girls, two Russians, a Roumanian and a Cuban. And three were orphans.

These schoolgirls were not insular. And without exception they were ladies. Half of them were the daughters of noblemen. Two had fathers in the Cabinet—a Tory Cabinet—one was the daughter of a great newspaper owner. Others were the children of diplomats, generals, eminent jurists. Most of them had traveled and knew something of the world—more than one might have boasted royal godmothers, and three had royal blood—collateral but legitimate.

But they one and all resented the coming of Ch'êng Tzŭ. And no one disputed it with a word or look when Marion Helmsely said, with scornful finality, "I do think we might draw the line at Chinese."

CHAPTER XXIII

IF Lady Mary, the next day, was asked less cordially than she usually was, to "come in to us, won't you?" she took no notice, and said quickly, "Yes, thanks, I'll be there."

It was during lunch that the invitation was given and accepted. The Chinese girl had not come yet, and no further mention had been made of her.

Lady Mary came into their sitting room later than she usually did. Their tea had been cleared away. And she came without the twins.

But Ch'êng Tzŭ walked beside her—slim and tranquil.

Short of being a Scandinavian blonde, she scarcely could have looked less like what the girls had expected.

Her skin was much lighter than that of the pretty Cuban toasting chestnuts at the fire, and except for her blue-black hair, she was less brunette than several of the English girls. In the half light of fire and shaded lamps she scarcely looked a foreigner in that rather cosmopolitan little gathering.

Her hair looked dusky, but not over glossy. It was free from unguents, braided closely about her head. And she carried no signal of her fabulous wealth, not one gem, not so much as a ribbon. She was dressed severely in unrelieved white—the material almost coarse. For she still wore mourning for Ch'êng Yün —the only relative she had ever known.

From her first coming she had conformed to English ways in almost every particular. She had done it at first because her great-grandmother had so enjoined her, but soon had come to like doing it. But every once in a long while Beatrice Ford had found some little point upon which Ch'êng Tzŭ would not conform. She dressed as an English girl, excepting only her shoes—and they were a compromise—and that she had a passion for thrusting things in her hair—for first choice, jeweled, beaded tassels that tinkled and shook. But she would not wear black for mourning, nor allow the coarse, white robes she chose to be trimmed in any way. And never a stick-pin, a flower or a tassel did she wear in her hair now.

"It scarcely looks comfortable," Mrs. Ford had pleaded.

"It is not intended to be comfortable," Tzŭ had told her. "I do not wish to be comfortable—now."

And that had ended it.

The Infanta Mercedes went up to Ch'êng Tzŭ, and held out her hand—partly it was good manners, partly it was impulse, and there was fellowship in it too. Beauty appealed compellingly to Mercedes always. And she was the first to recognize the rare beauty of the girl in the coarse white gown. Her princely homes in Spain were rich in masterpieces of old portraiture, not a few by Velasquez among them, and the girl standing beside Lady Mary reminded the Infanta of the loveliest Velasquez on the walls at home.

Tzŭ put her hand, it was like a warm yellow rose leaf, in the Infanta's hand, and thanked her with a smile. And when she smiled every girl there saw her beauty: it sparkled through the room. Lady Mary caught her breath at it, and more than one girl did too.

"I am glad that you have come," Mercedes said, and Elenore Selwyn hurried forward then, not because she was attracted, but because she was a "good sort," and said heartily, "Yes, we are very glad you have come."

Ch'êng Tzŭ dimpled. She rather wanted to say "Why?" But that would have been rude, so, instead she smiled again and bowed.

She rather doubted that they were glad that she had come—yet. But she did not resent it. For herself, it scarcely touched her, and she was a just soul, and knew how little an intimate group of Chinese girls would have liked to have an unknown English girl thrust among them, to share all their work and play, and, no doubt, to interrupt, if not spoil, their many interests.

Tzŭ sensed the embarrassment that the other girls were too socially accustomed to show. But it was there, and Tzŭ knew it was, and rather pitied it. She was accustomed to it—in others—here in England. In the quiet country rectory and countryside, she had grown used to noticing that every one or group to whom Mrs. Ford had introduced her was awkwardly embarrassed. And it had always amused her greatly. It did now. But of that she gave no sign.

"Do you like England?" Elenore asked desperately.

"Very much," Tzŭ replied truthfully, not allowing herself to smile—too much. But her eyes danced.

There was an awkward pause.

Hector broke it.

He stalked across the room, and rubbed ingratiatingly against Ch'êng Tzŭ.

She bent down and took him in her arms, and sitting down put him on her lap. And he began to purr.

Hector had broken the ice.

"Well! I never!" Lady Mary said.

"I'm blowed!" a girl confided to her chum.

No one had ever heard Hector purr before. No one had ever been allowed to nurse him before, since he was a very young kitten. And never before had any one been allowed to push friendship to the stroking point, inside an acquaintance of some months.

Lady Mary explained all this, and added, "I think you must be a witch, Miss Ch'êng."

"So?" Tzŭ laughed. "I think it is just your English cat that is very kind, and such a gentleman, that he too makes me welcome." She lifted the big beastie, and cuddled his head against her radiant, pomegranate face, looking across him laughingly.

Lady Mary—the least psychic of women—had a quick prevision of what a sensation this Chinese girl might make when the time came to introduce her. Lady Mary hoped she might be able to present Ch'êng Tzŭ herself. It would be a noble advertisement for the school—although happily it needed none—and it would be a personal pleasure. How would not a girl look when dressed to the greatest advantage who was so exquisitely lovely in that shapeless, almost hempen, thing? In brocades and tissues and jewels—and the Lady Mary Worthing was glad—rather meanly—to remember that the Chinese Minister's wife was not in England, to insist perhaps upon presenting Miss Ch'êng herself.

When the dressing-bell rang, Ch'êng Tzŭ had made three friends, the Infanta Mercedes, Lady Mary and Hector.

And one of them had gained a friend. Hector had.

CHAPTER XXIV

IN the next five years Ch'êng T'ien Tzŭ had many experiences, and made many acquaintances—not friends. The fault was hers, perhaps—for always something held her back.

She stayed nearly three years at Belgrave Square —it wasn't exactly Belgrave Square, but near enough to claim the hall mark—and spent two on the continent.

As soon as the girls forgave her for being Chinese—and they did it far sooner than they had intended, or quite approved of—she grew popular, and several of them loved her. But Tzŭ never attached herself to any one to the others' exclusion, and, unless a little to the Spanish Mercedes, scarcely to any one more than to the others. It was not that she held herself aloof. It was not that she was unfriendly. She was bright, gay and obliging always—half the life and merriment of the London house. And, if they all grew to like her, and some to love her, she grew, if a little more slowly—to like most of them. They were nice girls. And she met all their many kindnesses more than halfway and cordially. In their different ways—after the first strangeness and repulsion wore off—they were very good to Chinese Tzŭ, and for every kindness she was radiantly grateful.

Under sufficient provocation the Chinese are capable of great and ruthless cruelty. Often their vengeance is venomous and implacable. But no Chinese is capable of ingratitude. Not even Europe or European example can inoculate them with it.

Ch'êng Tzǔ was grateful to every one at Belgrave Square, but not one of them ever knew what she really thought of them. Lady Mary, several of the teachers, and the acuter girls, wondered about it very much, but they never learned. She gave no hint, and she treated all alike.

She laughed and romped delicately, she danced and sang, she worked tremendously, she tossed back jest for jest, and lavished gift for gift. But in some intangible way she seemed to live apart, her personality thinly, delicately veiled.

Even to Panü she expressed no preference for one schoolmate above another. Mung Panü had joined her at Lady Mary's soon after her own arrival.

Panü hated all English and all things English violently—and said so when she dared, which was not often. Tzǔ commanded silence, and the slave girl obeyed. To Panü, Ch'êng Tzǔ spoke only of China and in Chinese when they were alone, as they often were. They shared a room. And never to any one else, if she could help it, did she speak of China.

"Probably has forgotten all about the rummy place, and doesn't like to say so. She was only ten when she left, you know," Laura Kingsland said once to Inez, and Tzǔ, overhearing by accident, laughed softly to herself.

But Ch'êng Tzǔ had not forgotten China. She grew each day more at home in England. Month by month she found some new thing to like and respect in the English about her. But always she felt the hand of far-off China on her shoulder. Almost it seemed that each year she remembered her own coun-

try the more, and the more acutely, though each year
certainly weaned her more and more to the foster
arms of England. But between the country that she
remembered and the country in which she lived she
made few comparisons to China's disadvantage. And
twice she let a proud word slip that favored China.

In her first year at Lady Mary's a recalcitrant servant, dismissed for rudeness, created a scene, thrust
herself into the room where girls and mistresses sat
chatting, threatened Lady Mary, hurling at her
scurrilous, insolent abuse, and the crushing pronounce-
ment, "Call yourself a lady! You're no lady!" Some
of the girls were amused, some frightened, others—as
Lady Mary was—merely coldly angry. One mistress
waxed hysterical. Ch'êng Tzŭ grew pale with fury,
and her astonishment struck an unconsidered comment
from her usually careful lips.

Mercedes said to her, "How abominable!"

And Ch'êng Tzŭ replied, "It could not have happened in China."

But it could have happened in China—or something
very like it—and often did. For in middle-class China
a dismissed servant may stand just inside your gate-
way all day, and curse you shrilly, and, if a woman,
not infrequently does. But Tzŭ never had heard it.
Such things did *not* happen under the rule of Ch'êng
Shao Yün.

Some months later, Laura Kingsland—as highly
born as any English girl there—offended Tzŭ's Chinese taste far more than the harridan servant had
done.

Laura was easily the beauty of the school—with
lights of sheer gold in her rippling hair, eyes blue as

gentians, soft English roses in the snow of an almost perfect patrician face.

Balked of some indulgence she asked, one day when her parents had come to tea, Laura was openly rude to her mother, a white-haired woman as lovely as the girl.

Again the Infanta Mercedes commented, and again to Tzŭ.

"Laura is like a peasant cat. She ought to be beaten," the Infanta said.

"It could not have happened in China," Tzŭ said proudly.

"Nor in Spain," Mercedes added quickly.

But for this twice, whatever Ch'êng Tzŭ may sometimes have thought, no one ever heard her reflect on any English trait, nor on any one English.

She listened. She watched. She chatted. But all her chatting was impersonal.

Mung Panü lived in the school household just as Tzŭ did. Esprit de corps was one of Lady Mary's planks. No distinctions between the pupils were ever made at her school. And under her roof the Chinese mistress and the Chinese maid lived on a parity. But the Chinese difference between them neither ever forgot. Tzŭ ruled, and was absolute. That they ate together, worked together, and slept almost side by side did not strike them as strange or inappropriate. Chinese mistress and maid often share their rice, and bend over the same embroidery frame.

Lady Mary took "Miss Ch'êng" about with her a great deal. She always took the older girls out with her a good deal—a part of their preparation for their social duties to come. And it had been clearly stipu-

lated that she was to show Tzŭ as much as possible
of English life. "She had been educated in China
and, if necessary, her education would be completed
in China." And it was English ways that Madame
Ch'êng wished her great-granddaughter taught, and
would pay to have her taught.

Lady Mary sniffed a little at the idea of a girl of
ten having been educated, and educated in China, but
she made the desired bargain, and kept it staunchly.
And she soon became very keen to take Tzŭ about with
her. The girl was charming and charmingly behaved,
and her quaint appearance seemed an attraction. Lady
Mary, in spite of her chic clothes, had never been
spectacular herself, and she found the small social
eruption Tzŭ's entrance always caused, tonic and grati-
fying.

Mung Panü never went out with them. She stayed
behind, in their own room, and burned joss sticks.
But there was nothing startling in that, for half the
idle women in London burned joss sticks by now.

But Ch'êng Tzŭ studied in the ordinary way too—
and she read many books. Study is a Chinese instinct,
and the Chinese reverence books. Confucius said,
"You can never open a book without learning something." If that is true, Ch'êng T'ien Tzŭ must have
learned and stored a very great deal during these years.
For she had a Chinese memory, the most wonderful
of all memories.

After Belgrave Square she traveled on the continent
for two years—seeing all the usual places and many
that were unusual. She lingered where she was most
interested, and was presented and greatly vouched
for, at Rome, Madrid, St. Petersburg, Berlin and
Bucharest.

When Tzŭ came back to England, Lady Mary had her old wish. Lady Mary Worthing presented her old pupil—Miss Ch'êng—to the English Queen.

Ch'êng Tzŭ was her own mistress now. Before dying, Ch'êng Shao Yün had decreed it so, and none of the old woman's scattered progeny, absorbed into other clans now, had wished to dispute it, or had had power to do so. It was not unheard of for Chinese girls to be so placed, though more a Manchu than a Chinese custom. From Tzŭ's birth, her great-grandmother had determined the long-desired girl to be the next chief of the Ch'êngs, and there could be no question that at Ch'êng Yün's death, Ch'êng Yün's suzerainty had passed to Ch'êng Tzŭ. The details of the girl's European school-days, and of her school-days' guardianship, Yün had provided, and to evade or neglect any item of that provision no more occurred to Ch'êng T'ien Tzŭ than it occurred to Ch'êng Shao Yün to make her heir a ward-in-chancery, or any Chinese equivalent of it. She had hoped to live to greet Tzŭ on Tzŭ's home return, and to guide the earlier years of her re-Chinesed days, letting the girl study and even somewhat share her own methods of rule. But she had realized how precarious her own hold on life grew, and she had let life slip, and her own hold relax, content that Tzŭ would follow her will in all things, and in her footsteps. The King is dead. Long live the King! The crown and the regency never die. As little could the sovereignty of the Ch'êngs, or its queenship change. As she had been, Tzŭ would be. As she had done, Tzŭ would do. As she had reigned and *served*, Tzŭ would reign and serve.

Ch'êng Shao Yün had looked to Europe to do much for Tzŭ, and through Tzŭ do much for China, using

the bitter ingredient of a disliked alien race to medicine
China, as a pharmacologist employs bitter drugs to
purge a distraught human frame. But Yün had taken
no heed, turned no thought, to what Europe might do
to Tzŭ. To Ch'êng Shao Yün seed was everything,
soil but little, and foreign soil less than nothing. She
knew that transplanted flowers altered in vigor and
in character, but to her it was inconceivable that patrician Chinese seed could develop in any way along
new lines, be its transplantation what it might. Camel-
lias—and tangerines might change their tints—or even
deteriorate—but not a Ch'êng. The Ch'êng was im-
mutable, absolute, fixed. From Europe Ch'êng Shao
Yün feared much for China. But she feared it not at
all for Ch'êng T'ien Tzŭ. Among her friends were
several who had lived in Europe, and Europe had
tainted none of them. Shêng Liu had lived there, and
China had no son more Chinese than he.

Several things led Ch'êng Tzŭ to linger still in England after her program that her great-grandmother
had mapped out had been quite performed.

England tempted her.

She shrank from returning orphaned and detached
to an altered China.

And there had been no clear limit named to her
stay. She was to go to school. She was to travel.
And she was to see and study English life. So
much Ch'êng Yün had said clearly. But she had indicated no dates except the date of the girl's departure
from home. It was not Ch'êng Yün's way to announce a date until that date had come.

She was to go home. Of course!—She intended
to go home. But Ch'êng Yün was not waiting for
her there—and, for that and other reasons, she saw

no need to hurry. And her own inclination gave her no spur, but held her rather here where she had acquaintances—she had none in China—and where she had spent more than half her life. For she was twenty and a month.

So she took a little house in Mayfair, furnished it, and gathered a household about her, a household of English servants. Panü was the only Chinese in Tzŭ's entourage. And she engaged a chaperon so in every way impeccable that her salary ran into so large a sum that almost Ch'êng T'ien Tzŭ might have been said to nave bought her.

CHAPTER XXV

THE Chinese concentrate and they specialize: two of the secrets of their general efficiency, content and success. As individuals they arrive, because on their paths of life they so rarely turn aside—they pause to gather many a wayside flower, but they do not turn off into side paths to seek such blossoming, still less retrace their steps. They go straight on, and they rarely reach a *cul de sac*.

Had Ch'êng T'ien Tzŭ been now in China her life would have been direct and, in a superficial sense, circumscribed. She would have done one set of things: the things at once fitting her station and indicative of it. She would have known one dual set of people, the equals of her natural entourage, and its servitors and dependents.

But in London she lived more diversely. There she would have had her niche, and filled it. Here she was a looker-on, and she looked to the right and to the left, far and wide, pausing—and straying off—to look longest at whatever most amused her, as well as at what interested her most. But the distinction must be admitted a little hypocritical, for with her characteristically Chinese sense of humor, whatever amused keenly interested. Little came amiss to her young curiosity, nothing long or greatly balked her inherited gift for analysis.

In China she could have met on any parity, with any freedom or cordiality of intercourse, only one very limited class—women of her own caste. In London she met "everybody" now, and in the easy "give and take" of social intercourse rubbed shoulders of personality with many sorts and conditions of women—and men.

Her wealth, the rank of her sponsors and her carriage were her password into high and guarded places. Her baffling personality, the uniqueness of her appearance, of her story, of her entertainment—and of her loveliness, made her popular in the better class Bohemia so extraordinarily on the increase in London—increase of numbers, of influence, and probably of permanence.

Miss Ch'êng became a fashion and a rage—no high achievement perhaps in a milieu that has idolized an aged cowboy, and welcomed mountebanks and boors, a satiated society that prefers eccentricity to the best conventionality, and to dance (so called) in public restaurants—under the gaze of any who can pay the price—rather than to talk quietly in cool, private places.

Of what she thought of it all she gave no indication. No one knew, not even Mung Panü. But now and then some man, traveled and experienced in his country's civil service, wondered. And Shêng Liu tried several times to find out—in vain and anxiously.

She entertained sumptuously, but in European fashion. The rooms in which she received her guests were furnished in accordance with European custom, but more sparsely and more beautifully than can be claimed to be in strict accordance with European taste. But tucked away in odd parts of the house were little strongholds of Chinese decoration and furnishing. And Lady Mary knew—and Mrs. Marston suspected

—that whoever was welcomed into one of them had gained Tzŭ's respect and something warmer than the sunny coldness which was all she gave or showed to most. Lady Mary believed that that sunniness was a manner and a courtesy, the coldness a fact and a conviction.

She dressed as an Englishwoman—with a deft difference that was more individuality and love of the beautiful than Chinese. And too she wore her English clothes with a difference. They hung always. They never clung. Lady Mary knew that she wore always, day and night—usually, but not always, inside her gown—an exquisite bit of jade. Panü knew that it was a *ruyie*—but not that Ch'êng Chü-po had given it long ago to Ch'êng Ting Tzŭ.

As a schoolgirl she had worn shoes and slippers that copied somewhat English shoes. But now she always wore Chinese shoes—tiny, embroidered, jeweled things, that peeped out from her English skirts with an emphatic note of Cathay and of the history of its women.

And London never wearied of marveling at what the girl's maimed fragments of feet could do in those tiny, padded shoes. She played tennis in them. She skated in them. She danced in them—quadrilles and minuets. No man had ever put his arm about Ch'êng T'ien Tzŭ, or touched more than her fingers' irresponsive tips—and scarcely any English woman. The Worthing twins had kissed her as babies, and Tzŭ had suffered it. Edith kissed her still—sometimes. But Tzŭ had never kissed them. She abhorred the very sight of kissing, and this oriental instinct she wore about her as a veil. And, for all her bared face, the girl seemed veiled in several ways, definable some, others indefinable.

She dressed her black hair very simply and to a smoothness that was never, but for one brief season, fashionable in modern London. But Ch'êng Tzŭ still loved to stick flowers in her hair, and to hang jewels from it. Lady Mary's babies had loved—when Tzŭ put her mourning off—to play with the tassels dangling from above the tiny jeweled ears. All babies loved to do it, and still many did. Every baby adored Miss Ch'êng, and made free of her. Old people loved her—wooed to it probably by her unfailing Chinese deference to their years. Animals and birds were her veriest creatures. Wild home-sick things came to her at the Zoo, and looked at her with appealing eyes. And on the Embankment and the Terrace at St. Stephen's, gulls had eaten from her hand.

Doncaster House, built when ground in London cost less than now, was big and roomy. A regiment might have been billeted in the wide hall alone. But in tonight's super-crush, Lady Doncaster, panting in a purple dress, and with a purple face, was wedged tight among her suffocated guests. Her diamonds looked red with heat—all the jewels looked hot, and the crammed flowers were cooked—by electricity. Even Miss Ch'êng's long rope of pearls looked warm against her gown of silver brocade, and the tassels of smaller pearls hanging from her hair, and the great pear-shaped pearl on her forehead looked pink and winked warmly, more like the baubles of a geisha than the proud, imperial things they were. But the girl herself looked cool. Tzŭ liked the heat, and had no need to use her little fan—which was as well, for there was no elbow-room in Doncaster House to-night. Here and there the pattern of her silver-threaded brocade was touched with tiny beads of steel. Her long sleeves were thickly sewn with jewels of many colors. London had never seen Miss Ch'êng's arms—not even at Buckingham Palace. To-night, even in this hot crush, a number of women wore velvet, and hot-hued velvet—but no other woman would have thought to wear fur. But the chinchilla, wastefully cut into a design of curving scrolls, appliquéd on the hem of Ch'êng Tzŭ's skirt, looked cool and light. Her toilet conceded nothing to the heat.

Her manner conceded nothing to the crush, or to those that made it. Seven years ago, in her coarse dress of mourning white, her beauty had sparkled in the school-house room. To-night it looked a softer beauty, the pale glimmering of a moonstone. And her slow progress through the hot rooms was still and cold. Mrs. Marston, white-haired, white-gowned, was the more compelling figure of the two, and not because of her greater inches.

John Selwyn stopped to speak to Mrs. Marston, but did not even see the girl beside her, to whom the Austrian Ambassador was speaking. Lord Ashford was leaving as Mrs. Marston and the girl came in. But Miss Ch'êng saw Ashford, and turned a little and watched him as he chatted with her chaperon. The astute and practiced diplomatist neither saw nor suspected the interest in Tzŭ's eyes. It was the sudden interest of a Chinese woman, and only Chinese eyes could have pierced to it. And Chinese eyes did. A Chinese, dressed, like Miss Ch'êng, in European clothes, watching her intently, standing near, but not waiting or wishing to speak to her, saw it almost before it glinted slightly in her eyes and across her immovable face. And seeing it, Wang No frowned, and his delicate hand tightened on his fob.

Ch'êng Tzŭ saw her countryman a moment later, and sent him a Chinese salutation with her fan. And at that he had to come to her. He bowed before her coldly, and waited for her to speak.

"Good-evening," Tzŭ said, smiling for the first time that night—Miss Ch'êng's smiles were few, and they were home-keeping. "I sent you a message by Shêng Liu, Mr. Wang, did he not deliver it? I told him to ask you to call on us."

Again Wang No bowed ceremoniously. "Thrice honorable," he said, answering her in their native tongue, "the noble graybeard gave thy contemptible slave thy gracious command."

"Which you have disobeyed," the girl said with an amused shrug, and speaking still in English.

The man bowed.

Tzŭ gave him a level look. She could not have eyed him so in China. But then in China she could not have taken speech or heed of him at all. She often, but with discretion, gave acquaintances permission to visit her, but she never invited them. That this so excepted man refused to come—it amounted to that— amused her, but did not vex her, for she was a girl, and she knew the reason of his refusal, and knew that now as he stood before her, angry, disapproving, imperturbable and seeming cold, his blood was throbbing wildly in his veins, and his Chinese heart pounding sickly an old and world-universal agony beneath a well-cut, white English waistcoat.

"But I intend you to come, Mr. Wang. So I suppose I must get Mrs. Marston to ask you. You cannot refuse to obey a woman of her years, and a sash-wearer."

"There are no sash-wearers among these foreigners, jade-like maiden," he said coldly, speaking again in Chinese, "and thy contemptible worm can disobey any Englishwoman."

Ch'êng T'ien Tzŭ laughed—a tinkled laugh that was music, and had a sweet, soft tang of wild honey. Her laugh was less rare than her faint moonlight smile. But several men turned toward her at it as she moved slowly on with a tiny gesture of her fan which he could not disobey. And Wang moved beside her reluctantly, Tzŭ chatting to him almost merrily, in English, which he answered, as briefly as he could, ceremoniously and always in Chinese.

"Why are you angry with me, Mr. Wang?" she teased him presently. She was incapable of bantering with any Englishman. But she took a naughty and a very girlish satisfaction in flaunting this countryman of hers here in London, to whom she could not have spoken, scarcely permitted herself to think of, at home.

She had scarcely expected him to evade her question. Evasion is not a Chinese habit, though ignorance proclaims it so loudly. But his answer came more blunt than she had expected.

"Because you are here."

"At Doncaster House? Or in England?"

"Both."

A naughty pleasure rippled on her mobile face, and she turned it to him squarely. It was her rule, as well as her habit, to bear an impassive face abroad. Only Panü often saw expression on it. But she chose to toss even that veil carelessly aside now with Wang No, and no face is more mobile or more expressive than a Chinese woman's face so unveiled. It was an unveiled face Ch'êng T'ien Tzŭ turned to Wang No. And her eyes—wide open for once—were dancing.

"My honorable great-grandmother," but still speaking English, "decreed it."

"I know——" his Chinese words were longer and richly dressed with ceremonial courtesies and humble salutations—but his tone was crisp and hard. "But I believe that the most honorable noble Lady Ch'êng Shao Yün would think your task here now quite done, and would wish you to go home."

"Why do *you* stay?"

"The Son of Heaven commands it. My honorable father commands it." It was answer doubly enough for any Chinese to make, for any Chinese to hear. "But I go soon," he added.

Ch'êng T'ien Tzŭ shifted a little. "I like England," she said lightly.

Wang No said nothing, but his eyes said that he believed and hoped that she lied. And Tzŭ laughed again, and mocked him delicately with her fan.

"And," she told him, just a little sadly, "I might feel strange at home—after all these banished years. I should be lonely at home—now."

"Banished, indeed!" the man exclaimed. "I think you would not feel strange, at home—could not. Or if you did, it would soon pass. And you need not be alone there long."

Ch'êng Tzŭ veiled her eyes with their lids, to hide their quick triumph. Wang No had "declared" himself. Defiled—as she knew he held her by her English sojourn and junketing—English acquaintance, unveiled

face, unmaidenly practices, continental journeyings, yet
would Wang No, if they were both again in China, if
his father consented, send the matchmaker to her. And
it was no small triumph. A Chinese does not often
offer himself and his sons to a woman of whom he
disapproves.

"Perhaps! Who knows?" she said lightly, and released him with a courteous twist of the wrist that
held her tiny fan of jeweled gauze, and turned to greet
an English acquaintance.

She greeted many during the next hour, and let one
bring her an ice. As she listened and replied, now
to one, now to another, she kept wondering who the
man was that had gone away so soon after speaking
to Mrs. Marston. Ch'êng Tzŭ had watched him go.

At midnight she chanced again on Wang No.

She spoke to him in Chinese, and at it his eyes leapt
to hers, and his hand clenched upon his fob, and Ch'êng
Tzŭ, seeing and understanding, added something
quickly in English—for the minx was not unkind, and
she was highly bred.

They sauntered, walking as best they could, through
the still thickening crowd, toward a litle sheltered room
where palms grouped about a fountain. Tzŭ parted
the thick curtains that screened the doorway of the
hidden nook from the dense throng of guests, and
Wang followed her.

But the tiny pleasance was already tenanted.

Ch'êng Tzŭ's scrap of padded shoe made no sound,
and Wang's light English evening shoes made scarcely
more. The well-born Chinese are light of tread.

Tzŭ stiffened and stood stock still. Wang No saw
almost as soon, and he pushed protectingly in front of
her, to shield her from what was there to see.

On the fountain's broad, flat edge, a man and woman sat in unmistakable intimacy: a fair-haired woman with naked shoulders and uncovered arms, one hand—the hand that wore the wedding ring—lying heavily upon her companion's knee. And the man was handling her hair with careless, familiar fingers.

But they had heard Wang No's quick stepping in front of Tzŭ, and moved uselessly apart. The woman looked up with a startled, anxious face.

"Tzŭ!"

For answer Ch'êng Tzŭ turned and all but flung out through the curtains.

It was Laura who had called out at her. And the Englishman who had been caressing her accustomedly was not the husband to whom Ch'êng Tzŭ had seen her married not a year ago.

As the two Chinese came back into the outer room, letting the curtains fall again before the English intimates, they came directly upon Mrs. Marston.

Ch'êng Tzŭ caught at her chaperon's hand—Ch'êng Tzŭ rarely touched any one. "It could not have happened in China," the girl said sharply.

Mrs. Marston looked at her more amazed than her long social experience often left her—not because Tzŭ's words were meaningless, not because the girl's voice, in which the woman's acute ears had often detected scorn, was more full of scorn, and of scorn more bitter, than she had ever heard it, but because of the raging excitement in voice and girl. Tzŭ was trembling with it.

The woman looked from Tzŭ to the Chinese man —had he offended Miss Ch'êng?—But when she had looked at him Mrs. Marston thought not.

"Let us go!" Tzŭ said, more imperiously than the

woman had ever heard her speak—more imperiously
than Ch'êng T'ien Tzŭ ever had spoken before to any
one of Marion Marston's years.

"But Melba is just going to sing," Mrs. Marston
said feebly. "I was trying to find you to tell
you."

"I am going home at once," Tzŭ said, stamping one
red shoe. Then she laughed bitterly. "Home! I
mean back to Curzon Street."

Wang No followed them gravely to their carriage.
None of them spoke again till he closed the door upon
them.

Then—Ch'êng Tzŭ leaned forward a little, and held
out her gloved hand to him.

He took it at once. "Good-night," he said gravely.
And he said it in English.

It was to Mrs. Marston that he added, "May I come
to see you?"

Ch'êng T'ien Tzŭ answered before the other could,
"Will you come?"

"When may I?" And he smiled into his young
countrywoman's eyes.

"To-morrow at three," she said in their own tongue.
But in proud courtesy to the older woman, she repeated
her words in English. "When I wish you to leave us,
I will give you your guest tea in a Chinese room."

"Thank you," the man said gravely.

"Ch'ing, Ch'ing," Tzŭ said, as he stepped away.
And this time she did not translate it into "good-by,"
but left it his and hers—the intimate something, and
too, a claim, of Chinese to Chinese, in common banishment in an alien country.

They were turning into Curzon Street, and Mrs.

Marston was half asleep, when Ch'êng Tzŭ said abruptly:

"Who was the man that came up and spoke to you as we went into the Pompadour drawing-room?"

"Eh? Let me think," was the sleepy answer. But the woman was wider awake now than her voice. She had never heard Miss Ch'êng ask who any man was before.

"He was neither tall nor short. His hair, short as it's cut, is a little curly. He had a pink flower in his coat—daphne, I think. He is dark—for an Englishman."

Marion Marston was very wide awake indeed now. "Oh!" she replied indifferently, "that was Lord Ashford—Jack Selwyn. His cousin Elenore was at school with you. Haven't you met him?"

"I don't remember, if I have," Miss Ch'êng said indifferently. And Mrs. Marston drew a startling conclusion, because the girl troubled to add, and did it with a pretty, suppressed yawn, "One forgets so many people, in London."

CHAPTER XXVI

"WILL those Chinks talk? I wonder if they'd know either of us again."

"Tzŭ won't talk. I can't say about the man."

"Tzŭ! You know the she-Chink, then? Damn it."

"We were at school together for two years."

"Hell!" and the man kicked a little piece of lace and muslin viciously.

Laura picked up Tzŭ's handkerchief. "What does it matter, Dick? Half London knows."

"Probably half London suspects. But no one knows —until now. And we don't want them to," the man said moodily. "Can you square your negro friend?"

"I tell you Tzŭ will never say a word."

"I wouldn't want to bet on it."

"I would."

"Is she fond of you?"

"No, old dear, she is not."

"The devil!"

"Oh! do stop fussing, Dick. If I don't care, you needn't. And I tell you I know what I am saying. Wild horses wouldn't get a word about it out of her."

"What about the other Chink?" The man was not reassured.

"He may, of course," Lady Cooper conceded crossly, angry at an interruption that bid fair to end her evening's pleasure, and hotly humiliated that all his concern was so clearly for himself.

"Then you must square her, and make her square him."

"No one can *make* Ch'êng Tzŭ do anything," Laura said sharply. "I'd like to see any one 'square' her."

"Soft-soap and coax her. She's a woman."

"I shall never mention it to her," the woman said curtly. "I shall take my chance, and you'll have to take yours. What a hero you are! If you can't be anything but disagreeable, you'd better go——" she added a little pleadingly.

But he ignored her challenge, and spurned her invitation.

"Go! I should say so. We'd better both make tracks," he said sulkily, "and not together, either."

Meeting Sir Aston Cooper a little later, Dick David son greeted him heartily.

"Your wife was looking for you, in that big red room, a few moments ago."

"Was she? God bless my soul!" said the elderly baronet, even more delighted than surprised, and hurried off beaming.

And when he had found his wife he almost crushed her hand, and apologized profusely for having kept her waiting.

"Dick Davidson's one of the nicest boys I know," Sir Aston said as they reached home. "We must ask him to the Grange for the first shoot."

"Ask whom you like," his wife told him dully. " 'Nice' is about the last thing *I'd* call Dick Davidson."

"Darling," her husband coaxed, "don't be so prejudiced and critical. You are so particular."

Lady Cooper had been entirely truthful in telling Davidson that she would not approach Miss Ch'êng. But the night and the next morning brought other counsel, though certainly no other inclination.

She had no idea who the man with Tzŭ had been. He might talk. And she had no mind to throw away the ample convenience of Sir Aston's bank account for a man who she now realized clearly would avoid facing the catastrophe with her.

As she sipped her early tea she half resolved to go and speak with Ch'êng Tzŭ. She did not relish the task. If Tzŭ had been indifferent to her at school, she had very actively disliked the Chinese girl. But she had no fine feeling about it, and little sensitiveness. Some friends of her own race she would relish telling of it. Probably she would boast of it to two or three. It would have humiliated her to speak of it to others. But Ch'êng Tzŭ was only a Chinese. She had visited Miss Ch'êng several times, because every one else did that could, and because Tzŭ was the fashion now. But she despised the Chinese woman sincerely, and no more thought of her as an equal, or cared for her opinion, than if Ch'êng Tzŭ had been a Zulu, or a scullery maid.

She had picked up the handkerchief that Tzŭ had dropped, simply because all pretty, costly things appealed to her, and she had disliked seeing rose-point kicked by a man's boot, and had rescued it with no thought either of keeping it herself, or of restoring it to Miss Ch'êng. But she had brought it home with her, and it would serve as an excuse for an early call —at an hour she'd probably find the other alone—if she finally determined to go. She spread it out over her blue dressing-gown. What lace! Yes—she almost thought she'd go.

After breakfast she had a stormy scene with Sir Aston. A dressmaker's bill, of "unbelievable extravagance" he called it, had reached him with a peremptory note. He was very rich and very much infatuated. But even his income had its limits, if his infatuation had not. Sir Aston Cooper was very angry and he was frightened. Such preposterous conduct, uncurbed, might land a richer man than he in bankruptcy. He pleaded, stormed and threatened.

Lady Cooper did not plead. She brazened it out. She stormed too, and threatened. But she did condescend to coax at last. For she had more than this one bill for him to swallow. Her enormous allowance —his solicitors had called it "imbecile"—was overdrawn for six months, and she owed a thousand pounds at bridge.

She didn't cry. But he nearly did when she had told him all. And before he would write her the necessary checks she had to perch herself upon his knee, and stroke his face for quite a minute. She rather disliked doing it, she hated *having* to do it. And she was in a hurry. Dick was coming at eleven.

But the Hon. Richard did not keep his appointment. She waited for him almost an hour, then she rang for her car, and went to Curzon Street.

Miss Ch'êng's footman who opened the door had announced Lady Cooper before, and did not hesitate to announce her now. And before Ch'êng Tzŭ thought of such a possibility Laura was with her.

Neither moved to shake hands.

"You dropped your handkerchief by the fountain when you came upon us," the visitor said calmly, holding it out, "and I picked it up. Here it is."

"I am sorry you troubled." Miss Ch'êng made no sign of taking it.

Lady Cooper laid it on a table and sat down. "No, of course, I might have sent it. But I wanted to speak with you—about last night."

"Please do not do so." Ch'êng T'ien Tzŭ stood looking down coldly on the other.

Laura laughed. "Who was the man?"

Miss Ch'êng lifted her delicate brows slightly, but made no more reply.

"Who was the man?" Lady Cooper persisted, "the Chinaman who blundered in with you, into my little tête-à-tête?"

"Why?"

"Why do I wish to know? That's easy."

"Perhaps my Chinese intelligence is dense."

"I don't know anything about the general run of Chinese intelligence," Lady Cooper returned with careless flippancy—it was unassumed—"but *your* intelligence is not dense. No one's was ever less so."

Miss Ch'êng bowed.

"Who was he? Or tell me this—it's what I really want to know—will you vouch for him—for his silence?"

Ch'êng T'ien Tzŭ's face flamed red. "I vouch for my friend—to you?" And this time the hauteur in her voice got its angry message through.

"Forgive me, dear, if I sounded rude," Laura Cooper said prettily. "I don't quite know what I'm saying. I've had such a rotten time this morning. My husband was in a silly rage over a bill of mine, and some other things. And I had to sit on his lap and let him hug me before I got him tame——"

The Chinese girl—still standing—threw out one hand, as if to ward off a blow. "We do not speak of such things in China. Kindly go."

The English woman was the angrier of the two now. But she was growing frightened, and it held her. She rose and stood, cringing a little. "Yes, I've lots to do," she said weakly, "and you are busy too. I only came so early because I wanted to be sure of finding you, and finding you alone. I'm going now. But won't you please tell me, will the—the Chinese gentleman—your friend—say anything to any one—about last night?"

Miss Ch'êng smiled. "It did not interest him," she said.

"But will he tell?"

"He *is* a Chinese gentleman," was Tzǔ's cold retort.

"That means he will say nothing? I am so very anxious."

"It means, Lady Cooper, that he has forgotten it."

And Lady Cooper took the cue at last. "Good-by, Miss Ch'êng, and thanks."

At that moment a footman came in carrying a tray. It was Miss Ch'êng's rule that every guest admitted to her—no matter what the hour—was offered some refreshment. Tzǔ motioned the man away. And he went wondering, carrying his cakes and lemonade.

Again Ch'êng Tzǔ had got her message through.

"Are you going to cut me—if we meet?" Lady Cooper said from the door, laughing a little, and less anxiously than she felt.

Ch'êng Tzǔ answered gravely: "To do that would be a rudeness to Lady Mary Worthing, at whose home I met you."

And then the other went. She knew that she had been here for the last time. But she knew that Ch'êng Tzǔ would never do a rudeness to Lady Mary.

When she was alone Ch'êng Tzŭ rang again.

"Send Miss Vail to me," she told the man that came.

Ellen Vail was Miss Ch'êng's English maid. Panü was her maid and tire woman still. But Panü's needle-craft was slight. She had been learning other things when most Chinese girls of her class are being taught to sew. Vail had charge of their mistress's European wardrobe, and waited on her sometimes.

When the English maid came now, Ch'êng Tzŭ pointed to the lace handkerchief, and then to the fire. "Burn it—or take it away. I do not care which. I wish never to see it again."

CHAPTER XXVII

WANG came just as the clocks struck three.

Tzŭ received, and welcomed, him in a Chinese room. She chose to show him honor—and she felt it—her countryman and of her caste. And for herself she was glad to escape from England for an hour. She had even begun to change into a Chinese robe after lunch—she had eaten it alone. But she had thought better of that. To have received Wang No, wearing Chinese robes, her face unveiled, her eyes unabashed, would have emphasized how un-Chinese a thing she did in receiving him at all. The morning had left her nervous—morally unstrung. And to have met Wang No to-day, dressed as the women of their race dressed, but doing what no virtuous woman of her race, caste and years ever did, would have embarrassed her to-day she felt—lightly as she held Mr. Wang's disapproval and angry strictures, as a rule.

The morning had shocked and revolted Ch'êng Tzŭ more than last night's contretemps had. The sorry tableau by the fountain had filled her with an angry contempt for Laura Cooper. To the Englishman she did not give a thought, then or now. Ch'êng Ting Tzŭ would have thought—could she have known her—Ch'êng T'ien Tzŭ shamefully "advanced," but, for all her social enfranchisement, the girl was wedded to old prejudices, and had no taint—or leaven of "one self-same law for man and woman." What she had seen had given her for, and in, herself a sour humiliating sense of sex degradation. But the visit of the morning had seemed to her much the more horrible. That a woman, caught and seen as Laura had been the night before, should come out into the clear light of day, face the morning sunlight unabashed, present herself before an unspoiled woman, and ask a girl who had known her as a girl, ask an unmarried girl, to condone—and somewhat connive, was to Ch'êng Tzŭ immeasurably grosser than the dalliance by the fountain. Her gorge rose at it.

/What she felt about it all was a little unjust, and a trifle pharisaical—but the sweet good taste of it is undeniable. Such things happen in China sometimes. They happen everywhere. There is no race so guarded that womanhood is always safe even against itself. In China it happens very rarely, and, when it does, it comes from some great irresistible mutual passion, not from social laxity. And in that East scores over West. And in China it happens so rarely that Tzŭ had some excuse for saying that it could not happen there—but not quite excuse enough, for she had read deeply her people's history, and had read Chinese fiction widely, and must have known that in many Chinese novels just such misbehavior is recorded.

Ch'êng T'ien Tzŭ was not quite fair. And to-day, for the first time in years, she was consciously homesick. Probably she had always been a little homesick without knowing it.

Laura Cooper had set ajar for Wang No a door until now shut and barred against him.

Ch'êng Tzŭ was glad to see him—and told him so. And all their talk was of home and things of home. Mrs. Marston sat by the window, and made lace, but her thoughts were far away; and for the most part they did not interrupt her. She left them presently, and Mung Panü slipped in and sat down at Ch'êng Tzŭ's feet.

After Panü came Tzŭ spoke to him in their own tongue—and until he went English was not spoken again, scarcely remembered.

Mrs. Marston did not come back. She knew that Miss Ch'êng would send for her, if she wished for her. Tzŭ did not send.

The little Chinese room was heaven to Wang No. He had been racked with homesickness every hour of his long absence from China. When he slept he heard his mother call him, and the temple bells of home, the lanterns of wayfaring coolies on the mountain passes flickered in his closed eyes, he smelled the lotus on the lakes—and he woke in a sweat, and moaning, writhing, because he could not call out in answer to his mother.

This was China! And she he loved was here.

Two pillars of sandalwood, one beautifully planed to marble smoothness, one carved as elaborately as a lady's fan, supported the lacquer ceiling. A hand-woven rug of silk lay on the lacquer floor. Everything was elaborate; nothing was crowded. The ceiling was painted with homing birds. A great bronze crane held the jeweled incense-burner in his polished beak, his eyes were rubies, his feet were pink with claws of pale coral. There was lavishness of color, and no premeditated color-scheme—but the whole room had the tone of amber—partly from the sandalwood every-where: hanging from the ceiling in pierced lambre-quins, the open-work cornice, the screen inlaid with mother-o'-pearl, the great chair picked with turquoise, as was the couch of sandalwood, the stools and table, partly from amber colored cushions embroidered with orange chrysanthemums and lemon peonies, partly from a gold-stone brazier and the great yellow lily moving a little in the hot breeze that came from the open window. The cornice was a jungle of dwarf bamboo, rhododendrons, arbutus and loquat, with many a thistle and sharp-thorned briar. Monkeys and dragons and weird-faced imps peeped and played in that jungle of sandalwood. And open-mouthed dragons, gargoyle-like, held up each corner of the painted ceiling. A porcelain elephant, that might have been Pusien's, so richly was it caparisoned, stood on the floor, and held up on its back a great candlestick of yellow crystal taller than Ch'êng Tzŭ, filled with a great red candle. And smaller candles of red wax stood spiked (every Chinese candlestick is fitted with a spike) on the long, low table with the gong. From one corner of the ceiling hung an antique lantern of jade. Three silk scrolls on the walls—far lovelier than any kakemona of Japan, recorded a saying of a sage, the praise of a flower, and a couplet of the poet Li Po. On the fourth wall hung the one picture in the room (except for a miniature) and it needed not its beautifully executed idiographic lettering to tell its story or to signature it the brush-work of great Ma Yuan, for the herons lived on the silk, slaking their thirst at a living pool, one, wing-outspread, come a little later than the others, moving yet, looked up questioningly to a gathering cloud. The picture breathed. The miniature was a portrait of Ch'êng Shao Yün, as Tzŭ had known and loved her, but wearing robes and gems of state, painted for Ch'êng Tzŭ by an artist who had crossed China to do it at Ch'êng Yün's bidding. It was framed in cam-

phor wood carved and pierced. It stood on a slab of
solid gold, in a niche as in a shrine. And a curtain
embroidered with the crests of Ch'êng and Shao hung
beside the niche, ready at a touch to veil the picture
face of the old chieftainess. There was no door in
the room. Panels that slid back and forth shut its
privacy from the London house. The panels, too, of
the fragrant, amber-tinted sandalwood, were carved,
one with sprays of peach blossoms and cherries in fruit,
one with dragonflies and wild roses, one with hawthorn
in leaf and bloom, several with Buddhas in bold relief,
exquisitely, minutely chiseled. There was no imperial
yellow in this Chinese room of a London house, but
the room almost breathed the forbidden color, since
every other tint of the supreme color, except the one
Emperor-sacred shade, mingled in one delicious amber
glow. A piece of needlework—Tzŭ's—lay on the
couch. Her lute was on a stool.

This *was* China! And she he loved was here—a
Chinese girl, for all her hideous English dress, with
cherry ribbon twisted in her braids, a red flower in
her hair, and tiny clumping shoes that told each golden
lily but one human toe.

The clock struck five when Ch'êng Tzŭ bade Mung
Panü bring the guest tea.

When it came Wang drained his scalding cup, and
left her almost without a word. But his eyes spoke,
and Tzŭ knew that he would come again.

CHAPTER XXVIII

WANG NO often came again.

He made no further effort to resist the presence of Ch'êng T'ien Tzŭ.

But his race-blood was stronger than the clamor of his love, and he spoke no word to her that all the world might not have heard unmoved—unless racially moved—and he spoke scarcely any word that Panü did not hear—when she troubled to listen.

If what Wang sometimes said, in the little amber room, of Europe and of international things, might have angered, or even alarmed a listening Englishman, he said it but seldom. China was their theme.

And if Wang No had urged his suit with frank words, frank English fashion, he might have won Ch'êng Tzŭ.

But he could not. He loved her too well to do her that indignity. And his Chinese taste forbade it. He wooed her, heaven knows, and Ch'êng Tzŭ knew it, as did Mung Panü and Mrs. Marston. His devotion moved her—and an emotion in her presence that he could not always hide. But he spoke no word.

Ch'êng Tzŭ was kind to him more often than not. Sometimes she teased him. He met both moods with the same grave courtesy. And, if either moved him, he gave no sign—no sign added to those that despite himself escaped him occasionally in her presence, and that mastered him as often and in the same degree when she flaunted as when she was kind.

She wondered sometimes if she could have torn him from his determined self-control. But it never occurred to her to try. To have invited a man to woo her would have been as impossible to Ch'êng T'ien Tzŭ as to have taught one how to woo her, or to hint to any man how his wooing of her would fare.

The Chinese man and the Chinese girl met constantly now, in her house, and at the London whirl of functions. But since the night she had held it—gloved—out to him through her carriage window he had not touched her hand, nor had any garment of hers brushed against him. And they knew that their fingers would not touch again until their acquaintance had ended—in marriage or in parting.

Ch'êng Tzŭ wondered how it would end. They all did. And Wang No wondered most of all. The three English women who loved Ch'êng Tzŭ wondered how it would end, almost as anxiously as Wang No did.

Lady Mary thought that Wang would win. And she hoped it. She liked the man. Lady Mary hoped the wedding would be in London. She longed to attend it, and have a voice in the multi-colored functions. She even hoped that Mr. and Mrs. Wang might continue to live in London—at the Chinese Legation, perhaps. She was very loth to lose Tzŭ.

Mrs. Marston, who saw more of Miss Ch'êng than Lady Mary Worthing did, and far oftener saw her with Mr. Wang, had no idea what the upshot would be. She would not have hazarded a sixpence either way.

Nor would Mung Panü, who heard most of their talk—and with the added interpretation of understanding the tongue in which they spoke when alone but for her. And Mung Panü wished it, if possible, more

eagerly than Wang himself did. For she knew that
the marriage would mean a return to China. Mung
Panü would have sold her soul—if it had occurred
to her that she had one—in return for a passage to
China. To be back in China but for one moon she
would joyfully have given her rest of life. She loathed
each day of her exile more and more. She sobbed herself to sleep almost half her nights in an agony of
homesickness and despair. Ch'êng Tzŭ had repeat-
edly offered to send Panü back to China, and the slave
girl had ached to go. But her august lady Ch'êng
Shao Yün had charged her to stay with Ch'êng Tzŭ,
and stronger than her hate of Europe, stronger than
the terrible homesickness that tore and tortured her,
was the slave-girl's fealty to Ch'êng Yün. Mung Panü
would sooner have disobeyed the son of Heaven himself, or him who slept beneath the crystal tree at K'iuh-
fow, and whose name she might not speak, than have
disobeyed Ch'êng Yün living or dead.

Elenore Selwyn thought that Ch'êng Tzŭ would
never marry Wang No. And she was sorry to think it,
for she liked Wang—and liked him more each time
she met him. Attractions are even stranger than antipathies. Almost half our antipathies can be searched
out, and accounted for, but probably not a quarter of
our affinities can. Love is a slyer, subtler thing than
hate is; liking than dislike. And Elenore Selwyn was
the one English person, the one only thing in England, that Wang No liked. Not only liked her, but
he liked her warmly, and he respected her. It was not
her fault that she was English, and went about at
night with naked neck and arms—and Mr. Wang never
failed to remember it; all the English abominations
were England's—the fault of an abominable people, a

contemptible system, and neither in justice nor in Chinese chivalry to be laid at the door of Miss Selwyn. That she was as she was was supremely to her credit, the miracle of England, the one flower in a welter of weeds. Her friendship with Elenore was the one sole thing in Ch'êng Tzŭ's English sojourn of which Wang No approved. He always treated Miss Selwyn with a cordial deference, and tried sincerely to oblige and please her. And no one could be more charming than Wang No was when he cared to be.

Elenore thought that Tzŭ would not marry Wang.

Mercedes—she and her husband were in London for a few weeks—was sure that Tzŭ would not.

And so the restless shuttle of conjecture went. But it wove no woof.

Tzŭ expected to marry when she went home. She wished to do so, and intended it. She dreamed of it sometimes. For she was intrinsically feminine, quickly normal of body and mind, and her soul was sane.

She liked Wang No. To European blindness he looked "very much like any other Chinaman," but Ch'êng T'ien Tzŭ knew him handsome. And Shêng Liu valued him. And that Wang No loved her counted to her for much. It had to count, for she had come to ripe marriage years, and he was the only eligible Chinese man she knew. There were other young but adult countrymen of hers at the Legation, and she had had speech of all of them. But each of them was married.

Several of her schoolmates had married happily men of their own choice. And the happy thrill of it had reached Ch'êng Tzŭ, and a little moved her even while it shocked. It was impossible even for a Chinese girl of strictest caste to live as she had lived in England for ten years now, to see as she had seen, without having century-old ideals a little warped, inherited instinct a little swayed towards some freedom of personal choice, some opportunity of personal inclination.

Did she love Wang No?   No.

Could she?   Might she come to?   Perhaps.

His devotion touched her.   His ardor reached her. More than once it flushed her cheek, when he had left her—not before.   She knew that they were congenial. Slowly he was becoming to her—this courtly countryman of hers—what the girls had called their sanctum at Belgrave Square—"home from home."   And she knew that he was waiting, and panting, for her return to China.   It almost seemed as if Wang No was destined her by fate.   And yet——

CHAPTER XXIX

LORD ASHFORD pitched the letter from him with an oath that made the breakfast crockery shiver, and rammed his doubled fists into the pockets of his shabby bath gown.

"Shut it, you silly ass," Tom Granville said fiercely, fishing the offending epistle out of the slop-basin. The basin had considerable discarded tea in it. Tom shook the wet pages gingerly, and laid them out to dry, if they could, on the spotless damask. "Damn you, see what you've done, you blighter, made me spot my pretty dress."

"Blow you, and your silly clothes. Shy over the matches, can't you?"

If the peer's bath robe was nondescript and shabby, the warrior's matutinal raiment was fine enough to cover a regiment with rainbowed glory—a delicate confection of pink silk, embroidered with silver storks and butterflies of gold. The pink dressing gown smelled of violets and tobacco, and it made the guardsman's crimson head scream.

Captain Granville shied the matches over—and he shied them accurately. They landed neatly on Jack Selwyn's nose. And the silver match box was heavy and sharp-edged.

"You would, would you!" Ashford rose to battle.

They closed instantly, and wrestled mightily—shouting opprobrious epithets at each other, as they lurched interlocked about the room.

Burton—their man—came in hurriedly, but accustomed and unperturbed—and pounced—but with dignity—upon the table glass.

"You leave his love letter alone, Burts," Tom admonished.

"Damn the letter," the noble spluttered, his head pinioned under Granville's arm.

Granville released him—so quickly that he almost lost his footing—and drew back in shocked surprise.

"Don't let me hear you speak like that again of a lady's letter, you low old turnip—or I'll punch your head again."

"You haven't punched it first yet, you red-headed carrot! Lady! No lady'd write a thing like that."

"What's the matter with it?"

"Look, and see!"

Tom picked up the dampened sheets, and scrutinized them through his single eyeglass.

"Good lord, Jack, old bean, what a vermilion awful fist! You have my sympathy."

"Yes, ain't it!"

"Who the glory wrote it, Ashes? I can't read a word of it!"

"Of course you can't. Who the hell could? And eight pages of it, and probably important."

"Do you think she's going to sue you, old dear?" Tom stared at his friend with a commiserating eye.

"Probably not, you brilliant humorist. But I want to read it. I promised her——"

"Breach of promise! My poor, poor friend!" and the Hon. Thomas Stuart Granville sank into a chair, and began to moan piteously.

"Shut up that slosh. I tell you, we must read it. It's from my cousin——"

"Oh!" The news was dull.

—"and I promised her I'd give her anything in reason she chose, for her birthday, and, of course this is a little list of what she wants."

"Eight pages of it."

"Oh—she has generous ideas—if she can't write. And she trusts me. I say, Tom, a girl ought to be arrested who writes a fist like that."

"I quite agree," the young guardsman said cordially. "Couldn't her people afford a governess? Didn't they ever send her to school even? Board-schools are cheap."

Ashford took the letter up again, and began studying it disgustedly.

Tom sat down on the damaged table-cloth, and began eating out of the marmalade pot—the only provender that Burton had not yet carried away.

"Shut off stuffing, you pink old crocodile," Jack Selwyn said pathetically, "and try and help me make a word out here and there."

The warrior spooned the last of the marmalade into his mouth, threw the porcelain pot at Burton—as he came in. The man caught it gravely, and with unabated dignity bore it away.

Granville went to Jack, and studied—over his shoulder—the hieroglyphic page.

"Nell deserves brimstone."

"Who?"

"Nell—my cousin Elenore."

"You're a pretty brand of liar, Ash-bin. That's not from Miss Selwyn."

"Oh! isn't it! You know my cousin's handwriting better'n I do, of course."

"I have had a note or two from Miss Selwyn," Tom

Granville retorted coldly. "Her handwriting is beautiful."

Lord Ashford roared with laughter. "Nell's maid wrote any notes you had, old dear. Dean always writes Nell's letters. She must be away or something. Nell *can't* write, I tell you, any better than this flytracks. If she writes to a florist's for violets, they send her roses. She's given it up since her catastrophe with Lord Tunnicraft. The old boy wrote her an offer of love and coronet. And Nellie wrote back, 'Thank you kindly, no.' And he went out and bought her a ring—big square diamond set in platinum, and came round with it smirking—kissed Nell before she knew what was up, and tried to ram the sparkly on her finger."

"Don't be a disgusting beast," Tom said curtly.

"Give you my word it's true." Which it was. Elenore's writing had been the scandal of Lady Mary's school. "And from the day of that chaste salute to this Dean writes all Nell's letters—signs 'em even."

The guardsman moved to the window, and stood— his pink embroidered back to Ashford—gazing moodily across Hyde Park. Those "note or two" were inside the pink dressing-gown, in a pocket book, with a rose-bud he'd begged. And a lady's maid had written *t*hem! He'd kissed the handwriting of a lady's maid —rather more than once!

When they settled down presently to the business of the day, with valiant industry and the soothing aid of good tobacco, they contrived to read Elenore's letter—in places.

As her cousin had thought, it embodied her birthday demand. She wished to give a house-party, of her

very own—at Jack's place, Ashford Grange—"Aunt
Annie will chaperon"—the guests of Nell's selection—
she enclosed a list—"We needn't bother with that,"
Jack said tossing it aside—"and Jack was to be there,
of course, and be very, very good."

"That's all right." Lord Ashford was relieved.
"I suppose I'd better ask Nell if I may bring you along,
Tom. You're dying to come, aren't you?"

"Oh, not particularly."

"Who's lying now, you ruddy-headed lobster?"
Ashford chuckled.

Captain Granville blushed.

Lord Ashford rang the bell abruptly. "Where the
devil is the *Morning Post*, Burton, and the other
rags?" he demanded harshly when the servant came.
"Why the blooming Moses can't you allow me to see
the morning papers—when you've quite finished with
them?"

"Beg pardon, m'lord, your lordship's a-sitting on
them."

"Put them higher up then, another time."

"Very good, m'lord," the man said amiably.

"Pretty lordship you are!" The taunt came from
the window. Then came a plaintive cry—"Good
lord, look at this! All ruined with tea." And clutching tragically at his pink and gold and silver gown the
soldier began to sob like a little girl.

"Darn your blinking togs," was the heartless reply.
The guardsman sobbed but the more piteously.

But Ashford, engrossed in print, ignored him.

"For the love of Mike," the peer burst forth in
triumph, tossing the newspaper with a whoop of

ecstasy towards the ceiling. "Tom! Tom, me darlint, our nag has won!"

"Never."

"Honor!"

"The good old outsider!"

Pandemonium! The outsider—backed in freak and joke—had won by an hundred to one.

They rocked in each other's arms.

They sang.

They danced about the room together, shouting hymns to ragtime tunes—with Indian war whoops for Amens.

And the maiden lady in the flat above rapped on the floor—her floor, their ceiling—with a poker, and they heard her not.

The scene was typical. Ch'êng Tzŭ might have said of it that it could not have happened in China. But it happens in London every day.

And these were very gallant English gentlemen—staunch friends, fair foes, clean-limbed, clean-hearted English boys, thinking little evil, doing none—upright, true, not uncultured, not unthoughtful: lion cubs at play—splendidly whelped, and warranted to crash and muddle through every grim emergency of life. Both had served their country, in time of war; and stood ready to serve her again, to their last gasp. Jack Selwyn had deserved the honors he took at Oxford. Tom Granville had well won the V. C. he sometimes had to wear. They loved each other tenderly. They revered all good women, and pitied all who were frail. Tom had been wounded in battle twice. Both had been scarred in the hunting field. They loved their kindred and their King. They rode straight—and lived straight. And both stood ready to die for England any hour, and to do it blithely—and stood ready to suffer for it things far more hideous and sordid than any death, and to do it gladly and heroically for any number of protracted years.

The scene was typical.   So were the boys.

CHAPTER XXX

ASHFORD GRANGE, long and low, gray, red-roofed, mullioned-windowed—the loveliest but not the largest of Ashford's houses, sparkled softly in the early morning's silver sheen. Wide swathes of tender grass stretched softly green and newly washed between the flower-clotted gardens and the old gray house. And beyond the gardens stretched a cool paradise of trees. The girl plainly clad in gray linen, moving slowly with many a pause among the flowers, found, as she stopped to smile at him, the "bonnie lark," perched on a daisy's stalk, bending it "amang the dewy weet wi' speckled breast," a "neebour sweet," and he looked up at her with tiny friendly eyes, as if he thought her indeed a "companion meet," and ducked her a gracious salutation with his downy head as he sprang "upward blithe to greet the purpling East," and the "modest crimson-tipped flower" straightened itself up, shaking the tiny dewdrops from its rose-petaled head.

And the girl went slowly on through the tulips and the ferns, drinking the roses' wet attar-breath, weaving their red and pink and amber beauty into her soul, and moved towards the long cool vista that stretched through the trees.

Tzŭ had seen nothing in Europe that she had liked so much as this—nothing she'd thought so beautiful, or that satisfied her so, since she had left Ho-nan. Ashford Grange seemed to her indeed a "home from home." The house looked, she thought, a home. And with its long, low, irregular gray walls, its red sloping roofs, it reminded her of her home far across the world sprawling gray and irregular, low beneath curving, red, tent-shaped roofs. The pergola over there, hung thick with ramblers of every hue, and lacquered by the sunrise, was not unlike a paifang. The smell of honeysuckle came to her across the tall lilies. There were violets everywhere—as there were at home. Musk brushed her skirt, and her skirt beat sweetness from lemon verbenas and clove pinks. A bell called in the distance—it might have been a distant breeze-blown temple bell at home. The sound of rushing water, and the liquid trickling of a rill met somewhere, and kissed, beneath the hiding of the trees. And the new hour and all the perfect peace were hers. No other human creature seemed awake, certainly none was astir. She and the shy wild things of the place were all alone—she and they alone with the new day.

Ch'êng Tzŭ stretched out her hands in greeting to the sun, coming up to England and to her from China —on its way back to China—bringing her a message, taking a message from her. The sun was rising up from China—and, for that, and for its regnant self the Chinese girl kot'owed to it, before she stooped to gather a few violets for her breast. And the rising sun shot a shaft of radiant light through the perfumed air,—it fell at Ch'êng Tzŭ's feet, and kissed them.

The day called to her, the day and all its quivering things, and she called back to them. They claimed her. And she claimed them, and gave herself to them, as she curled down against a great oak tree, and took communion with Nature, drinking from its perfumed chalice, breaking its blessed daily bread; such intimate communion as occidental souls cannot take.

Europeans living in China, and living there with an un-European humbleness of sympathy to which she sometimes shows a little of her sceret, never cease to wonder, never slake their surprise, at how marvelously psychic the Chinese are. But they never suspect but the outer fragments of that marvel.

What occidental science to-day begins to whisper of Nature, Chinese soul-instinct has known always. Chinese poets, Chinese artists, Chinese sages have told it, and Chinese prince and peasant have received the message, and quickened to it. The Chinese have known for centuries that birds have immortality, that flowers have souls and hearts and "love the fresh air they breathe." Ch'êng Tzŭ knew that the roses loved the air that touched them, and that the air loved them. She knew that the dewdrops counted their petals, enjoyed their velvet, and that the birds gloated over their colors.

In Europe Confucius is credited the greatest Chinese, and the most far-reaching and potent force in Chinese life and thought—perhaps because "Confucius" is the only Chinese name that most educated Europeans know. Ch'êng T'ien Tzŭ scarcely presumed to mention Confucius's name. In China she could not have mentioned it at all. Ch'êng Shao Yün had never spoken it. But Tzŭ knew that not Confucius but old Lao Tze—another name she must not voice—counted in China for most, had taught China most. And it was of a saying of Lao Tze that she was thinking as she sat leaning against the great oak, with the English violets in her gown—his saying that: "The tree that needs two arms to span its girth sprang from the tiniest shoot. Yon tower, nine stories high, rose from a little mound of earth.   A journey of a thousand miles began with a single step."

Scrupulous in their observance of the intricate Confucian ritual, with all its long minutely prescribed ceremonial, the Chinese—loving freedom as no other people has, but holding soul-freedom as much, compared to physical freedom—soon wearied of the chain and cramp of the older philosopher's materialism and narrow elaborate rule, and turned for refreshment, rest and soul-growth to the rhythmed thought of Lao Tze's spirituality and to the Nature that it hymned: finding "books in the running brooks, sermons in stones," friends in flowers, counsel in the far-off hills, companionship in the white-crested water's foaming fall— peace and satisfaction without satiety in the blue sky and the breathing cloud.

Probably—in international thought—Confucius's name will always be the name most prominently associated with China—and largely too, though unspoken, most celebrated in China.   But a nicer estimate would give old Lao Tze pride of place.   The more visible observance of Taoism has become cheapened, degraded even, by its popular malpractices: crass fortune-telling and superstitious gibberish.   But the fine spirit of the great cult remains, permeating China with beauty, spirituality and sanity.   And perhaps it is the soul of Lao Tze that may yet preserve China from her last and crassest folly—the crime and stupidity of aping the pinchbeck ways of alien modernity, and substituting for the most ideal *and* successful democracy the world has known a mountebank and puritanical republic. Insanity is all but unknown in China, and conceivably it is so because Lao Tze still breathes out his healthy heart upon his people, and because they live so much with nature, holding with nature their greatest intimacy. Confucius was great-souled and great-minded. It was idiocy to belittle him. It is the mingling of their sages' teaching that has made the Chinese what they are: a contemplative *and* the most practical, indefatigable and industrious of all races; the only human race that has had the wit, the sanity and the culture to make of daily downright hard work a pastime, a culture and an art.

The Chinese love nature—scenery, birds, verdure, foliage and all the misted wonders of the air, for themselves, for what they *are*—with a loyal and an understanding love. Ch'êng Tzŭ loved the lark that had greeted her and left her, the daisy he had bent to a dew-bath in the grass, the violets at her breast, the lovely things she saw through the vista of the trees— loved them passionately—for their souls, their being, for what she knew they were and said and felt and thought and told her, even a thousand times more than she loved the beauty which was to her but their signature—as a hungry lover craves more to see his loved one's face, and touch it, to hold her hands in his, to feel her breath upon his cheek, than he does to find a letter from her in his post.

Dim in the distance a hill misty and gray in the early light, soft with willow trees, stooped down to a marshy meadow where kingcups grew and cuckoo flowers and purple flags, with violets and forget-me-nots edging a silent, tranquil pool. It reminded Ch'êng Tzŭ of a landscape of Ma Yuan's—perhaps easily the greatest landscape painter earth and art have ever bred—a long scroll of silk, that sometimes was reverently unrolled and hung for a few days on the K'o-tang wall at home;

a famous picture, and little Tzŭ had loved it passionately—remembering it she loved it now, and for it loved this English landscape, and understood it, the more, and felt and claimed it hers.

She thrilled to the breaking day. She felt nearer to China than she had felt in years. The soul of her womanhood was waking to consciousness as it had not before. And she felt happier, happier to be in England, more one with it, than she had ever done before.

A pale blue butterfly came hovering down and lit a moment on her hand. A tiny squirrel studied her from behind a clump of fern—and sent her a soft chattered friendly greeting before it scampered leisurely away.

Tom opened his sleepy eyes, and lay very still, staring in astonishment at Jack.

They had arrived so late the night before that they had seen neither Elenore nor her guests. A bursted tire, a recalcitrant crank, and a wrong turning had delayed them for hours. A somnolent and indignant footman had let them in, and they had tumbled as quietly as they could to bed—grumbling in whispers at each other because they had to share a bedroom. The Duchess—the "Aunt Annie" of Elenore's undecipherable letter—had even hinted, over the telephone, that it might be necessary to put a third bed in Ashford's room; Nell was so cramming the roomy old Grange with her birthday guests.

Tom watched Lord Ashford with astonishment that grew. The clock showed little more than six. Jack Selwyn—regrettably indifferent to habiliments as a rule, and incurably fond of his morning pillow—was brushing his hair with rapid assiduity, at the same time regarding his own face gravely in the mirror. His

tie was beautifully knotted. His flannel trousers were
immaculate, and he evidently intended to assume soon
a coat as immaculate, hanging ready on his bed, for
Tom saw a pink rosebud in the white lapel.

"What the hell's the meaning of it?"

Jack frowned at him through the glass.

"You go to sleep again. You're not on in this act."

Granville raised up on to an elbow, and propped
his head in his hand.

"I require to know the cause of this sudden lunacy,"
he said sternly—"brushing your hair as if you were
going to a fresher dance—at four in the morning!"

"It's gone six," Ashford said, curtly.

"And we didn't get to bed till after two."

Jack put on his coat.

"For the love of Mike," the man in bed remon-
strated, "tell me what is up."

"You turn over and go to sleep."

"Precisely what I desire to do. But my torturing
curiosity won't let me. Tell me about it."

"I couldn't sleep—I'm going out. It's a ripping
morning."

"Good Lord! Where did you get that flower? It's
fresh picked or I'm a turnip."

"You are—a mangel-wurzel."

"John Selwyn, you've been out already! And not
in those new flannels. You picked that rose. What
sent you back here to dress for a garden party, in a
very devil of a hurry too, and with a look of acute
anxiety on your pretty face?"

"I'd come and thump you, if I had time," the peer
retorted, scrutinizing a fresh silk handkerchief criti-

cally, and rearranging it in his coat pocket three separate times. "But I haven't, I'm in a hurry."

"So I perceive. Well! My aunt, kid, if I didn't know you never looked at one twice, I'd say it was a girl."

"It is a girl."

Tom Granville sat bolt upright in bed. But he was speechless.

Jack laughed. "I couldn't sleep, Tom, straight stuff. Got tired thrashing about on my bed, and hearing you snore in yours. So I got up. Thought I'd have a pipe in the garden. Well, I didn't—I picked you a rose instead—but when I realized how like hell you look in pink, I put it in my coat instead. And now I'm off. There's a girl out in the garden I want to speak to——"

"Which girl?" Tom asked shyly—he no longer thought the situation funny.

"I've no idea. I didn't see her face."

"Holy Moses! And you've dressed up like that! I say, boy, are you well? One of the maids of course, at this pagan hour——"

"I didn't see her face, I tell you, just a girl in a gray dress mooning about the garden, but it was not a maid."

"How do you know?" Granville demanded disgustedly.

"I saw her walk. It was a lady, the girl I saw out there with the flowers—no maid, more like a princess. And it was a girl. I know that, if I didn't see her face."

"Hope she's sixty—when you see her face——"

"No fear! I know. I say, Tom, old lobster, I wish

I knew who all Nell's asked. I may know her, and may not. But I can say 'Good-morning' to any one in my own garden. Ta-ta."

Granville listened to Ashford running down the stairs, then sank back into his pillows with an eloquent whistle.

CHAPTER XXXI

TOM whistled low and long. Here was news indeed. Jack Selwyn off before breakfast to talk to a girl in a garden—a girl whom for all he knew he'd never seen before. Gee whiz! What next!

He—Tom himself—had been in love for years, and he supposed everybody knew it. He was pretty sure Jack did. But Jack!—that was different. Jack was only twenty-four—almost three years younger than he himself. And Jack had never cared for girls—except his cousin Elenore—and that was just brother-and-sister of a very special sort. Her people had brought Jack up; their home had been his until he came of age. He and Nell had been inseparable since they were babies. Tom had fallen in love with a picture of her Jack had at public school, long before he'd seen Elenore herself, and had treated his fag with special amenity in consequence. But he knew that Jack had never bothered with any other girl. Of course, if he had put it to himself, probably he'd have said that Jack would go the marriage-way of most men some day. You were pretty sure to marry if you lived long enough. There were lots of girls—and girls were ripping. And Jack *was* twenty-four. But Tom never had put it to himself. It had never crossed his head. He had always thought of Jack—as far as it had shaped into thought—as a very desirable belonging of his own and Elenore's. And now the boy was off at six in the morning—"all dressed up"—after a girl. By Jove. Go to sleep again! Of course he couldn't go to sleep after this—who could! He wondered who the devil the girl was any way? Probably one of the maids after all. And then the drinks would be on Jack. Tom chuckled grimly. He rather hoped it was a maid. Jack's face would be worth seeing. Tom lit a cigarette, curled down more comfortably, and gave himself to tobacco and day-dreams—of Elenore.

This was Ashford's own room. A water color of Elenore smiled above the fireplace. What a face! English, fair, wholesome. How blue her eyes were! How well her head sat on her shoulders! How nice that soft brown hair! He wondered if she hated red hair as much as some people did. All the Granvilles had red hair. And probably—oh! damn it! He was a cad to take such a liberty as to think of that——

But the dream would not be driven away. And Tom Granville lay very still, his eyes riveted on a pictured face, his thoughts far away. He forgot to smoke. The cigarette burned steadily on until he dropped it with an oath. Tom was still sucking his finger when Jack came in. Jack's face *was* worth seeing: disgusted and thoroughly sulky.

"Hello, old bean! Sold?"

Lord Ashford nodded, and pushed the bell viciously.

"Scullery or tweenie, or only sear and yellow? You didn't stay long."

"I didn't stay at all. You wait till I see Nell Selwyn, I won't half roast her! What!"

"Wasn't she gracious?"

"Gracious be blowed. I didn't speak to her—when I saw her——"

Tom grinned. He was not ill-pleased.

"Tea—and look sharp," Ashford said snappily, as Burton appeared.

"Very good, my——" the man began, to break off and cross the room more quickly than he often moved. "Beg pardon, Sir, but are you afire?"

"No," Tom assured him, "but I have been. And probably the damned bed is."

That restored Jack Ashford's perturbed spirit.

"Set himself alight with his own head, Burts. He often does."

Tom found a boot, and flung it, as Burton left the room carrying a smoldering sheet.

"She was under the trees when I got there," Jack said more amiably, "sitting down—as if she meant to stay there all day. I got quite near, and had a jolly good look before she saw me. I don't think she did see me at all. Tom, she's a Jap!"

"A what?"

"Japanese, or Indian, or something rummy of that sort."

"Black, eh?"

"Good Lord, no! Not even brown. A good sight lighter than Mercedes de Piro was, or a Cuban girl that went to school with Nell. But she's a Jap or something of that sort."

"Lady's maid of somebody. My Aunt Susan's got a Jap butler, and he's top hole."

Ashford frowned. "No! I tell you this was a lady-girl."

"Lady-girl!" Tom chuckled at the odd phrase. "Well—you needn't bully me, if she is. And why didn't you speak to her then?"

"Didn't want to. Shouldn't have known what to say. She might have screamed."

"Funked it, eh? You'll need to get over that, my child. There's lots of them about now. I took a Maharanee in to dinner at Aunt Kate's last year— awfully interesting woman. Intelligent—what! We live in an advanced age, you and I, old dear. No London drawing-room is complete without an Asiatic. And I'm quite expecting to waltz with an African belle any day."

"I dare say! But I prefer English. Oh! there you are at last! Pour it out. And, I say, Burts, who all are here?"

Burton recited a page from the Court Circular.

"Thought I saw a Japanese—gentleman—out in the hall just now."

"No, sir," the servant told him, "I think not. There's no Japanese gentleman staying here, I think, except her Grace's pugs. But there is Miss Sheng, a Chinese lady."

"Hello!" Granville whispered.

"Chinese," Lord Ashford cried. "That's ten thousand times worse! You wait till I see Nell."

Breakfast was an elastic appointment at the Grange —eaten when and where you liked. The Duchess hadn't breakfasted out of her own rooms for twenty years.

Lord Ashford looked about him a little apprehensively as he and Tom went into the breakfast room. Tom saw it and grinned. Then Elenore came in through another door, and Granville forgot all about Jack Selwyn.

But Miss Ch'êng did not come. She breakfasted much later, eating fruit in her own sitting-room, while the Duchess ate steak, omelette and several other things in bed.

Ashford followed his cousin when she left the dining-room.

But his attack upon her was less direct and strong-armed than he had led Tom—and incidentally Burton —to anticipate.

"Who all are here, Nellie?"

"I sent you a list."

"Much good that was! You wrote it. Where's Dean?"

"In a sling. At least her right wrist is. She sprained it."

"Who's here—that I don't know?"

Elenore ran through a score of names.

"And who's Miss Sheng? I never heard the name before."

"Ch'êng," his cousin repeated severely. "Do try to say it correctly. And, Jack, I particularly want Tzŭ to have a really good time."

" 'Choo'? Who's 'Choo'?"

"Ch'êng T'ien Tzŭ is a dear. She was at Lady Mary's when I was."

"Not English, I gather from her names."

"Of course not. She is Chinese."

Lord Ashford whistled.

"Don't be coarse, Jack—if you can help it. Miss Ch'êng is very charming."

"Look here, Nell. I gave you carte blanche—I know that. But, great Scot, a Chinese girl, here with us! What is she—why——"

"My friend," Elenore said icily. "And your guest."

"Oh—all right—coz. Don't get the wind up."

"I don't intend to. I leave that to you. But, John Selwyn, if you are not nice to Tzŭ, I'll never speak to you again."

"Oh—all right—no need to go off the deep end." His voice was meek, but his face was sulky. "I say, Nell, can she speak English?"

"Better than you do—and everything else. You are taking her in to dinner."

"No, please, I can't do that. I say, Nell."

"Aunt Annie goes in last, of course. There is no other married woman here until to-morrow. Miss Ch'êng takes precedence. It belongs to her. There is no other girl here of her rank."

"Chinese rank! My hat! I say, what am I to say to her?"

"Just what you'd say to any other lady at your own table."

"Oh! I'll not forget she is a lady," Ashford said a little huffily. "I told Tom so."

"You said you didn't know her, pretended not to know her name even."

"No more I did. But I saw a girl in the garden this morning, in the distance, a—a foreigner—just saw her back—but I told Tom."

"Said it was a princess," Granville corroborated, joining them in the hall.

Elenore was mollified. "So she is," she said stoutly. "See that you treat her as such."

"Tennis?" Tom said ingratiatingly.

"If you like," Elenore told him. "Coming, Jack?"

"Thank you, no. I am about to search the library for a life of Confucius."

"I wouldn't, if I were you," his cousin said over her shoulder. "You couldn't possibly understand it."

Lord Ashford watched them moodily until they were out of sight. Then he turned on his heel and made for the stables.

"Chinese!" he muttered.

CHAPTER XXXII

LORD ASHFORD supposed he'd meet his dinner partner during the day. He hoped so. He wasn't looking forward to it—except disagreeably. But he'd like to get it over, as informally as possible, crash through the ice somehow, before the more formal hour —get his bearings a little as it were. Thank heaven there were some married women coming to-morrow. He wouldn't have to go through it twice. He supposed married women took precedence of any girl— even one who ate with chopsticks, or undoubtedly could, and was a granddaughter of Confucius himself.

But Ashford did not meet Miss Ch'êng until just before dinner was announced, though he heard her name all day long, pronounced by twenty tongues in twenty different incorrect ways.

There had been a riding party in the morning, and several girls lunched in their habits. Tzŭ among them. But she sat at the other end of the long table, beyond a barricade of flowers, and he caught no glimpse of the girlish face shaded by her broad hat. He thought the Chinese guest was not there, and wondered, but would not ask. Perhaps the Chinese did not lunch. He wondered if she ate meat.

When Ch'êng T'ien Tzŭ came into the long drawing-room—a great white, candle-lit room, John Selwyn caught his breath. There were eyes there that could not at first see, or focus rather, the loveliness in that unaccustomed type. But Ashford saw it at a glance.

In his wordless British way he worshiped beauty. His ancestors had collected pictures for centuries, and had spared no pains to make their beautiful holdings more beautiful. Lord Ashford was no mean judge of beauty: and he quickened to it always.

He quickened to Ch'êng Tzŭ as she stood a moment near the door. It might be hard to talk to her, but it would be good to look at her through all the dinner hour. And what an artist had designed that dress!

The face of Chinese age is full of extraordinary dignity. The faces of Chinese youth are extraordinarily lovely. This girlish face was the most exquisite that old storied English room had ever seen; radiant, patrician, gracious, tinted like a pomegranate flower. The twisting dress of crêpe, blue as forget-me-nots, hung and half clung falling from a band of turquoises an inch below her throat—a throat that was velvet just not white. He could see the lumps of rings under the loose long gloves. She wore no other jewels, unless those were real that blazed out from the tiny padded shoes that her gown escaped. The girl's black hair was braided about her proud-set tiny head, and above each ear she wore a little stiff bunch of forget-me-nots. He thought the Chinese had narrow slant eyes. This girl's were magnificently set, absolutely straight—fearless, unfathomable, sparkling now like deep brown diamonds. He had never seen anything to match the sure, exquisite penciling of her narrow eyebrows. And her mouth—there was no describing that—her mouth——

The Duchess beckoned him.

"This is my nephew, Lord Ashford, Miss Shen," she said.

"I saw you in the garden," he told her, as he bowed,

"this morning, Miss—Ch'êng," stammering a little at the name.

Ch'êng Tzŭ smiled frankly at her host. "Thank you for having such a beautiful garden, Lord Ashford," she said.

Ashford's gray eyes leapt—in spite of him—at Ch'êng Tzŭ's voice. English ears can never grow quite accustomed to Chinese voices. And there are a few of our English alphabetic sounds that the Chinese voice will not repeat, and some sounds we slur they cannot slur. When a Chinese man speaks our tongue the light timbre of his voice is always something unwelcome to our hearing—and the finer his birth, the lighter his voice. Ch'êng Tzŭ's pronunciation of English was almost English, the slight difference as intriguing as a tiny mole on a beauty's white cheek or a dimple in a baby's chin. And her voice, with a tiny ripple in it, like the natural ripple in some happy woman's hair, was very musical, like a scented flute, or an exquisite silver bell, low, clear and strangely sweet.

"Thank you, for liking it," he replied, with a slight grateful bow for which the Chinese girl liked him. Elenore's cousin was well-bred she thought. And she remembered that she had thought he looked that at Doncaster House.

He offered Miss Ch'êng his arm, half wondering if she'd take it.

Ch'êng Tzŭ took it very simply, and quite impersonally—as a queen might accept a chamberlain's—just touching his coat with her glove. But Ashford knew that the distance the girl kept was a natural aloofness and no pose. And, if he had thrilled to her beauty, he liked her for the distance that she kept. He wished his mother might have known this girl.

Elenore, who had been watching them a little anxiously, sighed with relief. She was very pleased with Jack. She'd knit him a pair of braces—and embroider them, or a very special tie. And then she gave her attention to her own escort quite whole-heartedly. Jack was a good boy.

He was still a somewhat embarrassed one. The garden had been a good opening. But the announcement of dinner had interrupted it—and he didn't know how to get back to it. He could think of no compromise between stark silence and the weather—as they moved to the dining-room. He took craven refuge in the weather.

Miss Ch'êng answered pleasantly, and showed none of the amusement she felt. Possibly she felt less than she would have felt at the conversational poverty of another man. She had not forgotten the man who had caught her interest at Lady Doncaster's, and had known that she had not.

When dinner began her host found himself in scarcely better small-talk fettle.

"Do you like England, Miss Ch'êng?" he asked rather desperately.

Ch'êng Tzŭ did not misunderstand, and, understanding, she did not resent the trite old question. Many an Englishman who'd taken her in to dinner had clutched at it as at a life-belt. She was accustomed to the embarrassment of Englishmen who met her for the first time.

"Most of it," she said laughing.

Jack Selwyn wondered which was loveliest, the white brightness of her teeth, or their perfect shape. Ch'êng Chü-po had wondered the same thing years ago when another Tzŭ had laughed at him first.

"It is almost half home to me, Lord Ashford—your England," Miss Ch'êng continued more gravely. And she added a trifle sadly, "In a sense I am without a country; I have been away from home so long—since I was ten."

"How jolly rotten for you." He said it impulsively.

Tzŭ nodded. "Yes—just that."

"But you remember China?"

"Yes," she told him, with an odd smile. "I remember China, Lord Ashford—quite well. I think China is not easily forgotten. And we Chinese have persistent memories—self-centered ones."

"I wish I had seen China." It was a new wish—brand new.

The girl divined that he was at a loss for subjects for chat. She liked him none the less for not being glib. And when he ventured a question or two, she told him of her country, and something even of her people—a rare thing for Ch'êng Tzŭ to do. She almost never could be led to speak of China unless alone with her sparse Chinese London acquaintance.

While dinner was still young she had put John Selwyn at his ease—partly by her quiet good-nature, partly by her magnetism—the magnetism to which children and all animals responded invariably.

He thought her hands the most wonderful things he had ever seen—and probably they were: tiny, flower-sweet things, exquisitely modeled, proud and dimple-nicked beneath a wicked weight of rings. Little quiet, tranquil hands that made him think of pale yellow rose leaves and of old French love-songs. He marveled that she had contrived to carry them about without breaking them. And he wondered what they felt like—and how it would feel to touch them, the funny little things!

Lord Ashford ate very little dinner. And the lady on his left grew more and more indignant. Her host scarcely remembered to speak to her once—and, when he did, what he said was not worth the trouble of hearing.

In the drawing-room after dinner Ashford went to Miss Ch'êng and stayed by her for a decent time. Not to have done so would have been rude.

The men in the smoking-room missed Ashford, an hour or so after the women had all said good-night. Granville volunteered to find him. He had seen Jack saunter off by himself some time before.

Tom ran Jack to earth in the library. Lord Ashford, long after midnight, was reading an article in the Encyclopedia Britannica—the article on China.

CHAPTER XXXIII

NOVELTY is stimulating. All men find it so. A great deal that Miss Ch'êng could do and do well, Ashford would have taken for granted in almost any English girl, and, taking it for granted, would have found it commonplace and tame. Tzŭ rode almost as well as he, matched him at tennis. So did Elenore. In Elenore he accepted it indifferently. In the Chinese girl it was unexpected, and gave him the tonic tingle of novelty. She played the piano admirably—which Nell did not—could give him odds at billiards, and beat him hands down at bridge. She distanced him hopelessly at chess. She was more widely read, and more deeply than he—and he had taken honors at the 'Varsity, and still loved books. She spoke French better than he did—and knew other European tongues of which he was all but ignorant. Man-like, this might have bored him in a plainer, older woman, piqued him in a pretty girl of his own race. But he found it vastly attractive in this dainty Oriental with the piquant, flower-like, girlish face, and the hands like pale yellow butterflies—and never tired of it, because it never ceased to surprise him.

Lord Ashford was too good a host to devote himself to one guest to the exclusion of others—though often inclination pressed manners hard—and Ch'êng Tzŭ was not the girl to allow it. But her racial loneliness gave her a prior claim which her host was not slow to yield. And accident threw them together oddly often, and each day pushed their acquaintance towards ripe and fruited friendliness.

Elenore smiled.

Tom Granville was troubled.

The house party shrugged and grinned—but only a girl or two did it acidly. They thought Lord Ashford might have been better employed.

Jack had given Nell carte blanche, and she had invited most of their guests for a long stay—three weeks. Jack had grumbled at the length when she told him. He grumbled to another tune now, and pestered Nell to "keep it going" for five weeks—or six.

An English man and a Chinese girl were in love. And inside a week every human being, except Ashford himself, knew it of him. What Ch'êng T'ien Tzŭ felt, or if she felt, no one, but she herself, could hazard. Tzŭ gave no sign.

But Tzŭ knew. And she was troubled even more than Granville was.

She had known at the Doncaster crush that for the first time in her life a man had interested her. And she knew that she came of a strong race whose women cared but once. But she had no mind to make a misalliance, even if this English man would bow his pride of race beneath a Chinese yoke. And she thought that he would not. She knew that Lord Ashford had lost his heart—for a time, at least, but she thought that he would not lose his head. She would marry, of course. A life less fulfilled was unthinkable. She would go home—soon now, and throw her lot in with her own people. To do less would be unthinkable. But she was here, through no fault or weakness of her own. "Character is destiny," Ch'êng Yün had taught her from her birth. Well—she would not fail or smirch her destiny. She was going back to China—home. But first she'd drink this cup—not to the dregs, not to the rich-scented purple depth, but sip the golden perfumed bubbles foaming at the rim. Fate had provided the shrine. Fate was a divinity—and she, Ch'êng Tzǔ, would taste but a lip-touch of the heady draught, before she spilled its richness out to soak and be lost on the English grass—a libation to China—would taste, just taste, that she might hoard its memory, and know sometimes its tang when she was alone in China. Alone in China! But she would not be *alone* in China—long! Ah, well—all she had done in Europe, even what she was doing now, had been commanded by Ch'êng Shao Yün. Who was she to know better than Ch'êng Shao Yün? That venerable queen-thing could do no wrong.

And Ch'êng T'ien Tzǔ went to the mirror and fastened honeysuckle in her hair. And at her breast she thrust an English rose—just opening pink.

The old butler hurried across the room unceremoniously, the pompous quiet of a lifetime torn away, and spoke to his master without prefix; man to man.

"Nero has broken loose."

"My God!" Ashford sprang up, his wine glass shattered on his plate.

A girl gave a little silly scream. A sillier girl giggled. Elenore Selwyn clutched the cloth.

Ashford turned to her. "Where is Tzǔ?" he snapped.

They all were there, all but Tzǔ.

Elenore choked. "She was picking cherries—in the walk. I left her there half an hour ago——"

"Has Miss Ch'êng come in? Can't you speak," John Selwyn cried, rushing from the room.

"Not yet, my lord, I've been in the hall for some time," a footman said.

They all crowded into the hall.

John Selwyn was pelting up the stairs. "Tom," he called over his shoulder. "No woman is to leave the house. See all the side doors shut and fastened, Bates. Stand by that front door, Tom. I want you in a minute. Tell the maids, Bates."

They heard him rush through the upper hall—break through a door. And he was running down the stairs again, a great whip and a thong dangling from his arm, loading his pistol as he ran. His face was white.

"Which way did he go?"

A stable boy—he had brought the word—answered. "He was headin' for the Cherry Walk, my lord."

Ashford swayed, an instant, and choked back a sob.

Elenore caught at him at the door.

"Jack," she sobbed, "don't hurt Nero unless you have to——"

"Not unless I have to," he said grimly as he ran. "Keep the women in, Tom, until I come back."

Granville nodded, and laid his hand on Elenore Selwyn's arm. And they stood together watching Jack rush down the path calling, "Tzŭ!"

Nell swayed a little. She was crying softly now. Tom put his arm about her, and led her into a sitting-room.

"Shut that door," Granville commanded as they went. "Watch through the window, Clark."

Jack's face had quivered a little when she had said, "Don't hurt Nero," and Elenore had thought she saw tears near his eyes as her cousin pounded down the stairs.

She knew, and Tom did, how Jack loved the dog; a great untamed mastiff whom scarcely the man who fed him dared approach—docile to his master, brute and bully to all other living things,—a terrible, vicious dog-monster, herculean in strength, lion-limbed, who should have been destroyed long ago—only Jack Selwyn could never have it done.

How had it happened? Who was to blame? And little children might be playing in the woods and meadows, and at the cottage doors. And Tzŭ was in the Cherry Walk.

A hundred men were hunting Nero now—men with whips and sticks. Farm laborers with forks, game-keepers well armed—their master and Nero's foremost in the chase.

Ch'êng Tzŭ was sitting beneath the oak tree where he first had seen her, her hat upturned at her side, filled with red and yellow cherries. Nero lay beside her, his great head pillowed on her lap, one paw—it could have killed a child; it had killed a sheep, and had shredded a stout barrow into tow—snuggled on her ankle. Tzŭ was eating cherries.

Jack tried to call him—but no sound came—he pointed his pistol, moved another step, a cautious step, tried again to rule his voice. And this time a sound came, a guttural, tortured sound.

Nero heard and looked up, beat his great tail a little on the ground—but made no other move, lifting his eyes, but not his head.

The girl looked up and smiled.

"We are having a pic-nic," she called.

"Hush!" Ashford gasped sternly. "No—for God's sake don't move."

Ch'êng Tzŭ laughed. "Are you afraid of my dog, Lord Ashford? I won't let him hurt you"—and she gave the great shaggy brute's head a proprietary pat.

How he got to them John Selwyn never knew. Ch'êng Tzŭ knew that he lurched as he came—the nozzle of his pistol still aimed steadily at Nero's head. The hand that held the pistol never wavered the tremble or the space of a hair. But the girl saw how gray his face was, and how it twitched.

He reached them. Down on his knees—his body thrown on the big dog's—his arm about the dog's throat—the lead was snapped on; with a superhuman effort—Nero had thrice his strength, and the man's strength was spent—he hurled the brute a little way from the girl, pitching him over onto his splendid tawny back. Nero lay quite still, upside down but content—with a pistol at his head, and gestured lazily one friendly paw.

"Please go," Ashford said hoarsely.

Ch'êng Tzŭ held out her hand. "Give me that gun——"

"I may have to use it. Go! but not quickly. He may try to spring."

Tzŭ cuddled back against the tree, and selected a cherry—two, on their slender, dangling stalks.

"I'm sorry if we've frightened you," she said. "But it's nonsense, indeed it is. He's quite a darling. He wouldn't hurt me for the world. No animal will attack or harm a Ch'êng," she added simply. "I think he knows I'm Chinese. And I know he knows I love him. He is my friend."

And at last Ashford believed it—and let the pistol

lay on the grass—but close to his hand. And Tzŭ
spoke more intimately to him than she had done before—told him things about her country and her people
that she had not told before—told him of her wonderful old great-grandmother, to whom wild birds came
when she called them, Ch'êng Shao Yün who had ruled
a great estate with a glance or a gesture, and whose
magnetism could conquer every four-footed wild thing,
and with a smile could make them come and crouch
and fawn upon her.

And Nero crept back and laid his head again upon
her knee, and watched her with adoring eyes.

And John Selwyn, Lord Ashford, knew that he
would give his soul to take the Chinese girl into his
arms, and hold her there.

CHAPTER XXXIV

"NERO'S done it!" Tom said dejectedly.

"I rather think he has," Elenore replied cheerfully.

Granville groaned—and missed his shot.

"Why do you mind so much?" the girl asked, winning hers, and throwing down her cue. She had won the game.

"Because it isn't natural. It's upside down and inside out. And those things never work."

"Tzŭ's splendid."

"She's top-hole. I'm not blaming Jack. I blame no one—unless it's the old lady over in China that you say sent her here to grow up where she don't belong, among people with whom she can never really mix—without a single friend or thing of her natural own. It wasn't cricket."

"No," Elenore said slowly, "Tzŭ doesn't mix. I doubt if she'd 'mix' anywhere, in China any more than here. But I like her and respect her more than any girl I know. And she is very lovable. We all loved her at school. I don't see how Jack was to help it—and after the other day."

"No more do I. I'd be in love with her myself, if I hadn't been in love already for ten years and more." He said it stoutly, and looked Elenore Selwyn square in the face. He tried to look her in the eyes—but Elenore was looking hard at the scoring board. "I can understand Jack being in love with Miss Ch'êng all right—that's easy—and I can understand Miss Ch'êng caring for him—lord, yes—if she does—that's not my trouble, but what my trouble is, what I can't understand—is how they are going to hit it off—after. That does me."

"Well," Elenore said, "it's up to them."

"I suppose it is," Granville agreed gloomily.

"Perhaps they won't risk it."

"Oh, they'll risk it. I know Jack."

"But I know Tzŭ—if any one—of us—does."

"It's up to Jack," Tom insisted.

"No," Elenore contradicted. "I think it's up to Tzŭ. My how it rains," she added as the storm crashed against the window panes.

"Yes, it's a nice drizzle," Granville said admiringly. He blessed the torrents that had been pelting down all day, and given him this hour.

There is nothing a novelist so dreads as making a proposal. And the dread is justified of its abortive children.

The proposal is every fictionist's Waterloo. In real life there are few proposals, and almost never one articulate. Men contrive without it—and women assist them. It is common knowledge that no woman will tell even to her bosom friend at the time, or to her children in the after years, what her husband said when he asked her to be his wife—not because every woman has this one nice reticence, but because he did not—say anything.

Captain Granville was made of manly stuff. He intended to propose to the girl he loved. And he intended to do it squarely—with crossed "t's" and dotted "i's." He thought it wasn't playing the game to do

Sitting safe in boudoir, drawing-room, or at bridge-table, Nero, providentially reënclosed, brought something of the jungle to them. Their London-jaded souls were more easily stirred than children's. "That terrible brute—so incredible that dear Ashford should keep him, and fond of him too—must be—and such a nice boy, and such a quiet dear thing—your deal, dear"—Nero and his escapade were a novelty—and a novelty less repetitional than the new Montenegrin dancer, or the last society divorce—"Mary Montecute, of all people, only fancy, *and* Lord Smythson!"

Two women left abruptly. "The brute got out once, and he may again any day. No one can say I am a coward, but I draw the line at being eaten by a mad dog." Several, more spectacularly mettled, begged Lord Ashford to introduce them into Nero's paddock, "and let me pat him," and were denied it. And men of the party, who had scarcely noticed Ch'êng Tzŭ before, regarded "the little Chinese girl" with new interest, and an affectionate respect. Any girl who could make friends with Ashford's beast was a damned good sport, if her relatives did eat rats and puppies, and carry their new-born female children to the top of the nearest hill, and leave them there to die.

Nero remained unavoidably ignorant of his happy advancement into the scintillating intellectuality of Mayfair social small talk. But he realized that his existence had brightened considerably. And, being a dog, he was grateful. Ch'êng Tzŭ took him for a long walk every day—even when it rained—Lord Ashford in close attendance on them both, in case of emergency. And the "clotted cream" of the stable boy's sarcasm, though a verbal inexactitude, was no exaggeration. Nero would not be killed. Nothing less regal than old age would usher him on high to be a mandarin—so Ch'êng Tzŭ told Ashford, and Nero corroborated her with a thumping tail—among the dogs who had joined their ancestry. But Nero would make no second unauthorized and unaccompanied escape. His paddock door would never be left unlatched and unguarded again. The head stableman, and two of his underlings had been dismissed.

"Aunt Annie" agreed with Captain Granville that Nero had "done it." But Nero had not. He was an accessory after the doing. Propinquity, novelty, and the one thing in human nature for which there is no analysis, the call of maid to man, the claim of man to maid, had done it—in as far as it yet had been done. Nero had convenienced and hastened—advanced it. But he was but a supernumerary in the play in whose essential cast there is rarely but two.

Moreover the now expectant house party stood a fair chance of disappointment. They counted on the announcement of a second, and more exciting engagement, but there was not a little probability that this preliminary first act would end an unfinished play.

Love at its strongest—is a mighty destroyer. It can shatter all things but one: self-control established and convinced.

Ch'êng Tzŭ, a quickening girl, home-sick for a home she'd scarcely known, and homelinesses she'd never known, heart-sick for soul-rights, lonely in exile— exile none the less exile for all the interest, soft garments, and jeweled comforts—ripe for happiness, had given him her heart almost at once—and she knew it. For long centuries the women of her race had loved at first sight—prepared for it by tradition and upbringing—the first sight of a husband's eager face when he lifted her crimson veil. Ch'êng T'ien Tzŭ—so alone in England, so socially exposed—had loved suddenly, as Ting Tzŭ—so harem guarded—in a Ho-nan court-yard suddenly had loved Ch'êng Chü-po. It was in their blood—a thing of fate and character, no un-maidenliness. But Ch'êng T'ien Tzŭ did not intend to become the wife of John Selwyn. And she believed that he would not seek it.

Ashford knew now that he loved Tzŭ—and he was amazed to find what a masterful thing love was. He wondered if it took many fellows by the throat as it had him; and he watched Granville with troubled, speculative eyes. He would have avoided Ch'êng Tzŭ now, if he could. But that was beyond his strength. He followed and waylaid her, and his assiduity was grave, without smirch or taint of flirtation. He came of a race that rode straight. He was incapable of any thought even, of flirtation, with this girl so alone and so trebly a guest, Nell's guest, *his* guest, and a guest of England. But both his judgment totally, and his taste somewhat, discountenanced his taking of a Chi-nese wife. He was willing that Tzŭ should know he loved her, indifferent if others did, but he did not in-tend to woo her.

The Chinese and the English are the two races rich-est and strongest in self-control—character is destiny. And it was improbable that the match-making ac-credited to Nero would succeed.

CHAPTER XXXV

A NOTHER day had come—so the clocks said. The storm still held, a deluge now that wrapped the Grange in blackness. Electric lights and dinner-candles were as necessary to satisfactory breakfasting as kidneys and omelettes were. The Duchess had ordered fires in all the rooms, and Elenore was disturbed for the success of her dance. For it must not be supposed that gossip and tobacco (about equally shared between the two sexes—the women smoked everywhere, and the men everywhere but in the drawing-rooms) were the only entertainment Elenore had provided for her guests. Gossip and nicotine undoubtedly were the roast beef and Yorkshire, but there were soufflés in abundance and in variety. There was dancing every night in the hall, in an improvised ballroom, for those who chose. To-night's was to have been a big affair—half the county invited. Elenore wondered how many, if any, could come through such a deluge.

"May I show you the pictures now?" Ashford asked as Miss Ch'êng left the table.

Of all he had Lord Ashford loved and knew his pictures best. Ancestor worship is not a conscious English trait. But that Chinese characteristic is deep-rooted in the family loyalty of many an English aristocrat, though it expresses itself but mutely and along lines distinctly non-Chinese. But as Ch'êng Tzŭ went with him from canvas to canvas the race-barrier between them seemed less to her than she could have credited even an hour ago. She realized—it was patent —that this man loved his great possessions—his homes and lands, his tenants, the treasures stored and cherished in old rooms, because his ancestors had gathered them together, and lived in them for him. He accepted his wealth, his high position, with the unquestioning simplicity of a well-bred, unselfconscious child. Above all, he loved his pictures—his face quickened at them as until now she had only seen it quicken for her. And presently she saw that he loved the pictures for what they told rather than for what they were, for the beauty they recorded rather than for the beauties of color and line that were their own. That drew the Chinese girl closer to him than she had felt before. But the pictures themselves left her a little cold. And he felt it, and presently he said so, and asked her why.

Ch'êng Tzŭ laughed a little—a little sadly but not unproudly, and sitting down on a wide, low window-seat, knotted her hands upon her knee, and answered frankly, with a gentle shake of her head that set jade and an opal quivering gently, "It is because I am Chinese, I think. Your pictures are very beautiful, Lord Ashford. But I think them dead. There is scarcely a picture in a gallery in Europe that seems to me quite alive, or quite to get its message through."

"Not even the Turners?"

Tzŭ smiled, and shook her head. "Color isn't movement. It isn't even life. Our masters spare color more than they use it. They never crowd a foreground, because their pictures are designed to make us look off and through them to the sky, and mist and hill beyond—to show us the loveliness beyond the silk even more than the beauty instanced on it—the soul beyond the line. Your pictures seem to me still-life— their clouds never shift, their atmosphere is paint, the water-wheels never turn, their torrents never break or foam, even the flowers in a valley, or at the gorge's edge, are like flowers in a woman's hat in a shopwindow, they never tremble in the wind, they don't grow, they are sewed on—most of all, I think, your pictures have no wind. And their foregrounds are clotted with a crowd of things that hold the eye from the better things beyond. Your pictures are still-life, ours are thought. Yours show the artist's skill, ours show us nature. In a landscape of Ma Yuan's you can hear the wind. Do I boast too much, Lord Ashford? You asked me to say."

"By Jove"—there was room on the window seat for two—"you have surprised me, though!"

"You thought there were no pictures in China?" She mocked him, but there was friendship in the mocking.

"Did you think there were many in Europe before you came?" Jack retorted. "Had you ever heard of the Sistine Madonna?"

The girl laughed merrily. "That's fair. No, Lord Ashford, I didn't know there was a Europe until I was eight, and my great-grandmother told me I was going there—and all I ever gathered of it in my own country was that it was full of soldiers and mission-aries and—and peculiar women. No, I had never heard of Raphael, of Turner or of Tintoretto. But I have been industrious here. And I have tried to study your art. In Europe pictures are gulped and talked about. In China pictures are read and felt. You would think our pictures rigmaroles. We think yours scraps. Our greatest pictures are long scrolls. We unroll and re-roll them bit by bit, and read them as you read a book. Ours tell a story, yours, at best, an incident. Ours show nature, as a man sees it stretching slowly through a wood or by a river. Yours cut a piece out of nature, and put it in a frame, and hang it up to dress a wall. Nature does not cut a tree and a brook out of her panorama and frame the fragment, and hang it on a wall, and say, 'Oh, look!' or a moment out of a life, and call it a story. Our figure-pictures are novels. Yours are short stories."

She left the window-seat and went back to his pictures—and found some pleasant truth to say of them one by one. And John Selwyn grew meek in his surprise at what she knew of art—an alien art. He had brought her here to show her his pictures, but she was showing them to him.

He lured her back to the window-seat, as soon as he dared, and when he asked it, Ch'êng Tzŭ told him something—not much—of Chinese pictures and of the artists who had painted them. He tried to follow her —but much of it was a little difficult, and all of it was embarrassingly new. The music of the girl's voice reached and pierced him, but like the European painters she'd strictured, not much of her message got through. He had never heard of great Ma Yuan or of Ku K'ai-Chih, and English ears find strange Chinese names hard to catch when heard for the first time, English memories find them even more difficult to remember. But he began to suspect something of how much this wonderful girl of twenty knew, and to surmise that her exquisite beauty of mind and person—the fine finish of each delicate feature—was but the natural, simple flowering of the long culture

of a great race—the imperial culture of an imperial
people. And he began to sense how little he knew
of many things of supreme interest and value. That
message at least—and she had no thought to give
it—Chinese Tzǔ did get through, as they sat together
on the window-seat, the storm beating on the panes, the
great gallery glowing with electric lights.

He still thanked God that he was English—as well
such English may—nothing could prick him there.
But a Chinese girl with crippled feet had jarred his
old insularity and cut it to the quick. She had stirred
his senses, and delighted his eyes from the first. To-
day she had quickened his mind, and had made to it a
gift.

In speaking of a picture she'd seen at home, a bull-
finch on a bamboo spray—Ting Yüch'uan had painted
it—Ch'êng Tzǔ suddenly said something in Chinese.
Almost he had laid his hand on those tiny apricot-
tinted fingers. At the Chinese words he drew back.
They stung him. And he felt the gulf between them,
and a cold wind from it in his face. He wondered
if Tzǔ had spoken Chinese—he had not heard her
do so before—to remind him of a distance that must
be kept.

Perhaps her soul had, or some spirit instinct of
her race. But if she had, she had done it unconsciously. She had not seen the half-approach of Lord
Ashford's hand.

"Have you been very home-sick here?" Jack said
gently.

"Home-sick? Scarcely that—at least not very. I
was so young. Home has been more a bright memory,
and a happy promise, than an aching need. But, oh!

so lonely. It has been hard, my loneliness—so cruelly alone."

"But you have friends here—of your own people?"

"None. My old tutor is in London still. But I see less and less of him. And we were never comrades. There is no one of my kindred here. I am the only Ch'êng in exile—I have a Chinese woman with me in London—a companion in some surface ways, but not a friend—a slave girl a few years older than I am. My great-grandmother had her educated well, that she might live with me here, and speak Chinese with me every day. She is near me always in London—in the house. But—she's a slave, a big-footed woman. I have no friends. And I have never had a playmate since I left home—not many then, for I had to work too hard. And I often long to play."

"But at Lady Mary's—you were there——"

"I had the twins—just babies—no friends among the girls."

"But surely—why Elenore loved you——"

"She was very kind to me. Most of them were. But I never knew any of them. And none of them knew me. I know no one in England."

Ashford was moved. "Your Chinese maid—I have not seen her—is she not with you here?"

Miss Ch'êng laughed. "Mung Panü? No, indeed. I have Vail, my English woman, with me here. She does not fit in, in an English servant's hall—Mung Panü. I never take Panü to a country house. How it rains, Lord Ashford. It's a gorgeous storm."

"Yes," he said heartily. He was grateful to the storm, as Tom had been. Then, "Your porcelains," he began—knowing, as he thought, something of them, and thinking perhaps to bear some share less ignorant in talk of them—and he would show her the Chinese vases in the yellow room some day—she would be delighted with them.

But Ch'êng Tzŭ pushed the porcelains aside with an almost contemptuous gesture of a jeweled hand. "Our porcelains are a minor art—just a reflection and a record of the worthier arts; something of a partial catalog," she said, moving to the door.

He dismissed the showing of the vases. "But, won't you stay a little longer—and tell me more?" he begged.

"I must go," the girl said. "I have a letter to write."

"Write it after lunch."

Tzŭ shook her head. "I shall be very busy after lunch, dressing for Elenore's ball."

"But you can't dress from lunch till dinner!"

"Every moment of it until tea. No dinner for me to-night. Just a biscuit and a tea-pot in my room. I make a Chinese toilet for to-night. It takes many hours."

"Why?" he said a little lamely—perhaps a little gauchely.

"Because I am Chinese, Lord Ashford. To do honor to Elenore—she was very good to me at school—and to do honor to myself. I am Chinese, and I do not wish my friends to forget it—if any one could be so blind——"

Ashford bowed, and drew aside—that she might pass and go.

CHAPTER XXXVI

JOHN SELWYN smoked more than was good for him that afternoon—and as a host he was so remiss that it amounted to not being one, and to a rudeness that was all the more because it was not intended.

No one saw him after lunch. Tom failed to find him when Nell ordered it. It was Burton that found him at last, and only Burton knew in what scant time, and how ill-temperedly Ashford had dressed for dinner.

Tzŭ in Chinese clothes! He wished she wasn't going to do it. He hated it. He wondered why he hated it. He wondered why she did it. Over his third pipe he concluded that he hated it because he foresaw how all the county apes would stare at her, and nudge and gibber, as they did at some new creature at the Zoo. It was a feeble and an unjust conclusion. It was years since any one of Elenore's well-born guests had favored the Zoo and not one of them was ill-mannered enough to nudge. Over pipe number five he concluded that Miss Ch'êng was doing it in rebuke of him, and to keep him in his place. Good Lord, she needn't have troubled. He'd thought of little but race-barriers for a week now. He told his seventh pipe that he didn't give a damn for that or anything else. And when Burton interrupted a last pipeful Ashford flung it away, and ordered the man to find a Johnnie who could sell decent tobacco, which the tobacconist in present possession of his patronage damn well didn't.

Ashford was mistaken about Tzŭ.   She was putting
on her Chinese robes in self-defense against self—
to remind herself, and, in a qualm of conscience to
show herself to him as she was.   But it was an act
of honesty, not an act of rebuke or warning.   It was
herself she feared, it was she herself whom she wished
to warn.   She trusted Lord Ashford not to overlook,
much less overleap the sharp-spiked racial barrier.
But it was her pride—and her alarm—to-night to lose
Miss Ch'êng, to be again Ch'êng Tzŭ the great-granddaughter of Ch'êng Yün—a girl born in Ho-nan,
going back to Ho-nan.

At the court of St. James she wore her native
dress—because it privileged her to cover arms and
neck—but she had not cared to wear it elsewhere,
except in her own house—and not there when she
had guests.   She still thought her own dress both
more comfortable and more beautiful than the dress
of European women, but for some reason, which she
could not have explained, she preferred to keep it
to herself.   Probably in this Ch'êng Tzŭ's taste was
at fault.   The European and American Christian
missionaries—the men in pigtails and second-hand
Chinese garb, the women dressed as amahs or Chinese
frail, were the sorriest sights and the silliest that the
much-seeing streets of Shanghai ever saw.   And
Ch'êng Tzŭ would have kept her Chinese maiden
state in Europe with more dignity in a Chinese dress.
But she had been sent to England when a child—and
by the time the choice of her garments had been
altogether in her control she had grown accustomed
to wearing clothes such as all the girls about her wore.

But to-night she would be a looker-on in England,

and attend an English function as a Chinese guest, in her true colors.

Ch'êng Tzŭ had never dressed her own hair—and her English maid had never dressed it in Chinese style. But between them they accomplished it at last. A Chinese coiffeuse might have looked at it askance, but Vail thought it quite Chinesey. Secretly Tzŭ wondered if it would keep up. But wonderful as it was, it was secure enough. Vail was no bungler. The diamonds and the yellow honeysuckle sprays, the dangling pearls, the carved and glimmering jades, the tassels, and the pins encrusted with blue kingfisher feathers were fast and safe in an immovable foundation.

The jade-green wide-legged trousers, embroidered with wistaria in its natural colors, the overrobe of rose, fur-edged, a jeweled dragon on each side, the vest of crimson crêpe powdered with diamonds, and the top-coatee of clear, soft blue sewn with pearls— a paneled, almost skirt-shaped garment that hung almost to the lower edge of the jade-green trousers— and all the jewels of her station blazing about her, made a picture such as few there had ever seen before. The little hands were lost beneath their rings. And gems enough to enrich any crown in Europe might have been spared from her breast and not been missed. A messenger had brought most of them from London the day before. Miss Ch'êng had brought no such an array with her to the country house.

These were not the treasured jewels of the Ch'êngs, or any part of them. Ch'êng Yün had not deemed it necessary to send heirlooms to Europe—though she had yielded to little Tzŭ's request for Ma Yuan's herons. But Yün had sent before her death, a case of ornaments new-bought, in readiness for the first attendance of Miss Ch'êng at the English Court. Tzŭ had never worn so many before—and these were not a half. Her tiny fan had taken an artist a year to paint, an ivory-carver a year to stick. The tiny shoes were red as dye could stain satin, and to-night they were plainer than she often wore, their brilliant color not cloaked by embroidery or ornament—except for a cluster of loose-hanging pearls that clicked as she walked. Tzŭ wished to emphasize her feet.

She was dressed now—all but the paint. The paints, red, white and rose, lay ready on their tray of glass. Vail waited for her mistress' order, half hoping that Miss Ch'êng intended to paint herself. A touch of rouge, an eyebrow pencil, liquid cream, enamel—Vail was deft enough with those—but these Chinese pigments she doubted her skill to use. Ch'êng Tzŭ did intend to paint herself. She put her hand out— and drew it back, blushed a little—and walked away. She would wear no paint. She couldn't do it. Loyalty and self-revelation had gone far enough. And she made no doubt she'd look strange enough to English eyes. She almost looked strange to her own.

Tom Granville saw her first, and hurried to her. "By Jove," he exclaimed, "you are some picture. You ought to wear this sort of thing always."

"I believe I ought," Tzŭ smiled, but there was sadness in her smile.

Ashford had been watching for her for some time —since before the first guest came. It still rained with unabated fury, but the county had come. The great rooms were crowded now.

Jack saw her as she smiled up at Tòm, but he did not come to them at once, but stood and watched her. This suited her best—he saw that at once, and recognized it with a selfish pang. The barrier hardened and was higher. But his senses ached, as a sick man's for the fragrance of a flower. This was a new Tzǔ— but even lovelier than the one he knew. He saw that. But even more a girl apart. Was this the girl who had ridden with him neck to neck, and taken a hedge more carelessly than Nell, who knew more of the books in the library than Nell did, as much of his own pictures and flowers and crops as he? Was this the girl who spoke his tongue, and had lived among his people since she was a child? Then he realized, with a throb of pleased but dazed surprise, that she looked to him less un-English so—more like some delicate brunette girl of his own race wearing "fancy dress." He had seen Elenore as a Turkish lady, an Indian princess and a Persian Houri,—though he suspected a Houri overdressed,—and half the women of his acquaintance in what they thought Eastern dress. Tzǔ scarcely looked strange to him. He went to her then, and offered her his arm with, "My dance—please."

"I do not dance, Lord Ashford."

"But you will—a quadrille—you always do," Captain Granville insisted.

"No—not to-night."

"But why not?" Elenore's fiancé persisted.

"Chinese ladies do not dance," she told him. "We hire our dancing-girls, or have slaves to do it."

"But you are in England," Tom blundered on.

"No," Ch'êng Tzǔ said, "I am always in China really."

"Then let me find you a seat," Ashford begged,

offering her his arm again, "where we can watch the nautch."

"Yes, I shall like to watch," Tzŭ answered. "Will you take me to the Duchess? She said I might sit with her, when she had smiled the county in."

But, because she was in Chinese dress—and her hands bare, she would not take his arm—or even Captain Granville's, whom she treated with a lighter camaraderie than she did any other man. She walked between them through the rooms—until they found the Duchess, flirting with the Dean—or so the Duchess said, and the Dean did not contradict her.

Men—and women too—buzzed about the Chinese girl, but no one seemed surprised at her dress. English society has few surprises left it. And no one seemed to notice those jade-green trousers. Why should they? Half the girls there rode in divided skirts—or less. And Tzŭ's trousers were almost as wide and far less revealing than the latest thing in English skirts. Cut to show her shoes, still they kept her stockings private, and were almost hidden by the rose and dragoned tunic. It was a gorgeous, jeweled, girlish figure that paused beside the Duchess when it had curtsied a little proudly to Mr. Dean. But no man spoke presently in the smoking room of her jade-green wistaria-embroidered garment. None thought of it. There was a virginity that veiled this Chinese girl as a cloak, or the miraculous raiment of Saint Agnes. And not the coarsest coster in the East End or at the Docks could have mistaken or disregarded it. No man had ever thought a rudeness of Ch'êng T'ien Tzŭ.

The Duchess studied her hair with a buying eye, and planned a tableau at Albert Hall for a pet charity.

Lord Ashford left them soon. He came back more

than once, but not to stay long. He must play host to-night—in his own house—Nell's dance. But each time he looked at Ch'êng Tzǔ he wished the more that Sargent might paint her so—or some lesser great who would not scorn to repeat minutely each thread of those embroideries, each pearl and jade, and that the picture might hang forever his—in the gallery up-stairs where she had told him of "fluidity of lines," "atmospheric effects," old chaps with remarkable names, and the soullessness of Turner and Tintoretto.

CHAPTER XXXVII

IT was in the garden, almost where he had seen her first, that the end came—the first great punctuation in two lives. Tzŭ was sewing—she often sewed —sitting on an old bench, a little shaded from the sun, the flowers blazing for yards about her. The day was fiercely hot, and the few guests still remaining kept to the dimmer comforts of the house. But the Chinese girl loved the sunshine, and drank its hot wine as greedily as the flowers did.

Lord Ashford was not looking for her when he came upon her. He had weighed it all—realizing his dilemma at last—and he had decided against it. That he believed—as he did—that Miss Ch'êng would repulse any suit of his—but whetted his desire to urge it. He came of stock that took joy in difficulties, loved untying international knots with suave diplomacy, loved still better cutting them with a ready sword. He liked resistance—his metal rang to it. But he had himself in hand. And his judgment told him nay. Ch'êng Tzŭ had crept into his heart. He doubted if time or any other woman could ever oust her from it. Last night—balancing it all, fighting it out—he had sickened a little at the thought of life lived out without Tzŭ. His heart clamored for her. His arms ached for her. But, if life without Tzŭ seemed to him now a something of emptiness, and a pain, life with her he saw as a difficulty and a personal satisfaction embittered by much! That their marriage would be the social sensation of an hour revolted him, but it did not dissuade. For himself he desired this girl above all else on earth, beyond every other possibility of life. The soul-barriers between them he would risk. They might be absorbed and cease to be, in the intimacy of married companionship, begun in love and lived in loyalty—if not, for him, her sweetness and her charm would be compensation enough. But for one thing, of which he tried not to think, Tzŭ was perfect in her lover's sight. But his pride of race was a loyal devoted pride, not a selfish pride. As an Englishman he now saw no abhorrence in marriage with a Chinese wife. As a Selwyn he did. To put it bluntly—as he was clean and man enough to put it to himself—he reasoned that he had no right to subject the current of his family to something of abnormality. For himself he would accept a Chinese wife—he craved such a wife now, eagerly—but he shrank from a Chinese mother of his children. His children had a right to ask of him—to demand of him—an English mother. His ancestry had its rights. His descendants had theirs. Even for himself—selfishly he shrank from the thought of calling children of parentage so strange, his. He loved Ch'êng Tzŭ. Would he love her children? He desired her. He did not desire the children she might bear. He faced it squarely. He made his resolve. After Nell's wedding he would travel: travel the one panacea for every young Englishman at bay if he has bank account sufficient. Well— it's a wholesome safety-valve, and admirable treatment for half the ills of flesh and hearts and heads and nerves, if not always the last proof of grit. His mind made up he went to bed—but not for some time to sleep.

He breakfasted early and went off with Nero for a tramp. But the growing heat drove man and dog back after an hour or so. He put his dog into its quarters, and, feeling another man for his exercise, and not a little braced and comforted by his resolve, turned down the path that skirted between the trout brook and the tulip beds, where the lilies-of-the-valley and the heliotrope too, kept their fragrant state,— turned down the path and saw Ch'êng Tzŭ darning butterflies into a piece of crash.

She was his guest.

Might he sit down?

He was her host. Of course he might.

"Do you never feel the sun, Miss Ch'êng?"

"But of course I do. That is why I came out—to feel the sun—that and the flowers. I don't know which I like most."

"Do you know which flowers you like best?"

"Indeed I do not. One day some, others another day. To-day the heliotrope, I think, and those little round lily bells. You like the roses best always, Lord Ashford."

"How do you know?"

"Because you are English."

"So proscribed as all that are we? But you are wrong for once. I like wall-flowers best."

"Yes,—they are perfect," Tzŭ agreed. And how like a flower she looked, he thought, a delicate, sun-loving flower—as brilliant as the day itself, as exquisite as the little white lilies sending their perfume to mingle with the perfume of the heliotrope. She wore European dress again—a dress that was just suggestive of the Orient, but less bizarre than many English women wore that season—a season of Japanesque effects and Muscovitish influences. Tzŭ wore dull, clear blue to-day—probably every woman sun-hidden in the shaded house was wearing white—but above the low-cut neck and the slashings of the tunic brilliant embroidery showed—great cut-out flowers of many colors that some mandarin might have worn a century ago. Her shoes were poppy-red (they matched her lips) encrusted with jade and silver threads. But she wore no ornament in her closely wound braids to-day. And he noticed that for once she had no fan.

A giant lady-bird inched across the path. "Look what a big one," the girl said pointing towards it with her shoe.

Ashford nodded, and looked away. The deformity that he knew snuggled within that little Chinese shoe— was always a revulsion to this Englishman. He never saw that pretty Chinese shoe without visualizing the hideousness within. He chid himself for the liberty his thought took with that poor little maimed naked foot, a mangled stump of what had been a foot. But he could not mask the thought. He shrank from the thought, and knew that he would shrink from the veritable sight—from seeing what was to him her only defect—a terrible defect. And then he cursed himself again for the caddish liberty he took.

The girl caught something of the shadow on his face.

"It seems terrible to you?" she said simply. "It does to me sometimes. England has done that one un-kindness to me. And I think that I shall hate it—and to think of how it hurts them—when they bind my baby daughters' feet."

Ashford flushed a little—but it was impossible to

misunderstand her.   Her maidenliness was unmistakable.   But he bit his lip a little, man-like a little
dashed, because her saying that told him that she
considered marriage with him impossible, or, ever more
probably, had never thought of it at all.

Ch'êng Tzŭ did not catch his thought this time,
and chatted on happily.   For thousands of years the
girls of her race have spoken to each other of such
things quite simply.   They speak to no man, the
maidens of Ch'êng Tzŭ's caste.   They are born for
marriage, and live in preparation for it.   Maternity is
the apex of every Chinese girl's hope.   The tiniest
girl toddling across the sheltered courtyard longs for
and loves the babies she is some day to bear her
unknown lord.   And she prattles of them as innocently
as of her dolls.   And, because for thousands of years
the women of her clan had had no casual speech with
men, transplanted Ch'êng Tzŭ spoke to men as she
did to women.   Even Lady Mary had been unable to
impress that habit away.   But it had mattered but
little, since the nature of the Chinese girl was crystal-
pure, and all her speech immaculate.

"But it hurts less than you would think.   The little
bones are so soft then, like supple cartilage.   And we
have our opium pipes, you know.   Oh!   It is a good
thing our opium, much better than your English beer."

"You do not like beer?"

Ch'êng Tzŭ made a face.   "Let us not speak of it—
on such a day.   But oh!   I like your English flowers."

Well—let her talk about the flowers.   Flowers were
safe enough.   He had no excuse to leave her yet.   And
he had no wish.   Another hour with her in the old
garden his mother had loved—she'd taught him to walk

in the cherry-walk—would be but one memory more to treasure—and to curse.

"Tell me of your flowers," he said.

"At home? We have all your flowers, I think, in Ho-nan, and many that I have never seen in Europe. Oh! I shall be good to the flowers, when I go home. It hurts me to see how flowers are neglected here. Two things hurt me here—where I have had such kindness, and admire so truly—the way you treat flowers, and the way you treat women."

"Women! By jove. I say, Miss Ch'êng, you are pulling my leg."

"It is a thing I do not do."

"But English women rule the roost now. Why they'll have the vote yet, I think."

Ch'êng Tzŭ shrugged a pitying shoulder. "The vote!" she said with indescribable contempt. "And men speak rudely to them sometimes. I have heard it."

"How do we mistreat our flowers?" Ashford said hurriedly. He felt safer with the flowers.

"You do not make friends with them. You never even speak to them, or listen to them."

Lord Ashford was speechless. But he tried to look less dumbfounded than he felt. And Tzŭ talked on. She loved her theme. She liked her listener. Every Chinese woman is a born chatterbox. Ch'êng Tzŭ had kept her tongue tied for ten long years. But an affinity she did not analyze, an attraction she could not resist, a propinquity that both soothed and stimulated, and a place that had seemed to her from the first something of "home," gave her a feeling of easy comradeship, and a naturalness that until now she had left behind—in Ho-nan.

And in that hour Jack Selwyn learned more of Ch'êng Tzŭ—and more of China—than he had in the picture gallery. Because he loved her, and too because there were artist and poet in his convention-cloaked soul; he understood her, and learned in an hour what few Europeans ever learn—he learned what a living, throbbing intimacy the Chinese have with nature, an intimacy so quick and convinced that the Chinese know that flowers have loves and hates, the wind and mist temper and mind, birds souls, and every natural phenomenon or plant or tree or creature, friendships, destiny and immortality.

"And that is what I mean by being good to the flowers. One of our Emperors"—even now, though for centuries he had been a guest on high, she did not speak his name—"I often make obeisance to his spirit for it—used when the flowers were budding, to have music made to them, that they might enjoy it, and be the more beautiful and fragrant when they bloomed. Was it not a great and gracious thing to do? When I go home, I think I shall do that. Yes, I shall have the flutes played and the guitar to all the baby flowers, and the young mother flowers, when the Feast of Lanterns is near—when I go back to Ho-nan—soon."

And the man saw that Ch'êng Tzŭ's thought was in Ho-nan as she spoke.

He bent toward Tzŭ, and laid his hand softly on hers. "Tzŭ," he said, "you must not go. Stay here with me."

The girl's face quivered. She paled, and then she flushed. She looked him shyly, bravely in the eyes—her eyes were full of tears, and at that his filled—and then she spoke.

"My lord," she said.

CHAPTER XXXVIII

THE garden swayed about them. The flowers were nothing to Ch'êng Tzǔ. She had forgotten China. He had forgotten England. Why not? There was no longer Earth—but only Heaven, the reeling music of the spheres, and life's great elemental passion.

An hour ago no man ever had touched her ungloved hand. And now a man had kissed her lips—her lover had kissed her mouth. A Chinese girl had learned what kissing was—and found no displeasure in it. It could not have happened in China.

He held her close. He put her from him a space to drink her loveliness the better, to learn anew her face.

When he found his voice, and could spare his lips for mere words, and said to her the passionate, tender things that men say at such hours, perhaps she heard, perhaps she understood. At least she understood his voice, and the message of his touch. And when he begged her, "Speak to me, Tzǔ!" she looked up with a great shyness, and said, "My lord——" as Ting Tzǔ had looked up, and said to Chü-po in a Ho-nan court-yard once.

No one had taught Ch'êng Tzǔ the immemorial phrase of Chinese womanhood—the vow of life-long fealty, Chinese-old when Cæsar came to Britain. San-pan women use it on boats in the crowded harbors and on the Chinese rivers. Peasant women say it, wading ankle-deep in the wet paddy fields. Probably Ching

Kimi's mother said it to Kublai Khan almost a thousand years ago, and surely Tze Hsi said it in her crimson-veiled girlhood to Hsien-Feng—the great oath of Chinese wifehood, rarely broken or smirched, telling a people's history, telling perhaps the secret of that people's strength—and giving perchance in all the turmoil and welter of ill-considered change and bastard upheaval, a nation's best promise, sanest hope of recrudescence and permanence.

Ch'êng Tzŭ said it, because it came—said it instinctively. And, had they known it, the old Chinese words were to them a promise—and a menace—of much.

"My lord," the girl said when he bade her stay with him. "My lord," she whispered when he laid his face upon her hair. And when his kisses crushed at last too sweet upon her lips, she pushed him from her, laughing a little, and rebuked him tenderly, "My lord!" And then Ashford slipped down, one knee on the path, at her feet, and laid his head upon her knees, crushed her hands to his lips, kissed the blue tunic's linen hem, and called her—as indeed she was— at least to-day—"My Queen."

The house-party, a remnant now—heard it cordially. To-morrow the last of them were leaving. And they would take with them two new things to talk about —the terrible adventure of Lord Ashford's awful, murderous dog, and the English nobleman's engagement to a Chinese girl "who eats like one of us, dear, fabulously rich, and wears such clothes, ripping good fun." Yes, on the whole, the County liked it—even if Mr. Dean did shake his head a little sadly—and the London papers liked it even better, good for any number of varied, almost sensational, and quite inaccurate, silly-season pars.

Captain Granville was distressed—but hid it. Elenore was hopeful, and cried a little. The servants were vexed—it seemed to them a lowering of their caste. The Duchess was neutral but kind. She had a high-bred gift for minding her own immediate business, a gift the fairies do not always bestow with the strawberry's pretty leafage, she had no foolishness to weep for milk already spilt. She could stand it, if Jack could; the girl was lady-like, and, best of all, was a compatriot of her Grace's own dear darling doggies. China and Japan were all one to Ann, Duchess of Killshire.

Three Chinese in London, when they heard it, liked it less. Shêng-Liu frowned at the *Morning Post,* and then turned to the editorials. Shêng-Liu shared the Duchess' attitude to milk already spilled. Wang No cried out in rage, threw himself upon the ground and writhing there clawed a rug until its worthless tatters looked as if some wild beast had shredded them. Mung Panü liked it even less. She made no sound. She gave no sign. But her despair was great and cold. She had failed her mistress Ch'êng Shao Yün —that crime not less, but more, because the lady Yün no longer lived. Only suicide was left for Mung Panü—she would not live on in England, she could not go home without Ch'êng Tzŭ with whom Ch'êng Yün had bade her stay. Suicide alone, remained— but first she'd kill the English lord that had stolen Ch'êng Tzŭ's sanity and despoiled her pride. And the slave woman meant both these gruesome, desperate acts, and intended them calmly.

John Selwyn and Ch'êng T'ien Tzŭ were very happy.
From his first word Tzŭ had had no doubt. And he
had none now. Ecstasy and content had taken the place
of reason and of doubt. If doubt still skulked near—
ready to his call—he never looked doubt's way. To
have doubted now would have been disloyal to Tzŭ,
unchivalrous to the woman he had chosen and wooed,
the girl so alone in England but for him, so soon to
be his wife. Loyalty was irradicably of his blood.
He was chivalrous with the perfect quiet of long generations gone and to come.

Ashford urged almost immediate marriage. (Was
he afraid to wait?) Tzŭ consented readily. It was
her Chinese instinct, that marriage should precede
courtship. She agreed readily, and left all the rest
to him.

The enormity of the girl's wealth aggrieved him.
When he told her so she smiled and said that when
she was his wife Shêng Liu should journey to China
for her, and give back her vast estate to some kinsman
of her blood—unless indeed some act of her great
grandmother's had already confirmed it to Ch'êng
Wên. Tzŭ thought that was not so. And it was not.
Wên would have his ample fortune—through his wife
—but not before their marriage.

Two days they spent in their garden, with the
flowers. And then Ch'êng Tzŭ hurried back to London—the time was brief—and John gave himself up
to lawyers and bailiffs.

In the month that followed, they met but twice.
And from each of these short times Miss Ch'êng
returned to her letters and her dressmakers with a
dimpling face, and from them her lover took a deeper
contentment, a strengthened assurance—which had

needed no strengthening—that he had made no mistake, and he rested on it as on a great rock.

When they were together she yielded herself to his caress more than a Chinese girl should have done. But Fate had thrust her far from China when she was but a child. She yielded herself to his caress less than any English girl who loved him would have done—granting Ashford but a tithe of what Elenore Selwyn granted to Tom. But Tzŭ had centuries of Chinese conduct and ideal behind her. And John Selwyn did not love her less, long for her less, because of the distance she kept.

Ch'êng T'ien Tzŭ loved with a great love. It surged and claimed her. Ashford was splendidly lovable —and she had known—beyond formal acquaintance— no other man.

And in the soul-things, the traits of character, that deeply matter, the Chinese and the English are of all races the two closest of kin.

And the girl was greatly softened, all the delicate hardness that exile and loneliness had crusted on her warmed and gone. And her love was exquisitely loyal. An unsavory matrimonial cleavage enthralled Mayfair just then. "Mary Chester of all people! *And* Lord Westlake, dear! What are we coming to?"

But Ch'êng Tzŭ made no comment—least of all, "It could not have happened in China." She thought it. But the phrase would not pass her lips again.

No one saw Wang No.

Mung Panü watched and waited, and plotted.

Tzŭ's wedding day was fixed for mid-October, Elenore's two weeks later.

Early in October Lord Ashford kept his birthday

at Ashford Manor,—the largest, stateliest, of his places, a terraced, feudal place, that looked a castle and a fortress with its draw-bridge, moat, and turrets.

Tzŭ spent his birthday there, trebly chaperoned by the Duchess, Mrs. Marston and Lady Mary. No one of her race was with her, but Nell clung to her lovingly. And Ashford's kin and friends were gathered from all the Kingdom to wish him luck and to meet his bride.

Ashford Manor sheltered by trees and hills, on the warm South coast, faced the sea. And it was warmer now than October often was even here.

Ch'êng Tzŭ had not seen this new home of hers before. She admired it greatly. Any girl must have done so. But she thought that she should love the Grange best always—perhaps, because—and she told Jack so; and he caught her to him, and kissed her.

She had come just before lunch, and was to leave the next day after breakfast—they not to meet again until she went to him in Church.

London had wondered how and where Miss Ch'êng's wedding would be. She had often attended church with the other girls at Lady Mary's. But Lady Mary knew, and so did all the girls, that nothing of the Christian faith had ever claimed Ch'êng Tzŭ. She had spoken of it to Ashford some weeks ago, and had told him how entirely, in observance, she wished to follow him. And he had kissed her, and said that that was quite all right, and had added that his wife need never play the hypocrite. John Selwyn was no zealot. Loyalty and riding-straight were a nearer religion to him than was his church.

London wondered if Miss Ch'êng would have a Chinese wedding. London rather hoped she would.

And Fleet Street and all its E.C.4 offshoots prayed heaven it might—and polished up their cameras.

But when he spoke to her of the where and how, she said, "In your Church—just as your mother was." And had added, smiling in his face, "You would make a queer sort of 'Chinaman,' Jack, so I intend to be altogether an Englishwoman."

Tom was booked best man, of course.

Captain Worthing was to give the bride away. Lady Mary had suggested the Chinese Minister—but Tzŭ had smiled, a little sadly, and shaken her head.

Tzŭ was to be married in a traveling dress—she could not bring herself to begin her new life in the white that Chinese widows wear—and there was to be no reception. But it would be a very splendid traveling dress, and the church a dream and feast of flowers.

Ch'êng Tzŭ wore no rings now—only the one great gem that Jack had given her.

He had begged that to-night she would wear her Chinese dress again—and she had promised, not too willingly, that—well, perhaps she would, for the last time.

And when she came to him, in the library, as he had begged, there was compromise most un-Chinese in her Chinese toilet. She wore only one color, a lemon that showed her skin almost white. Her robe was long; it hid her feet. Her hands were gloved— only one ring stretched her left glove out of shape. And the pearls were twisted English-fashion in her hair. And she wore no other ornament, except an English rose that he had picked for her. And, most un-Chinese of all, a train was slung free from her shoulders, a long, straight train of lace, lemon-lined.

"Take me into the garden, Jack," she said. "We've almost half an hour to spare."

"No," Ashford told her—his first refusal of any even hinted wish of hers—"not until after dinner, dear. There is something there you must not see, until after dinner."

Tzŭ laughed and went with him to the drawing-room, and was very gracious to his guests. And all the men admired her mightily.

CHAPTER XXXIX

N OW," Ashford said, following her from dinner, leaving Granville to shepherd the tipplers at the table the women had left.

Vail at Lord Ashford's order was waiting for them in the hall. He took the wrap the maid had been holding, and tucked the soft, silvery chinchilla about Miss Ch'êng, caught the long lacy train over one arm, put his other arm about Ch'êng Tzŭ's shoulder, and led her so along the hall, out through the door onto the wide stone loggia.

The moon rode high and clear, cutting the dark, distant sea with a wide belt of rippled gold; but the moon looked far and pale; a painted inanimate thing compared with the thousands of living lights that glowed on every branch of every tree. Even the tall autumn flowers had every plant its tiny lantern. The terraces were picked out with light, the outlines of the great house sparkled with blue and green and ruby lights. Each tree and shrub was heavy with a fruitage of radiant lanterns. They swung fairy-like above the grass. A junk of lanterned lights rode on the moat. The draw-bridge was jeweled with a net-work of lanterns, each lantern lit.

It was a carnival of colored lights. Half the shops in Britain that stocked Chinese lanterns had been ransacked for these. An army of decorators had hung them up, busy at it from sunset till now. Round paper lanterns, tall cylinders, odd shaped ones, great

273

and small, alone, festooned, in flower-like groups, bouquets of lanterns—and every lantern lit, solitary lanterns skillfully suspended as if floating in the air, crinkled lanterns, boat-shaped lanterns, smooth lanterns, painted lanterns, tasseled lanterns, fluted lanterns, bell-shaped lanterns—from every point and crevice, where string would catch or wire hold, some Chinese lantern swung and glowed; for glowing acres the old place glittered with their light.

Her lover felt Ch'êng Tzŭ tremble.

"I thought you'd like it, dear," he whispered fondly. "Isn't it beautiful!" he said exultantly.

On the hill slope where the great yew trees grew a monster paper dragon sprawled radiantly, its mouth yapping one trunk, its tail strangling another. Ch'êng Tzŭ saw it, and shrank back a little against the wall.

Ashford did not see her close her eyes. She was shutting out the sight—the sight of this costly, tawdry display that he had planned and had made for her. She was watching another carnival of light—the Feast of Lanterns as she had watched it last in Ho-nan, her childish hand in Ch'êng Shao Yün's. And she felt the hand of China clutching at her heart—and the Chinese blood surged madly through her veins.

"Look, dear," he said as a pagoda suddenly flashed out on the tennis court. Then a bridge—twisted, camel-backed—spanned the dahlia bed.

And Tzŭ looked, and understood, and slipped her hand again in his, and smiled up at him. "Thank you, Jack," she told him softly, "you are very, very good to me."

And when the others came out, she still left her hand in his, and let him keep his arm about her shoulder.

And when they "oh'd," and "ah'd," and "my'd," and "dear me'ed" and the women screamed a little with delight, she joined softly in their praise, and was very gracious.

They scattered presently, running here and there to exclaim again at this, cry out at that; and Ch'êng Tzŭ let Lord Ashford lead her down the steps, and about the grounds.

Looking up at the Manor house, they some distance from it now, she saw flying from the old round tower, where she knew his race's pennant had flown in Cœur de Lion's day, a Chinese flag fashioned of paper lanterns.

Ch'êng T'ien Tzŭ caught her lip beneath her teeth, and her face was pinched and gray.

Jack Selwyn was happier than a schoolboy, and prouder even than kings are said to be.

Lord Ashford's pretty Chinese fiancée was the gayest—though not the noisiest—of all the gay gathering in the drawing-rooms. The sweetness of her smile, the sweetness of her voice were irresistible. The Duchess was pleased. Lady Mary was proud of Ch'êng Tzŭ. Captain Granville determined that it was all right, after all. And several women liked Miss Ch'êng who had not liked her before.

There was dancing, after supper, in the great white ballroom with its thousand candles, its ropes of roses, and a string-band in a gilded balcony.

Jack put his arm about her. "With *me!*" he whispered—and Tzŭ kept step with him. It was a waltz they played—the musicians up in the open, begilded balcony—a slow waltz tune, a tender throbbing thing, more like a passionate love-song than a dance.

From her mullioned, ivied window Ch'êng Tzŭ watched the moon go, and the sunrise come.

"It's colder, very much colder," Ashford told her. "I've put fur rugs in your car."

Tzŭ was cloaked and hatted. Her gloves were on a chair. Lord Ashford would take her to the waiting motor-car, of course,—and stand and watch her go. Mrs. Marston was already in the car. Ashford had drawn Tzŭ here—to say "good-by" more privately.

"Our last good-by," he whispered, "until——" his voice choked a little.

"Our last good-by," Ch'êng Tzŭ said. Her voice was like a silver bell. Her eyes were very tender.

At the library door she turned and pushed back a little into the room.

"Jack!" she said. She took his face in her little hands, smiled again into his eyes, and kissed him lingeringly.

Ch'êng Tzŭ had kissed him on his lips.

John Selwyn trembled—and his eyes flashed his gratitude. He could not speak to her.

Only the flowers in the garden knew how often he had kissed Ch'êng Tzŭ—on face, on hands, on hair, or sweet, curved crimson lips, and only a man's heart and a girl's knew how tenderly. But Ch'êng Tzŭ had never kissed him before. And she had kissed him on his lips.

He trembled, and he could not speak to her.

Ch'êng T'ien Tzŭ had given him her first kiss. She had suffered kisses, plump, impersonal baby kisses from the twins. She had felt his kisses, and had not shrunk; after the first she had not felt them strange. A race-prejudice, a natural abstinence founded in a people's innate taste had kept her from returning the English baby kisses she had endured, or at the best accepted, but never welcomed—it had not kept her from a pleased acceptance of the lip caresses of the Englishman she loved. But Ch'êng Tzŭ had never kissed before.

If the Chinese lose much in missing one of Love's intimate, tender communions, possibly they gain even more in escaping the degradation and the cheapness of the indiscriminate, casual, meaningless—or worse— kissing that is a crime and an ill-taste of races whiter skinned—and whiter of blood.

That first kiss said more than the man who trembled at it could ever know. Mothers sometimes kiss sons so, whom they send for the first time forth to battle.

CHAPTER XL

FROM the sea—past the hop fields of Kent, on into Surrey, up towards London, the luxurious motor sped—Tzŭ under the fur Lord Ashford had wrapped carefully about her, huddled back against her cushions, gray-faced, drawn lipped. Neither woman spoke. Mrs. Marston looked at the girl shocked and amazed. How terribly ill she looked. What was it? No quarrel with Lord Ashford—not even a misunderstanding. The look he had given Tzŭ as he heaped the rug about her had been unmistakable, and she had seen the girl's eyes drink it in almost greedily. What on earth had happened—and in an instant? Tzŭ had been all right as the motor moved. Before it reached the lodge her face had looked like death—or worse—and aged incredibly. Miss Ch'êng must be terribly ill—some desperate seizure. Well—they were rushing to London, and to home—and home and bed were the only place for any one who looked as ill as this. Poor thing! How terrifying—and the wedding day but two weeks off! Mrs. Marston was experienced, and she was sensible. She pushed a cushion a little more comfortably behind Miss Ch'êng's head, lowered a window—and waited quietly. To her surprise the girl walked beside her steadily when the car stopped at the door in Curzon Street and went upstairs naturally. And at lunch she seemed so much herself that the older woman thought with relief that the seizure had passed. But she was anxious. Ought she to write to Lord Ashford? She had been his mother's closest friend. But she knew how Miss Ch'êng would resent such a liberty. She would wait till morning.

And in the morning she wondered if by any possibility she could have been mistaken, deceived by some trick of the frosting October air. Ah! perhaps that was it! The change of temperature had been appalling. It had chilled her to the bone—and made her almost nervy. And Ch'êng Tzŭ had never liked the cold.

Ch'êng Tzŭ went from breakfast back to her own room and rang for Mung Panü.

"Come here," she told her. "Come close. We go home at once—to Ho-nan—just you and I. No one must know. We go to-night. Pack nothing of my English things. I forget England when I reach our boat. You understand?"

"My honorable mistress," Mung Panü spoke in Chinese, as Tzŭ had done, they always spoke to each other so. "Thy worm understands." And she tried to keep from her voice the joy racing through her veins. She regretted that she need not kill the English lord. She was glad she need not commit suicide. But all else was nothing to the thought of going home—to see her people, to live again a normal life, to live decently, eat decently, be decent again, with decent people in a decent place,—to see the buffaloes pulling the water-wheels, to crack the melon seeds between her teeth, to sit and gossip, in the women's courtyard, to hope again for marriage—Ch'êng Yün had promised it on their return, marriage well-dowered, a first wife's place in some well-reputed farmer's house, or a merchant's. Oh! she would pack! And she'd be swift and secret. No need to caution her—Mung Panü bent down and laid her forehead on Ch'êng Tzŭ's shoe.

A lawyer for whom Miss Ch'êng had sent—she had written notes busily the night before—was closeted with her for an hour—inscrutable when he came, inscrutable, unperturbed still, but greatly puzzled when he went.

And after lunch Tom Granville came.

Ch'êng Tzŭ saw him in the Chinese room in which Ma Yuan's herons hung.

"I am going home to China," she told him almost without prefix. "And I have sent for you—because I trust you."

"Jack——" he began.

"You will tell him for me"—Ch'êng Tzŭ's lip trembled a little—"after I have sailed. I cannot write to Lord Ashford, Captain Granville. I cannot see him again. I cannot tell him good-by. I told him good-by yesterday, in the library at the Manor," she added with a quivering smile—all the Chinese immobility torn from her face by the pain that clutched her heart.

"But—does Jack know?"

Ch'êng Tzŭ shook her head—sadly. "Nothing. But I knew—I knew that I was—telling—him good-by. I knew—when I saw the Chinese lanterns illuminating all the house and place."

Tom Granville stared his amazement—too dumbfounded to speak, too puzzled to say, "Why?"

But Ch'êng Tzŭ told him.

"But they were not Chinese lanterns," the girl said passionately. "You might hunt the bazaars of Honan for such lanterns! Perhaps coolies may hang such at their marriage festivals—or some strolling players at a village theatrical—I cannot say. But the dragon—the dragon was a worm. It was a travesty of China

—a mockery—almost an insult to the most sacred festival of China. And he had done it for me!" A sob escaped her—but she choked its fellows back. "And just such travesty," Ch'êng Tzŭ continued sternly, "our life together would be, a disappointment, racial insult, and clash—where only love was meant. There can be no marriage between East and West—I know that now."

"He loves you dearly," Granville said.

"And I," Ch'êng Tzŭ said, "love more." She turned away—towards the window.

Granville waited.

'Ah, well! we both are brave. It will pass. And—in the meantime—the gods help us both—his God him, and my gods me!"

"But the fifteenth——"

"Our wedding day! I shall be at sea. And you must be with him."

"I don't think Jack will get over it," the Guardsman told her.

Tzŭ smiled sadly. "Oh—yes. He is a man. He will care—again. I shall not."

"Are you sure that you are doing right?"

Ch'êng Tzŭ drew a stool, and sat down near Granville, and faced him, her hands knotted on her knee —her right hand almost lamed with its weight of rings, John Selwyn's ring alone on her other hand. "Quite sure. I wish that I could doubt—if only for an hour. I would give my soul to be back where I was two days ago. But I understand now. Then I only felt. I must keep faith with my blood. And I must keep faith with—Jack——"

"But, I say! This will be a nasty jolt for him!"

Tzŭ smiled, and the Englishman turned his eyes

from the sorrow on her face. "It will hurt, I know.
Ask his forgiveness of that, for me. It is a kindness
that I do him, Captain Granville. If I did not know
that, I could not have the strength. I cannot tell you
what my revulsion was, or the hideous sickness of it,
when I saw that English garden hung with those lanterns. I cannot explain. Only a Chinese could understand. It took me home, as surely as the P. and O.
will do."

"But—think how it will hurt Jack," the man pleaded,
—"and the shame of it—all the talk—and all that. Is
there no other way?"

"No other way," Tzŭ said; "there never is but one
right way—and usually," she added with a sigh, "it is
the hardest way of all."

"But I must find Jack," Granville said desperately.
"He must have his chance. He would never forgive
me, if I let you get away without seeing him—and, if
you do, he'll be after you on the next boat."

"You forget. He went to Paris last night. No
one has his address there but I. I shall be gone before
you can find him." Granville groaned. "I have forgotten nothing, I think, Captain Granville. I have
sent Mrs. Marston for a week-end with her sister. I
have given my English maid a holiday. My lawyer
has been here. He will close this house—and all those
things——"

"He will follow you," Granville said doggedly.

"Not when you tell him what I ask. You must not
let him follow me, Captain Granville—and it would be
of no use. I shall not waver."

"By Jove," he began bitterly, "you are asking——"
he halted.

"A great deal of you—a hard thing. I know. But

you will do it—for Jack. It will hurt him least from you. Tell him what you like—as much or as little as you like—just what you think will hurt him least. Cure him quickly, if you can. Say *anything* of me or from me. Help Jack! That is why I sent for you."

"And you, Miss Ch'êng?"

"Thank you," she said—and for a moment her eyes brimmed. "I go back to China—to do my work. I do not know what it is. But I know that it is there—something my great-grandmother destined me for. And every true Chinese is needed at home now. I have forgotten China! But it has called me back. These last few weeks I've scarcely known what was happening there. Even the throne may be in peril—from what the papers say."

"And if it is—what can you do? A girl——"

"I am Chinese. At least I can wait and watch—keep one homestead in China loyal—and Chinese. It is not European armies—or even European statescraft—that I fear for my country, but the increeping of European thought and ways." She laid her left hand on her breast, and looked down at it. "I shall not send back his ring," she said, "or anything that he has given me. It does not seem to me a nice thing to do. He will understand. And—I want to keep my ring—and to keep it will hurt no one—but me—yet. Some day, perhaps, I must put it away. But—I wish I might give you this—but he would know it—and remember. We want him to forget." She pointed to the Herons. Captain Granville mumbled an attempted thanks, and said that he was just as much obliged—which he was. He thought Ma Yuan's herons "rummy birds."

"Good-by." Ch'êng Tzŭ held out her hand.

And Granville left her.

He felt deuced queer. He had always liked her.
And he foresaw high-jinks before him—with Jack.
But in his honest English soul he was sturdily sure
that Ch'êng Tzŭ was right. And his English spirit
liked her Chinese pluck.

CHAPTER XLI

IT was the only "good-by" Ch'êng Tzŭ said in England.

At night time, in rain and cold, they went silently from the house, and slipped away in the dark.

Ch'êng Tzŭ did not speak once to Mung Panü in the motor.

In wind and rain, in sleet and angry hissing storm, the car sped on to the seaport town. But the angry storm was nothing to Ch'êng Tzŭ. Her heart was keeping tryst in an English garden, with red roses at her feet, and a man's hand on hers.

And it was less than nothing to Mung Panü—Mung Panü was gossiping in a courtyard, cracking melon-seeds between her sturdy little white teeth, giggling while the women hung a red veil about her painted face—waiting for the flowery bridal-chair to come.

They went from the motor to their cabin. Tzŭ sat silently and immovable on the couch. Panü huddled on the floor at her lady's feet. Neither spoke.

And when—at last—the great boat moved, neither made a sign, or showed to know it.

Tzŭ would not look again at England. But she knew that her struggle had but begun—and that she must fight her lonely fight for years—perhaps forever. She had as little illusion concerning the hardness and the pain and of the struggle before her as she had of its wisdom and its justice. Ch'êng Tzŭ was in torture. And her heart cried out for England—where she had known her red-rose hour of love.

She was going back to China.

But she had left her man behind her.

Mung Panü dug her nails into her flesh when the vessel moved, that she might not cry out with the ecstasy that throbbed in her at the first throb of the engines. She was going back to China—where pork was fit to eat, where the poorest coolie woman could make a curry and dress a salad, where man respected woman, and the sun knew how to shine, flowers how to grow, fruits how to ripen. She was going back to gossip in the courtyard—she was going back to home.

From Southampton to Hong Kong the two Chinese girls scarcely spoke, and Ch'êng Tzŭ never left the cabin.

She was veiled when they landed.

They stayed a week in Hong Kong. And Hong Kong did Ch'êng Tzŭ good—because it angered her, and the anger braced her.

China's tragedy had fallen. The Manchu had been dragged and beaten from his throne. A republic had been proclaimed! The very coolies at their barrows looked to her like cockneys; and some of them were dressed so—Chinese merchants were dressed like Brixton bank clerks or house-agents at Hanwell—and Chinese gentlemen wore tweed and broadcloth with gardenias in their button-holes.

They carried her across China in her palanquin. Much of the journey the railways could have speeded. But Ch'êng T'ien Tzŭ would have none of them. She traveled as the Ch'êng women had traveled for two thousand years. And her nostrils quivered to the smell of Chinese flowers. Her face flamed back at it when she saw the brilliant fire-weed flaming on the gorges. She saw flowers she had never seen before, and she recognized and hailed them. Why not? They had bloomed for her blood for untold centuries.

She was heavily veiled when they carried her through the South Gate.

The cymbals clashed—a temple bell was tinkling from the rhythm of its mallet in the distance. A wild duck screamed above a sycamore tree. And her people crowded by the path-side, prostrating themselves before her litter. The Ch'êng had come home.

Ah Söng rose from her mat, and tottered from the courtyard, and held out her withered hands in reverence and in greeting. And the retainers called it a miracle—for Ah Söng had not left her mat for many moons.

In the morning when she walked through the garden to the silkworm house, four-footed creatures came and rubbed against her sleeve, and clawed her, and a host of silky doggies danced and yapped about her, clamoring for her notice—gold and amber coated doggies of the stock from which English King Charles' spaniels had been bred—gold and amber silk-haired doggies, descendants of Ti-tô-ti, who was playing pranks on high now, while his venerable bones moldered near the coffin of his mistress in the graveyard of the Ch'êngs. And the little yellow children ran and tumbled to her skirts —and the larkspurs nodded to her, and the poppies, and the yellow lilies on their polished stalks.

She gave the babies sweetmeats, and she gave her gods an oath.

And as soon as she could do it decently she gave Mung Panü a loud and a sumptuous bridal cavalcade: for Ch'êng Shao Yün had promised it, and Ch'êng

Tzŭ longed to be rid of the girl who had been with her in England—the girl who reminded her of England.

She needed no reminding of England—with its granges and its gardens, its manors and its roses, and its clean-limbed, blue-eyed men.

Ch'êng T'ien Tzŭ knew that she would not forget. And often in the twilight she wondered how long John Selwyn would remember.

For Ch'êng Tzŭ knew that in Asia or in Europe a man rarely remembers, a woman never forgets.

And she was glad that he would forget—for she was generous and big.

A Chinese man followed Ch'êng Tzŭ from England. But when the elder Wang sent the matchmakers to her, she sent them back to him with many a costly present and a wealth of honied words—and a message saying that her honorable great-grandmother had betrothed her long ago. She did not know that this was true, though Shêng Liu—at her request returning soon to her service—could have told her; but she allowed herself the courteous lie because it was a kindness.

Ch'êng Tzŭ did not purpose to keep Shêng near her when he came—he had been too close to her in England, he had known Lord Ashford—but to charge him with watching home events at Pekin, at Hankow and at Shanghai, and to have his advice and service near at hand, should she need them.

Captain Granville had said truly that she could do nothing to stem the débâcle of her country. But she kept her Chinese state in Ho-nan, and held her home a stronghold, nursing there a tiny mustard seed of loyalty that might grow some day into yellow verdure that would spread, and cover all the festered gashes in the China that she loved.

All that Ch'êng Shao Yün had done before her, Ch'êng Tzŭ did—and more.

But the Chinese girl was homesick for the England she had left—with a sicker aching than she had ever felt in Europe for the courtyards and the garden of her childhood. It was here in China that she learned how much she had liked England. And every day she had to fight her heart.

It was struggle, struggle all the way. Often her heart grew faint, and the little ring-heavy, apricot-tinted hands grew cold and listless. But her will never grew faint; and neither heart nor will failed her.

She had been alone in England—until a man had kissed her. She was alone in China now—more alone than she had been in exile. In London and at the Vicarage she had warmed herself with thinking of the going-home to come. Now she knew that she should never go back—to England. And there was no one to whom she could speak of her trouble—or hint. But for her, the courtyards of the ladies were empty, never clattering softly with the footfall of golden lilies, never ringing with the laughing of the children or the babies.

Worst of all, perhaps—she did not always feel quite at home here. Gardeners transplant seedlings when the young roots—still lightly fixed in earth and flexible —feel little pain from the fingers that uproot them: or the gardener waits until the plant has reached a sturdier growth, and can take new grip with seasoned strenuous fibers of the second ground. Ch'êng Tzŭ had been transplanted too late or too soon: too late to take honest root in England, too soon to take—as Wang No had—none there. And a fiber of her being still bled and perished for the homeland of the Selwyns.

Or perhaps even worse was her entire lack of companionship with any of her own caste. But she found her solace and her strength, as the Chinese always do, in a fellowship with nature. Whatever her hand found to do, she did with her might, cherishing her heritage and enriching it—spreading, slowly, silently the subtle propaganda of her hope and ambition for the healing of an Empire. But she made playmates of the daisies, and took counsel of the clouds. She listened to the winds, and leaned against the bamboo and the oak-trees, sitting—for hours—silent, a communicant with nature, on the grassy slope where the spotted tiger lilies quivered by a lazy, lagging river, on the moss-worn rocks where the pink arbutus glistened with the spray the rushing, tumbling cascade threw it, and the wild white roses told that this was China, and perfumed the air for leagues.

But, if she took communion with the grasses and the stars, Ch'êng Tzŭ neglected no material interest of her little kingdom.

The very by-products of her piggeries had her earnest consideration and her strict supervision. She watched over her school, her granaries, and her factories. Her tea-plants knew her. She bred a new rose in her gardens, and a new dye in her vats. She added the juice of cherries to the crushings of her peaches and her apples, making a sweetened wine that sold well in Shanghai, and reminded her when she sipped it of the tang of sherry she'd tasted after soup in London. She gathered fortune from her soap trees and silver from her bees. She watched and taught the girls that sang at their embroidery frames while the great silk flowers grew from their needles. Scarcely a day but she lingered with her artists—the ivory-carvers and the men who wrought in bronze, those who mixed the lacquer's sumptuous colors, and those who spread it, and the master-workers who inlaid the trays and boxes with silver and with gold, and those who inlaid the great lacquer screens with mother-o'-pearl and lead, and framed them with carved cut-out lace of camphor-wood and sandalwood and jasper, those who encrusted ornaments with the blue Kingfisher feathers, and the patient workers in malachite and cornelian. She directed the lantern-makers and the lantern-painters, painting one sometimes herself. To the silkworms' houses she went oftenest, lingering longest, watching and directing and dreaming. When the new eggs pulse out from the mother-moth's bursted belly she flutters down to death. In that myriad child-birth every mother dies. But such death is not without its beauty. And in the Hereafter in which every pulse shall be perpetuated, every atom gathered up and perfected perchance those mother-moths will find a longer flight and a compensation. Ch'êng Tzǔ believed so.

She was careful of her women, and very tender to their babies. She tended the sick, and gave their milk-names to the new-born. And all her people feared and loved her. And the little gold and amber pug-doggies fawned upon her shadow when they saw it.

The girl fought. And she took counsel.

Her conscience was her task-master, but her conscience approved her. And her character—bequeathed her by Ch'êng Shao Yün—was her destiny.

CHAPTER XLII

ON her mat Ah Söng lay dying.

In a last obedience to Ch'êng Shao Yün she had lived on these few years longer than Ch'êng Yün. For nine years were but few in the long tally of Söng's days.

Born a Shao slave, gifted from the cradle with second-sight, early skilled in simples, widowed after a few moons of marriage, her son had been born a month before the birth of Shao Yün, and had died in the cottage by the wayside just as the girl was born to the great house. Pitying the slave so doubly bereaved, knowing her trustworthy and skilled, Shao had called her to his wife, and had bidden her to her first attendance on their new-born daughter. The slave-woman took the baby in her arms, and the child took instant root in the torn heart, and had grown there —with a hold that had never loosened. Every hour since then Söng had been in attendance on her lady Yün. She was in attendance on her now—husbanding her last breath and her last strength to obey Shao Yün's last command. Life had ended for Ah Söng when it had ended for Ch'êng Shao Yün—but duty and obedience had remained. And she had breathed on to perform them.

The blind slave-woman had been invaluable to her lady, and chiefly had been so through two assets of personality—not her fidelity, for fidelity is a commonplace in China, a matter-of-course, to be had on every hand—her silence and her second-sight. Almost all Chinese have psychic gift, and they have it in a quality above all other peoples. But among the Chinese there is no uniformity of psychic gift—all have it, but in degrees greatly differing. And it sinks to its lowest degree, and is smallest in quantity, in the professional psychics—who, in China as elsewhere, strain and fray it thin, and often to nothingness. Blind Ah Söng was psychic far beyond the average of her country's genuine and unspoiled psychics. And she had never overused, or overtold her gift. It came to her, she never sought it. And even of normal, everyday things she had been all but speechless—unique in this in a country where women are more incessantly talkative than they are anywhere else, and where their license of speech has no limit.

Ah Söng had lost her physical sight in the service of Shao Yün—in Kwangtung long ago. At the Feast of Lanterns, little Yün had run, clapping her hands, towards a gilded fish-shaped lantern that had caught fire, as the pretty painted things often do, and always to the watching crowd's noisy ecstasy. A flaming fragment had caught her scarf and flared up to her throat. But Ah Söng had caught the child in her arms, and smothered the fire against her own breast, beating it out with her own face. Yün had taken no harm—beyond the ruin of a little festal finery, but Ah Söng had lost her sight.

She had only done her duty, and no one held it more—she herself least of all. But even so it had counted for another link between slave and mistress, and had served Ah Söng for many a privilege; for no Chinese is ever ungrateful. Heaven forbid that we should praise them for it. No praise is due. For it is merely that to a normal Chinese ingratitude is an impossibility.

Söng's sense of touch had been increased by her loss of sight. Everywhere the blind see through their fingers. She could embroider. She could detect the slightest variation of shade in silks or tissues. She could card silks accurately, and even pick up with the needle's eye the fine end in the broken cocoon, and wind it off and reel it with a hand that never wavered or mismoved; she knew a change of temperature before the thermometers could record it. She was invaluable in a dozen ways in the worm-houses. And blind Ah Söng almost as much as Ch'êng Shao Yün herself had achieved for one estate—in a province of inferior and wild silks—a sericultural preëminence that was acknowledged in the fabric markets of the world.

And her hearing had been as extraordinary as her touch.

Ah Söng lay dying on her mat, and Ch'êng Tzǔ sat on the floor beside her—and held her hand.

For weeks the old slave had not spoken, and had scarcely moved.

Now she raised herself a little, and turned her sightless eyes on Tzǔ. And Ch'êng Tzǔ slipped an arm about the wasted form, and listened while Ah Söng told her—pausing often for breath, but missing nothing of the message she had lingered to give—all that Ch'êng Shao Yün had planned and hoped in sending Tzǔ to England.

She told again the story—the glorious unbroken story of the women of the Ch'êngs. She told again the old tradition that when China's need should be sorest, China's fate lowest, a Ch'êng woman should give herself and all her days to China, saving her country, restoring it to brighter, firmer greatness. She told how Ch'êng Yün, as Ch'êng Yün's father before her, had sensed, and then seen clearly, China's peril from foes without and dolts within, and seeing, had set herself to avert—and when that failed had dedicated Ch'êng T'ien Tzǔ to restore.

"It will not be in thy time, O jade-like. But it will come. Nurse the pearl-like seed of China's sanity within thy breast—suckle it as a mother a babe. This is no time to strike. That time is far. But keep one bit of China Chinese. Let no alien influence creep within our gates to taint and poison. Bar socialism and anarchy out—with thy soul; if need be, with thy body. Love is the greatest force. Love China well. Wealth is almost an omnipotence. Thy great wealth can buy thee undisturbed seclusion for thy people, and the privilege to govern here as thou likest. Keep China alive in thy domain. Keep thy courtyards clean and garnished with old things. Keep the home life in the thousand huts true and sweet with old ways. Let thy men and thy women and all the little children live as their ancestors lived. Lean on our sages. Learn from the foaming waters, the quivering flowers, the mantling sky, the great trees and the whispering breeze. Keep the Feast of Lanterns. Keep it each year more sacredly: it is the very soul of China—China cannot perish while the Feast of Lanterns lives."

She rested.

Then Ah Söng told of Ch'êng Yün's death (not calling it that), details that Tzǔ had not heard before.

Ch'êng Shao Yün had spent a busy morning with the lacquer-workers, and in the silkworm houses. Towards sunset she had gone to watch her reapers at the grain, encouraging and admonishing them—join-

ing in their labor even—for there was little in all
the vast estate that she could not do better than her
serfs. She had sickened there, at the harvest, among
her people—her patient people who feared and loved
her. She had cried out in sudden pain, and had swayed
a little on her feet. And they had run to catch her,
but she had driven them back with an old imperious
gesture. And even in her dying they had not dared
to disobey her. A little longer she had stood so, leaning on her ivory staff—Ti-tô-ti whimpering at her
feet. Then she had spoken some last direction to the
reapers, a message to the charcoal-burners. And her
last speaking had been of Ch'êng Tzŭ and of China—
while pain had twisted her face, her voice sweet and
clear even while death choked it. Then a great joy
had lit Ch'êng Yün's face, her stick had fallen at her
feet, and she had stretched out her arms towards the
sunset, and had cried out, "My Lord!" and had fallen
among her golden grain. They had carried her across
the acres she had ruled, through the gardens she had
loved, across the courtyard that had been hers since
a bride, through the chamber in which she had borne
her children, and had laid her on the dais in the Ko-
tang. And at midnight, Ti-tô-ti had gone to her on
high, and they had coffined him at her feet, and not in
the dog's cemetery, feeling that his heart-break deserved it, and that their lady would so have commanded
them.

Again Ah Söng rested.

Then she spoke again.

"Wait. Watch. Work. And always watch. The
time will come. China cannot perish. Thy slave's
toothless gums have sucked the honey of China's sacred
breath, since great Ch'êng Shao Yün's most honorable

father was a toddling boy, and I can taste it in my hour of glad departure. China is immortal, lady. Immortal bees gods-sent stored that imperial honey from the flowers of heaven. Store it here. Keep it alive, *and unpolluted,* here in thy home—the bridal home of celestial Shao Yün."

The slight form was growing a little heavy in the girlish arms that held it.

Tzŭ thought Söng dozed. She laid her face against her slave's. Ah Söng smiled, and made a sign of obeisance with one feeble, claw-like hand.

Then—it was the last—she told of what Ch'êng Shao Yün had sacrificed; Chü-po, Lo Yuet, and then the companionship of Tzŭ,—Tzŭ, the girl-child so-waited-for, so-despaired-of, so riotously welcomed, so passionately loved, so tended, so yearned over, and missed in such long torture when Shêng Liu had taken the child to England, leaving Ch'êng Shao Yün bereft —alone in China, grieving but invincible. With laboring, straining breath dying Söng spoke of the marriage Ch'êng Yün had planned for Tzŭ—that Tzŭ might remain a Ch'êng, be the mother of Ch'êngs, and live and rule while she lived, here in her ancestral home.

With a convulsive spasm of her spent strength, Ah Söng raised herself again a little on her lady's arms, and, with again the gesture of obeisance, laid her hand on her lady's sleeve.

Death rattled in Ah Söng's stiffening throat.

Ah Söng had gone, to be again in attendance on Shao Yün.

Ch'êng Tzŭ took no counsel of the necromancer as to where or how the body of the blind woman should be laid.

They carried Ah Söng—to clash of cymbals, beat of drum—incense drenching her costly coffin—through the avenue of stone figures that denoted the approach to the tombs of nobles—noble figures, beautiful in execution and significant in subjects—mandarins, ministers of state, sages, priests, tigers and warriors, camels, and elephants, dragons and sheep, horses, dogs, birds and troubadours, colossal in size, standing on slabs of onyx, bronze and porphyry—to the family burial ground inside its guarding belt of great cypress trees. and laid it beside the tiny tomb of Ti-tô-ti at the feet of Ch'êng Shao Yün.

Ch'êng T'ien Tzŭ walked behind the coffin of the slave.

And on the temple wall Tzŭ put a tablet marked, "Ah Söng, the Slave of Ch'êng Shao Yün."

CHAPTER XLIII

A ND when the Feast of Lanterns had passed Ch'êng
Tzǔ sent the matchmakers to Ch'êng Wên. And
she sent Shêng Liu with them, and charged him to tell
Wên *all* he knew of her stay in England—and to remind Ch'êng Wên that, even if he did not wed her, by
the will of Ch'êng Shao Yün—as it now proved—Yün's
adopted son would have great wealth, and that, while
Ch'êng Yün's wish for their marriage was clearly indicated, she had not enforced it by formal betrothal;
they both were free.

Wên did not like what Shêng told him of Ch'êng
Tzǔ's engagement to an Englishman. But he had no
idea of the detail of actual acquaintance customary
between fiancés in England, and Shêng Liu felt no
need to explain it. Even so Wên winced, but he put
it from him—and sent the matchmakers back to Ch'êng
Tzǔ with his troth and a long length of gifts.

But the actual marriage took long to do. Tzǔ had
kept her year of mourning for Ch'êng Yün, as best
she could, in England. But she kept it here again in
China, and with a fuller punctilio. And before she
could wed with Ch'êng Wên, by adoption now her
kinsman, it was obligatory that she herself should
cease to be a Ch'êng. To become in marriage a Ch'êng
she must cease to be a Ch'êng maiden. A Chinese
must not marry one of his own family name. It is a
law sometimes evaded—but not by such loyalists as
she. The new republican dispensation had cast the old

299

law aside perhaps. But as to that, she neither knew nor cared. She gave neither courtesy nor heed to the new edicts—scorning even to know them. For her every old law was more stringent and more sacred than it had been—and she would fulfill and obey it to the last article.

She gave herself in adoption to Shêng Liu—who, though neither rich nor powerful, belonged to a family as noble as her own. And the ratification of the adoption, and all its forms took time.

But at last the marriage was accomplished.

When Ch'êng Tzŭ found that Wên her husband loved her, he did not find it hard, she took up that added cross, and bore it meekly. Presently she came to bear it gayly. His companionship was pleasant. And their children brought her content.

Presidents came and went in China, but in Ho-nan, Ch'êng Tzŭ watched, waited and worked. And in her domain the Manchu still reigned.

She served her lord meekly, but she ruled him. Shêng Liu knew that the new movement might have lured Ch'êng Wên had not his wife so held him in her keeping. But Wên knew no will but Tzŭ. He ordered—under her—the tilling of her fields, he lived her life, he thought her thoughts, and, for her bearing of his children, he worshiped her.

And she knew that for her life was better so. But she had a memory in her heart—sometimes a hidden secret sweetness, sometimes a pain that rankled.

She sometimes wondered what had come in England —to those she had known. But she was loyal to her own determination; and she never learned. She sent a thought to old friends sometimes—but she never sent a message, or let one reach her.

But within her gates no word might be spoken that disparaged the English land she'd lived in. As the years passed she compared the two countries and the two people shrewdly, and for a woman, strangely without prejudice. And each day she grew more confirmed in her conviction that China and the Chinese excelled. But she saw a spiritual kinship in them—the Chinese and English,—at their best and smiled to think how droll it was that none else had ever seen and sensed that kinship.

She lived the life of a great lady of the old feudal days. No I Kung Moy ever saw her face unveiled. Only Ch'êng Wên ever saw the face that once an Englishman had kissed. Ch'êng T'ien Tzŭ lived more strictly conventional than Ch'êng Shao Yün had been.

Sorrow touched her sometimes. But she was not unhappy.

She lived for China's regeneration. She believed it. She watched for it, waited for it, and worked for it tirelessly. And Ch'êng Wên was her good right-hand. Every hour of all her days was packed. That was part of her unswerving patriotism of which her husband was but an appanage—dutifully served, scrupulously, as a Chinese wife should serve.

Her sorrow for her country dwarfed her sorrow for herself. But even in her country's woe and peril, its momentary degradation, she saw a promise and a hope. In the universal dismay and resentment at the alien encroachments—now too potent to be overlooked even by the common people—she saw and hoped a knitting up of the scattered loyalties that heretofore had made the individual Chinese devoted to family, clan and province more than conscious of national needs or national duty.   She knew that her countrymen were fundamentally pacific.   But she knew how they could fight—their history told it—that patient, plodding people—and she smiled grimly, quoting to herself a Christian text she'd learned in England, "Beware the fury of a patient man."   And her longing burned for the day when China should turn and rend the intruders from without and the usurpers from within.

Travel is the test of patriotism—a terrible, acid test sometimes.   But Chinese patriotism is justified to pass through it unaltered and enhanced.   Travel and foreign sojourn had served to strengthen and quicken the patriotism of Ch'êng T'ien Tzŭ.   She gloated over her country.   She yearned over her people.   And all the old Chinese traditions lived and glowed in her heart. She was more intensely Chinese for the years that she had spent in England—more uncompromisingly Chinese than Ch'êng Shao Yün had been.

When Tzŭ's little daughter was three and a moon, Tzŭ's son was born.   And when she snuggled the little downy head against her face, she thanked Kwanyin Ko that she need never apologize to her son for having brought him into life disfigured and discounted by mixed race-blood.   She knew that she might have loved her boyling even a little more perhaps if—but she kept the thought in leash.   And she knew too that in another way she must have loved her son a little less had any blood of Europe flowed in his veins, must have respected him less, been less proud of him, and been less glad in motherhood—less rested—if——

Ch'êng T'ien Tzŭ sat lazy in the grass beside the quiet river where Chü-po had sat the day Ting Lo brought Ting Tzŭ to visit Ch'êng Ping-yang. A single narcissus grew beside a stone. The sun was fading to the twilight. A crane, on the other bank, was drinking peacefully, throwing the woman and her babies a friendly glance, as he lifted his long neck to let the liquid coolness trickle down his throat.

Her girl was playing with her girdle. Her boy was sleeping in her arms. Far on the hoary mountains a bell tinkled from the striking of its mallet. Buddhist monks were trooping in to prayer. From somewhere on a hillside—nearer, clearer a gong sounded: in a convent on the hillside Taoist nuns were going to their rice. The gods of China are a brotherly crew, and live in amity on high; and creed smiles on creed, rarely clashing, in the land of the pagoda.

Ch'êng T'ien Tzŭ often came here—and here no one ever sought her. That was a law. To-day she found it very good to rest here, and watch the narcissus petals grow gold then pink in the "good-by" of the sun, for Tzŭ was frankly tired to-day. The Feast of Lanterns was at hand, and from dawn she had been toiling with her women, giving directions to her men.

The little girl—"Flower o' Jade" was her milk name —was very quiet. Across the river a bird called to his mate.

Tears gathered in Ch'êng T'ien Tzŭ's eyes. The ripple of an old pain and an old parting crumpled her face. She laid her face down on her baby's, hiding it on his. "Jack," she said with a sob. And the child woke, and the little Chinese girl wondered, at a word they'd never heard before.

Ch'êng Tzŭ rose and shook out her wide crumpled trousers, and moved towards the house, one baby clinging to her hand, one cuddled at her neck; went smiling, carrying them to their women, went in to serve her lord meekly at his rice.

And the soul of Ch'êng Shao Yün lived and ruled in the homestead of her clan.

THE END

Popular Copyright Novels

AT MODERATE PRICES

Ask Your Dealer for a Complete List of

A. L. Burt Company's Popular Copyright Fiction

Adventures of Jimmie Dale, The. By Frank L. Packard.
Adventures of Sherlock Holmes. By A. Conan Doyle.
Affinities, and Other Stories. By Mary Roberts Rinehart.
After House, The. By Mary Roberts Rinehart.
Against the Winds. By Kate Jordan.
Ailsa Paige. By Robert W. Chambers.
Also Ran. By Mrs. Baillie Reynolds.
Amateur Gentleman, The. By Jeffery Farnol.
Anderson Crow, Detective. By George Barr McCutcheon.
Anna, the Adventuress. By E. Phillips Oppenheim.
Anne's House of Dreams. By L. M. Montgomery.
Anybody But Anne. By Carolyn Wells.
Are All Men Alike, and The Lost Titian. By Arthur Stringer.
Around Old Chester. By Margaret Deland.
Ashton-Kirk, Criminologist. By John T. McIntyre.
Ashton-Kirk, Investigator. By John T. McIntyre.
Ashton-Kirk, Secret Agent. By John T. McIntyre.
Ashton-Kirk, Special Detective. By John T. McIntyre.
Athalie. By Robert W. Chambers.
At the Mercy of Tiberius. By Augusta Evans Wilson.
Auction Block, The. By Rex Beach.
Aunt Jane of Kentucky. By Eliza C. Hall.
Awakening of Helena Richie. By Margaret Deland.

Bab: a Sub-Deb. By Mary Roberts Rinehart.
Bambi. By Marjorie Benton Cooke.
Barbarians. By Robert W. Chambers.
Bar 20. By Clarence E. Mulford.
Bar 20 Days. By Clarence E. Mulford.
Barrier, The. By Rex Beach.
Bars of Iron, The. By Ethel M. Dell.
Beasts of Tarzan, The. By Edgar Rice Burroughs.
Beckoning Roads. By Jeanne Judson.
Belonging. By Olive Wadsley.
Beloved Traitor, The. By Frank L. Packard.
Beloved Vagabond, The. By Wm. J. Locke.
Beltane the Smith. By Jeffery Farnol.
Betrayal, The. By E. Phillips Oppenheim.
Beulah. (Ill. Ed.) By Augusta J. Evans.

Popular Copyright Novels

AT MODERATE PRICES

Ask Your Dealer for a Complete List of
A. L. Burt Company's Popular Copyright Fiction

Beyond the Frontier. By Randall Parrish.
Big Timber. By Bertrand W. Sinclair.
Black Bartlemy's Treasure. By Jeffery Farnol.
Black Is White. By George Barr McCutcheon.
Blacksheep! Blacksheep!. By Meredith Nicholson.
Blind Man's Eyes, The. By Wm. Mac Harg and Edwin
    Balmer.
Boardwalk, The. By Margaret Widdemer.
Bob Hampton of Placer. By Randall Parrish.
Bob, Son of Battle. By Alfred Olivant.
Box With Broken Seals, The. By E. Phillips Oppenheim.
Boy With Wings, The. By Berta Ruck.
Brandon of the Engineers. By Harold Bindloss.
Bridge of Kisses, The. By Berta Ruck.
Broad Highway, The. By Jeffery Farnol.
Broadway Bab. By Johnston McCulley.
Brown Study, The. By Grace S. Richmond.
Bruce of the Circle A. By Harold Titus.
Buccaneer Farmer, The. By Harold Bindloss.
Buck Peters, Ranchman. By Clarence E. Mulford.
Builders, The. By Ellen Glasgow.
Business of Life, The. By Robert W. Chambers.

Cab of the Sleeping Horse, The. By John Reed Scott.
Cabbage and Kings. By O. Henry.
Cabin Fever. By B. M. Bower.
Calling of Dan Matthews, The. By Harold Bell Wright.
Cape Cod Stories. By Joseph C. Lincoln.
Cap'n Abe, Storekeeper. By James A. Cooper.
Cap'n Dan's Daughter. By Joseph C. Lincoln.
Cap'n Erl. By Joseph C. Lincoln.
Cap'n Jonah's Fortune. By James A. Cooper.
Cap'n Warren's Wards. By Joseph C. Lincoln.
Chinese Label, The. By J. Frank Davis.
Christine of the Young Heart. By Louise Breintenbach Clancy.
Cinderella Jane. By Marjorie B. Cooke.
Cinema Murder, The. By E. Phillips Oppenheim.
City of Masks, The. By George Barr McCutcheon.
Cleek of Scotland Yard. By T. W. Hanshew.

Popular Copyright Novels

AT MODERATE PRICES

Ask Your Dealer for a Complete List of
A. L. Burt Company's Popular Copyright Fiction

Cleek, The Man of Forty Faces. By Thomas W. Hanshew.
Cleek's Government Cases. By Thomas W. Hanshew.
Clipped Wings. By Rupert Hughes.
Clutch of Circumstance, The. By Marjorie Benton Cooke.
Coast of Adventure, The. By Harold Bindloss.
Come-Back, The. By Carolyn Wells.
Coming of Cassidy, The. By Clarence E. Mulford.
Coming of the Law, The. By Charles A. Seltzer.
Comrades of Peril. By Randall Parrish.
Conquest of Canaan, The. By Booth Tarkington.
Conspirators, The. By Robert W. Chambers.
Contraband. By Randall Parrish.
Cottage of Delight, The. By Will N. Harben.
Court of Inquiry, A. By Grace S. Richmond.
Cricket, The. By Marjorie Benton Cooke.
Crimson Gardenia, The, and Other Tales of Adventure. By
Rex Beach.
Crimson Tide, The. By Robert W. Chambers.
Cross Currents. By Author of "Pollyanna."
Cross Pull, The. By Hal. G. Evarts.
Cry in the Wilderness, A. By Mary E. Waller.
Cry of Youth, A. By Cynthia Lombardi.
Cup of Fury, The. By Rupert Hughes.
Curious Quest, The. By E. Phillips Oppenheim.

Danger and Other Stories. By A. Conan Doyle.
Dark Hollow, The. By Anna Katharine Green.
Dark Star, The. By Robert W. Chambers.
Daughter Pays, The. By Mrs. Baillie Reynolds.
Day of Days, The. By Louis Joseph Vance.
Depot Master, The. By Joseph C. Lincoln.
Destroying Angel, The. By Louis Joseph Vance.
Devil's Own, The. By Randall Parrish.
Devil's Paw, The. By E. Phillips Oppenheim.
Disturbing Charm, The. By Berta Ruck.
Door of Dread, The. By Arthur Stringer.
Dope. By Sax Rohmer.
Double Traitor, The. By E. Phillips Oppenheim.
Duds. By Henry C. Rowland.

Popular Copyright Novels

AT MODERATE PRICES

Ask Your Dealer for a Complete List of
A. L. Burt Company's Popular Copyright Fiction

Empty Pockets. By Rupert Hughes.
Erskine Dale Pioneer. By John Fox, Jr.
Everyman's Land. By C. N. & A. M. Williamson.
Extricating Obadiah. By Joseph C. Lincoln.
Eyes of the Blind, The. By Arthur Somers Roche.
Eyes of the World, The. By Harold Bell Wright.

Fairfax and His Pride. By Marie Van Vorst.
Felix O'Day. By F. Hopkinson Smith.
54-40 or Fight. By Emerson Hough.
Fighting Chance, The. By Robert W. Chambers.
Fighting Fool, The. By Dane Coolidge.
Fighting Shepherdess, The. By Caroline Lockhart.
Financier, The. By Theodore Dreiser.
Find the Woman. By Arthur Somers Roche.
First Sir Percy, The. By The Baroness Orczy.
Flame, The. By Olive Wadsley.
For Better, for Worse. By W. B. Maxwell.
Forbidden Trail, The. By Honorè Willsie.
Forfeit, The. By Ridgwell Cullum.
Fortieth Door, The. By Mary Hastings Bradley.
Four Million, The. By O. Henry.
From Now On. By Frank L. Packard.
Fur Bringers, The. By Hulbert Footner.
Further Adventures of Jimmie Dale. By Frank L. Packard.

Get Your Man. By Ethel and James Dorrance.
Girl in the Mirror, The. By Elizabeth Jordan.
Girl of O. K. Valley, The. By Robert Watson.
Girl of the Blue Ridge, A. By Payne Erskine.
Girl from Keller's, The. By Harold Bindloss.
Girl Philippa, The. By Robert W. Chambers.
Girls at His Billet, The. By Berta Ruck.
Glory Rides the Range. By Ethel and James Dorrance.
Gloved Hand, The. By Burton E. Stevenson.
God's Country and the Woman. By James Oliver Curwood.
God's Good Man. By Marie Corelli.
Going Some. By Rex Beach.
Gold Girl, The. By James B. Hendryx.
Golden Scorpion, The. By Sax Rohmer.

Popular Copyright Novels

Golden Slipper, The. By Anna Katharine Green.
Golden Woman, The. By Ridgwell Cullum.
Good References. By E. J. Rath.
Gorgeous Girl, The. By Nalbro Bartley.
Gray Angels, The. By Nalbro Bartley.
Great Impersonation, The. By E. Phillips Oppenheim.
Greater Love Hath No Man. By Frank L. Packard.
Green Eyes of Bast, The. By Sax Rohmer.
Greyfriars Bobby. By Eleanor Atkinson.
Gun Brand, The. By James B. Hendryx.

Hand of Fu-Manchu, The. By Sax Rohmer.
Happy House. By Baroness Von Hutten.
Harbor Road, The. By Sara Ware Bassett.
Havoc. By E. Phillips Oppenheim.
Heart of the Desert, The. By Honorè Willsie.
Heart of the Hills, The. By John Fox, Jr.
Heart of the Sunset. By Rex Beach.
Heart of Thunder Mountain, The. By Edfrid A. Bingham.
Heart of Unaga, The. By Ridgwell Cullum.
Hidden Children, The. By Robert W. Chambers.
Hidden Trails. By William Patterson White.
Highflyers, The. By Clarence B. Kelland.
Hillman, The. By E. Phillips Oppenheim.
Hills of Refuge, The. By Will N. Harben.
His Last Bow. By A. Conan Doyle.
His Official Fiancee. By Berta Ruck.
Honor of the Big Snows. By James Oliver Curwood.
Hopalong Cassidy. By Clarence E. Mulford.
Hound from the North, The. By Ridgwell Cullum.
House of the Whispering Pines, The. By Anna Katharine Green.
Hugh Wynne, Free Quaker. By S. Weir Mitchell, M.D.
Humoresque. By Fannie Hurst.

I Conquered. By Harold Titus.
Illustrious Prince, The. By E. Phillips Oppenheim.
In Another Girl's Shoes. By Berta Ruck.
Indifference of Juliet, The. By Grace S. Richmond.
Inez. (Ill. Ed.) By Augusta J. Evans.

Popular Copyright Novels

AT MODERATE PRICES

Ask Your Dealer for a Complete List of

A. L. Burt Company's Popular Copyright Fiction

Infelice. By Augusta Evans Wilson.
Initials Only. By Anna Katharine Green.
Inner Law, The. By Will N. Harben.
Innocent. By Marie Corelli.
In Red and Gold. By Samuel Merwin.
Insidious Dr. Fu-Manchu, The. By Sax Rohmer.
In the Brooding Wild. By Ridgwell Cullum.
Intriguers, The. By William Le Queux.
Iron Furrow, The. By George C. Shedd.
Iron Trail, The. By Rex Beach.
Iron Woman, The. By Margaret Deland.
Ishmael. (Ill.) By Mrs. Southworth.
Island of Surprise. By Cyrus Townsend Brady.
I Spy. By Natalie Sumner Linclon.
It Pays to Smile. By Nina Wilcox Putnam.
I've Married Marjorie. By Margaret Widdemer.

Jean of the Lazy A. By B. M. Bower.
Jeanne of the Marshes. By E. Phillips Oppenheim.
Jennie Gerhardt. By Theodore Dreiser.
Johnny Nelson. By Clarence E. Mulford.
Judgment House, The. By Gilbert Parker.

Keeper of the Door, The. By Ethel M. Dell.
Keith of the Border. By Randall Parrish.
Kent Knowles: Quahaug. By Joseph C. Lincoln.
Kingdom of the Blind, The. By E. Phillips Oppenheim.
King Spruce. By Holman Day.
Knave of Diamonds, The. By Ethel M. Dell.

La Chance Mine Mystery, The. By S. Carleton.
Lady Doc, The. By Caroline Lockhart.
Land-Girl's Love Story. A. By Berta Ruck.
Land of Strong Men, The. By A. M. Chisholm.
Last Straw, The. By Harold Titus.
Last Trail, The. By Zane Grey.
Laughing Bill Hyde. By Rex Beach.
Laughing Girl, The. By Robert W. Chambers.
Law Breakers, The. By Ridgwell Cullum.
Law of the Gun, The. By Ridgwell Cullum.

Popular Copyright Novels

AT MODERATE PRICES

Ask Your Dealer for a Complete List of
A. L. Burt Company's Popular Copyright Fiction

League of the Scarlet Pimpernel. By Baroness Orczy.
Lifted Veil, The. By Basil King.
Lighted Way, The. By E. Phillips Oppenheim.
Lin McLean. By Owen Wister.
Little Moment of Happiness, The. By Clarence Budington Kelland.
Lion's Mouse, The. By C. N. & A. M. Williamson.
Lonesome Land. By B. M. Bower.
Lone Wolf, The. By Louis Joseph Vance.
Lonely Stronghold, The. By Mrs. Baillie Reynolds.
Long Live the King. By Mary Roberts Rinehart.
Lost Ambassador. By E. Phillips Oppenheim.
Lost Prince, The. By Frances Hodgson Burnett.
Lydia of the Pines. By Honorè Willsie.
Lynch Lawyers. By William Patterson White.

Macaria. (Ill. Ed.) By Augusta J. Evans.
Maid of the Forest, The. By Randall Parrish.
Maid of Mirabelle, The. By Eliot H. Robinson.
Maid of the Whispering Hills, The. By Vingie E. Roe.
Major, The. By Ralph Connor.
Maker of History, A. By E. Phillips Oppenheim.
Malefactor, The. By E. Phillips Oppenheim.
Man from Bar 20, The. By Clarence E. Mulford.
Man from Bitter Roots, The. By Caroline Lockhart.
Man from Tall Timber, The. By Thomas K. Holmes.
Man in the Jury Box, The. By Robert Orr Chipperfield.
Man-Killers, The. By Dane Coolidge.
Man Proposes. By Eliot H. Robinson, author of "Smiles."
Man Trail, The. By Henry Oyen.
Man Who Couldn't Sleep, The. By Arthur Stringer.
Marqueray's Duel. By Anthony Pryde.
Mary 'Gusta. By Joseph C. Lincoln.
Mary Wollaston. By Henry Kitchell Webster.
Mason of Bar X Ranch. By E. Bennett.
Master Christian, The. By Marie Corelli.
Master Mummer, The. By E. Phillips Oppenheim.
Memoirs of Sherlock Holmes. By A. Conan Doyle.
Men Who Wrought, The. By Ridgwell Cullum.
Midnight of the Ranges. By George Gilbert.

Popular Copyright Novels

AT MODERATE PRICES

Ask Your Dealer for a Complete List of
A. L. Burt Company's Popular Copyright Fiction

Mischief Maker, The. By E. Phillips Oppenheim.
Missioner, The. By E. Phillips Oppenheim.
Miss Million's Maid. By Berta Ruck.
Money Master, The. By Gilbert Parker.
Money Moon, The. By Jeffery Farnol.
Moonlit Way, The. By Robert W. Chambers.
More Tish. By Mary Roberts Rinehart.
Mountain Girl, The. By Payne Erskine.
Mr. Bingle. By George Barr McCutcheon.
Mr. Grex of Monte Carlo. By E. Phillips Oppenheim.
Mr. Pratt. By Joseph C. Lincoln.
Mr. Pratt's Patients. By Joseph C. Lincoln.
Mr. Wu. By Louise Jordan Miln.
Mrs. Balfame. **By Gertrude Atherton.**
Mrs. Red Pepper. By Grace S. Richmond.
My Lady of the North. By Randall Parrish.
My Lady of the South. By Randall Parrish.
Mystery of the Hasty Arrow, The. By Anna K. Green.
Mystery of the Silver Dagger, The. By Randall Parrish.
Mystery of the 13th Floor, The. By Lee Thayer.

Nameless Man, The. By Natalie Sumner Lincoln.
Ne'er-Do-Well, The. By Rex Beach.
Net, The. By Rex Beach.
New Clarion. By Will N. Harben.
Night Horseman, The. By Max Brand.
Night Operator, The. By Frank L. Packard.
Night Riders, The. By Ridgwell Cullum.
North of the Law. By Samuel Alexander White.

One Way Trail, The. By Ridgwell Cullum.
Outlaw, The. By Jackson Gregory.
Owner of the Lazy D. By William Patterson White.

Painted Meadows. By Sophie Kerr.
Palmetto. By Stella G. S. Perry.
Paradise Bend. By William Patterson White.
Pardners. By Rex Beach.
Parrot & Co. By Harold MacGrath.
Partners of the Night. By Leroy Scott.